WHEN THE DOGS ATE CANDLES

WHEN THE DOGS ATE CANDLES

A Time in El Salvador

by
BILL HUTCHINSON

UNIVERSITY PRESS OF COLORADO

Copyright © 1998 by Bill Hutchinson
International Standard Book Number 0-87081-475-3

Published by the University Press of Colorado
P.O. Box 849
Niwot, Colorado 80544

The University Press of Colorado is a cooperative publishing enterprise supported, in part, by Adams State College, Colorado State University, Fort Lewis College, Mesa State College, Metropolitan State College of Denver, University of Colorado, University of Northern Colorado, University of Southern Colorado, and Western State College of Colorado.

The paper used in this publication meets the minimum requirements of the American National Standard for Information Sciences — Permanence of Paper for Printed Library Materials. ANSI Z39.48-1984

Library of Congress Cataloging-in-Publication Data

Hutchinson, Bill, 1947–
When dogs ate candles: a time in El Salvador / by Bill Hutchinson.
    p.   cm.
    Includes index.
    ISBN 0-87081-475-3 (hardcover : alk. paper)
    1. State-sponsored terrorism — El Salvador.   2. Human rights workers — El Salvador.   3. El Salvador — Politics and government — 1979–1992.   I. Title.
HV6322.3.S2H87 1998
972.8405'3'092 — dc21
[B]   97-48727
                                     CIP

10   9   8   7   6   5   4   3   2   1

For Lori
You came with me once to El Salvador
but were there with me every time.

Sometimes in the barrio where we lived, we would wake up in the morning and find a body in the street . . . someone we did not know. All day it would lie there. No one could afford to buy candles, so someone would put a tin can by the body, and people would put in a few cents until there was enough to buy candles. Then we would put the candles around the body and light them to honor the person. When the candles went out, the dogs would eat the wax.

— Carlos Cartagena
A Salvadoran Refugee

CONTENTS

FOREWORD

For a dozen years beginning in about 1980, El Salvador gripped the soul of tens of thousands of North American gringos. Most had been similarly tormented by the war in Vietnam during an earlier decade, from 1965 to 1975. The terrible paradox of such beautiful and impoverished people in foreign lands suffering so much violence, with our own powerful government participating as accomplice to that suffering, caused enormous anguish.

Already the pain of El Salvador has dulled. For most, the very memory is threatened. More recent violence — in Iraq, Liberia, Somalia, Chiapas, Haiti, Bosnia, Rwanda, New York City, Waco, Oklahoma City, a mosque in Hebron, a marketplace in Jerusalem — has numbed our sensitivity, diffused our focus, and too often reinforced a false sense of superiority and self-righteousness.

But El Salvador holds invaluable revelations for the people of the United States and all who seek peace. If the long struggle for freedom is between memory and oblivion, we must not let El Salvador del Mundo slip from our consciousness, or our conscience.

The power and importance of this book is that it captures indelibly the human aspects of the struggle in El Salvador in the most intimate and personal way from participants of several persuasions. You will come to know Salvadorans who risked and sometimes lost their lives to protect their own people from the terror of governments, and you will come to know a few good neighbors from the North who sought to protect the defenseless poor, their Salvadoran champions, and victims on both sides of the struggle. Jesús, as a justice of the peace, identified a thousand mutilated bodies, then later used that knowledge and evidence to protect the living. César, a soldier, killed with the death squads, then later struggled, with limited success, to overcome his own fear and threats to his life to disclose how the death squads — the *escuela de música* — worked, and how the U.S. government wrote the score.

As long as this book is available, the tragedy of El Salvador, where courage and compassion outfaced savagery and terror, can be remembered through its reading and its lessons learned. Few writings offer so much. Bill Hutchinson succeeds because he tells this tale simply, with love and honesty and generous admiration for real heroes, and a few others, whom most of us otherwise would never know.

During the century and a half between the two William Walkers, the dominant facts in the lives of the people of El Salvador have been the interest and acts of the United States. The first William Walker, the "grey-eyed man of destiny," an audacious filibuster, briefly reigned in Nicaragua. His government was recognized by the United States as he reestablished slavery, ordered English the official language, and sought to extend an empire over Central America, all in a few brief years during the 1850s.

The second William Walker served as U.S. ambassador to El Salvador before and after 1990, when Herbert Anaya was murdered, Mirtala López suffered body- and soul-breaking torture for seventy-two hours at the hands of the Treasury Policy, and many other events described in this book occurred. Jennifer Casolo, a young American churchwoman was arrested, charged with aiding the guerrillas and concealing a huge cache of arms in her backyard in San Salvador to be used by guerrillas in the urban fighting there in late 1989. She was quickly released by President Cristiani. Ambassador Walker helped secure her release. Lori Berenson, another young American who worked with the poor in El Salvador, was convicted of "treason" and is now serving a life sentence in Peru at an elevation of 13,000 feet, all because she tried to help that country's poor. In Lori's case, the U.S. ambassador failed to help her, although Berenson was tried in secret in 1996 before a hooded military tribunal and permitted no defense.

From the Monroe Doctrine to the present day — through scores of U.S. military interventions; gunboat, big stick, and dollar diplomacy; good-neighbor policies; and alliances for progress — the United States has sought to establish its power over the region, its peoples, and its economy. Near the middle of this long epoch, internationalist idealist president Woodrow Wilson's corollary to the Monroe Doctrine prohibition of European political and military intervention in the Western Hemisphere proscribed

European concessions and finance, allowing the United States to monopolize the fruits of the region. When El Salvador and Costa Rica complained to the Wilson administration about the growing U.S. presence in the region, a presence focused on Nicaragua, which separated the two countries, they were offered protectorate status to assure their stability.

When El Salvador and Honduras protested a U.S. bilateral treaty with Nicaragua for a U.S. naval base in the Gulf of Fonseca, which all three countries border, and prevailed in 1916 in the decade-old Central American Peace Court, which had been funded in part by Andrew Carnegie, the Wilson administration simply ignored the court's decision. This act destroyed an institution designed to resolve disputes in the region by legal process. The United States preferred reliance on its superior force.

By the 1980s, when it could no longer dominate Nicaragua, the United States had decided Nicaragua did not have sovereignty over the Gulf of Fonseca after all and threatened to intervene if Nicaragua used the gulf for commerce with El Salvador. But the U.S. attitude toward international law had not changed. When the International Court of Justice at the Hague agreed to adjudicate Nicaragua's claims from the 1980s against the United States for mining Corinto Harbor, shooting at the air control tower of Nicaragua's international airport, and funding Contras to kill its people, the U.S. delegation walked out, leaving the World Court impotent in the face of the superpower's noncompliance.

Throughout this era, U.S. policy was — as candidly, if secretly, noted in 1927 by Robert Olds, assistant to Secretary of State Kellogg of the famed Kellogg-Briand Peace Pact — to "control the destiny of Central America," where governments the United States "supports stay in power while those we do not . . . support fall." In January 1932, El Salvador suffered the infamous Matanza, the murder of 30,000 men, women, and children, which was prologue to events fifty years later. Never at any point during the twentieth century did the U.S. government respect the sovereignty, rights, welfare, or lives of the people of El Salvador. The horrors described in these pages are more evidence than you want of this truth.

With the fall of the Somoza government in Nicaragua in 1979, the United States, claiming to fear the spread of communism, stepped up its role in El Salvador. A military *golpe* installed a new government in El Salvador three months after the flight of Somoza, which soon degenerated into greater violence than even its predecessor.

At that time, more than half the population of El Salvador was illiterate. Per capita income was under $700 a year. The country ranked fifth in the world in malnutrition, even though half the population lived on lush rural farmlands. Two percent of the population owned 60% of the real estate — and nearly all the arable land. Within several years, close to 10% of the population fled to the U.S., to cities like Houston, which is closer to San Salvador than it is to Los Angeles, San Francisco, or New York, where Salvadorans also migrated.

On January 22, 1980, a peaceful demonstration of more than 200,000 in San Salvador was fired on by the army, killing 49 and wounding hundreds. Archbishop Oscar Romero, radicalized and, in the eyes of the populace, sainted by the violence and his unexpected elevation in the Catholic Church, denounced the government in weekly sermons heard on radios throughout the country. He publicly declared that the "most repressive sector" of the military was in control, and he opposed even nonlethal aid from the U.S. to the Salvadoran military. In his last sermon, the day before he was murdered, he said, "No soldier is obliged to obey an order contrary to the law of God. . . . Thou shalt not kill." He was assassinated on March 24, 1980, as he led prayers in the chapel of the cancer hospital where he lived. At his funeral, 75,000 mourners were dispersed with grenades and rifle fire, leaving more than 30 dead and 400 injured.

During a major military operation in May 1980 that included U.S. helicopter support, Salvadorans fleeing to Honduras were caught by the Salvadoran army at the Sumpul and Lempa Rivers and blocked by the Honduran army from entering that country. A priest later described the scene at the Sumpul, where more than 600 dead were covered by "so many vultures pecking at the bodies that it looked like a black carpet." Weeks later, while visiting refugees at Virtud, a refugee camp near the Lempa in Honduras, I witnessed stragglers carrying the wounded across the river. They feared that the Salvadoran military was in hot pursuit and that the Honduran army would force them back.

That same spring, our "human rights" president, Jimmy Carter, requested $5.7 million in additional military aid to strengthen the Salvadoran army. Congress appropriated the funds the week after Archbishop Romero's murder.

In November 1980, six leaders of the guerrillas' political wing were murdered and mutilated. On December 2, 1980, three Maryknoll nuns and a lay volunteer from the United States were raped and murdered after being seized on the road from the airport to the capital. This warranted only a two-week suspension in U.S. aid. In early January 1981, two U.S. labor union leaders were murdered in the coffee shop of the hotel where they were staying in San Salvador. These people, like the meddlesome volunteers from Marin who are described in this book, were inconvenient to the governments of El Salvador and the United States alike.

The Reagan administration, which took office on January 20, 1981, was determined to hit the ground running in El Salvador. The country would be a test case for rolling back communism. U.S. ambassador Jeanne Kirkpatrick solemnly declared Central America to be "the most important place in the world for the United States today." New levels of support for a right-wing government in El Salvador and new strategies to destroy the opposition were pursued for eight years.

In December 1981, hundreds of Salvadorans, mostly women and children, were murdered at El Mozote by troops trained in the United States. U.S. diplomats including Thomas Enders and Elliot Abrams participated in denials and the cover-up, and the Salvadoran army, with its U.S. advisers, blocked physical access to the site. More than a decade passed before the slaughter was verified.

During this period, I witnessed, before losing count, more than 400 young Salvadoran soldiers in fresh green uniforms disembark at the airport in San Salvador from a specially marked Boeing 747 after training at Ft. Benning, Georgia.

A U.S.-forced election in 1981 consolidated, as intended, right-wing power and U.S. influence and support. By then, there were already 180,000 refugees in the region, several hundred thousand Salvadoran émigrés in the United States, 150,000 displaced persons in El Salvador itself, and more than 40,000 dead. There were no absentee ballots, no real alternatives on the ballot, and pervasive fear and violence. Such is our passion for democracy. Notre Dame–educated José Napoleón Duarte was elected president, and ARENA, the party of Roberto D'Aubuisson, a renegade military officer accused of assassinating Archbishop Romero, won control of the National Assembly. Duarte was defeated in the next election by the ARENA candidate.

By October 1982, U.S. ambassador Dean Hinton estimated that "30,000 Salvadorans [had] been murdered — not killed in battle, murdered."

On the fourth anniversary of the assassination of Oscar Romero, I marched with the Mothers of the Disappeared toward the unfinished cathedral, which Joan Didion called "the clearest political statement in Salvador." Before his death, Oscar Romero halted the building of the cathedral until the poor of the nation are properly housed. The police attacked the marchers, knocked down and beat mothers and other women. A poster the marchers carried, colored blood red with a portrait of the archbishop, quoted an article of his faith: "A mí pueden matar, pero que quede claro que la voz de la justicia nadie la puede callar ya" (You have the power to kill me, but it remains clear that no one can silence the voice of justice).

Several years before the November 1989 army murders of Jesuit scholars at the University of Central America in San Salvador, Father Daniel Berrigan visited El Salvador and established lasting friendships with his fellow Jesuits there. Taken to a meeting with the Mothers of the Disappeared, he reported in his book *Steadfastness of the Saints*, "We stood there among the mothers, confounded, put to silence." It was difficult for him, he recalled, "to stand there consciously, a citizen of the U.S., [with] the stigma of our wars and incursions and racism on me," difficult "to stand in shame and borrowed hope."

In 1991, with a peace agreement in place, FMLN leaders resident in San Salvador, U.N. vehicles everywhere, and the Truth Commission in the final stages of releasing its reports, I went to El Salvador to plead for the release of several persons imprisoned on charges of criminal libel. They were printing and circulating detailed accounts of the role senior military officers played in the murders and repression of the past twelve years. The accounts, which included photos of the officers, were drawn from interviews with victims and from the records of human rights organizations like the Human Rights Commission of El Salvador. The officers were still in power. They brought the charges of libel themselves. Their anger and hatred were intense. Officials in El Salvador, the U.S. government, and the Truth Commission knew, or had access to, more information of criminal conduct than survivors and courageous journalists could ever hope to compile.

At dinner with Mirna Anaya one night, she and I noted the similarities between the commission's early documentation of the victims and this later, also heroic, use of devil's ink to expose the perpetrators. Though the prisoners were released, the presses were stopped.

Justice has been called truth in action, but truth must out for action motivated by it to occur. The struggle for truth never ends. If the truth does not come out in time, it will be stillborn.

In 1982, peasants in Chaletenango whose village had been attacked by the army asked me to carry messages that they were alive to relatives who had fled and were believed to be in a refugee camp on Catholic Church grounds near San Salvador. Shortly after I entered the refugee camp the following day, a bus and several vans arrived with a group of forty or fifty refugees from a village on Guazapa Volcano that had come under army attack. Among the dozen who were seriously injured, several were dying from their wounds. Half the group were children or infants. All attention turned to the wounded or dying. Several nurses dressed wounds, and a doctor did what he could for the severely injured. There were cries of pain and cries of sorrow. After a death, there was even greater wailing and crying. For several hours, the newly arrived children and babies seemed as stunned as the adults, all of whom were women, except for several older men.

As twilight fell, hundreds of children from the refugee camp, intoxicated by the cooling air, the witching hour, and their own childish energy, began to run in waves across a large open field, shouting with joy. Children in the Guazapan group, still huddled with the wounded and shocked adults, began to notice the other children as they ran and shouted. One by one, they began to slip away from the weeping and moaning of the adults and the wounded to move toward the field. Soon nearly all the children from Guazapa who had left dead friends and relatives earlier that day, traveling huddled with wounded dying villagers who were their only surviving contact with the past, were immersed in the waves of running, shouting children that in the dim light looked like wind rippling over a ripe wheat field.

I thought then that this is how we survive our violent tragedies. The children overcome crippling pain and grief to carry on in their turn. But I thought, too, that generations of the poor of El Salvador and other oppressed countries had suffered similar destinies and would continue to do so unless some profound change occurred.

This book can help achieve such change. As you contemplate what is revealed here, three questions will arise. Within the answers to these questions rests most of the hope for change that can end the cycles of violence, repression, deception, and greed that characterize so much of human history.

We see in these pages that some people are able to act with vision, courage, and compassion to help others and make a lasting difference. For Kate and Bill and so many others to set aside their own lives and interests and to offer themselves to protect impoverished and endangered Salvadorans is a powerful testament to our capacity to love. For Brian, so young, strong, and agile, to risk his life and lose his limbs in an effort to tell the people of the United States that they should not let their government ship arms to a violent tyranny in El Salvador reveals the existence still of true patriots who will sacrifice all to make their government righteous.

How can millions more be motivated to understand such efforts, support them, act on their own initiative, and demand that those values prevail?

Some people can endure the cruelest physical, psychological, and emotional suffering, the greatest human and material losses possible, yet hope for and seek truth and reconciliation. Herbert, Mirna, Mirtala, and Jesús risked everything to expose the murderous repression of a government ruling by force of arms and assassination. Herbert gave his life, Mirna and Mirtala lost family, and Jesús escaped by the grace of God, but all sustained the hope that peace and economic justice are possible, and all continue their struggle for truth and reconciliation to this day, with no desire for vengeance.

How can millions more learn from these acts that power is in the people and be emboldened to join the struggle that needs only their commitment to prevail?

Some people dare ask that their country be honest and just in all its acts, that it be as good a neighbor in the community of nations as individuals ought to be in the communities where they live. Both the Human Rights Commission of El Salvador and the Marin Interfaith Task Force on Central America addressed the wrongful conduct of their own and other governments and acted at their peril to protect life and human rights from arbitrary government violence. Barbara Boxer risked a promising political career in an effort as lonely as that of the volunteers. Knowing that neither the intentions of government nor the human condition in El Salvador has significantly changed, knowing that the poor still suffer, they persevere.

How can a new generation renounce militarism and exploitation and act on the faith that true patriotism demands that government respect and protect the rights and welfare of others as the sure way to peace?

Unless we come to understand from the lessons of the Salvadorans — and so many other sad histories — that our commitments and conduct have too often been desperately wrong, a global society will become the death squad of humanity.

Ramsey Clark
New York, New York
August 1997

ACKNOWLEDGMENTS

Many thanks to Kate Bancroft, who introduced me to El Salvador in so many ways and who translated the interviews I conducted in San Francisco and El Salvador. Kate's assistance did more than augment my inadequate Spanish; her friendship with those we interviewed made possible their candid disclosure. Thanks also to Kathy Kadane and Robert McAfee Brown for their critical readings, which strengthened the manuscript, and for the way in which they live their lives. I am also grateful to Jan Bauman, Suzanne Bristol, and Amy and Tom Valens for finding and sharing their photographs and to Anna Maria Spiker for proofreading the Spanish expressions in the text.

Finally, thanks to Suzanne Bristol, who co-directed the Marin Interfaith Task Force on Central America in the early days, and in the process became my fast friend.

In Loving Memory of
Herbert Ernesto Anaya Sanabria
1951–1987

WHEN THE DOGS ATE CANDLES

INTRODUCTION

It began for me in the sanctuary of the First Congregational Church in Berkeley, California, on one of those October days made for outdoor activities. Not many people could have persuaded me to squander a perfectly lovely Bay Area afternoon inside at Berkeley First Church. Maybe only one person — Bill Eichhorn, who happened to have been the one to ask me. The subject was Central America — specifically, El Salvador — and only someone I loved and respected could have dragged me across the bay to spend an afternoon listening to people speak about something that interested me so slightly. El Salvador. A country between Mexico and South America where my government engaged that of the Soviet Union over yet another piece of unfamiliar turf. That is what the U.S. government did in many far-flung corners of the world — with no complaint from me — and that is what I understood to be happening in El Salvador. Bill Eichhorn, my minister, wanted me to be concerned about it. So I went, gazing longingly at the sailboats heeling and tacking across the water as the girders of the Bay Bridge flashed by. It was 1984.

Fourteen years and fifteen-odd trips to El Salvador later, my insides have been rearranged, I myself have been ordained, and I spend my evenings here in Sonoma, California — one of the truly blessed places on God's blue earth — longing for El Salvador and the people there who have come to inhabit my imagination through no design of their own. How did this happen?

It all began that afternoon in Berkeley. John Fife spoke. His church, Southside Presbyterian Church in Tucson, Arizona, was the first in the United States to declare its real estate a sanctuary for the Salvadoran refugees who spilled in great hordes across the Rio Grande in the early 1980s, exhausted and broke from their transcontinental journey from their homeland, traumatized and grieving over what they had experienced and witnessed there, desperate

1

enough to leave all that they knew and loved to take their chances in the land that sent the bullets and bombs that killed their sons and daughters and reduced their villages to smoking rubble. Charlie Clements spoke, too. Charlie had been an air force pilot in Vietnam, had recoiled from that experience into pacifism and the practice of medicine, had eventually humped a backpack of sutures and antibiotics into El Salvador and there tended to the sick and wounded in guerrilla control zones.

Between them on that October afternoon, John and Charlie managed to insinuate into my brain the disturbing notion that what was happening in El Salvador was more a struggle between rich and poor than between East and West. They also spoke of massacres and death squads and decapitated corpses, U.S. advisors and military aid, and many other things about which I did not want to hear.

Afterward, I reeled out into the dusk with an armload of books — some thoughtful member of the Peace Commission of the Northern California Conference of the United Church of Christ peddled them from a table at the back of the sanctuary — and set about in the weeks that followed confirming everything they had told me. The kinds of gruesomely deliberate practices that I associated exclusively with Nazi Germany were being visited on peasants and priests and labor organizers and human rights workers in a tiny Latin country no bigger than the Bay Area in size or population, a tiny Latin country that enjoyed nearly unlimited logistical and financial support from my government and hence from me. This was a Holocaust happening in my time, on my watch.

I slept poorly and drank a lot of beer. And I asked myself again and again, what should I do?

Bill Eichhorn, good friend and pastor that he is, noticed my travail and nudged me one step further. He gave me a form letter that had landed on his desk. The Dominican sisters up the road in San Rafael had taken a Salvadoran family into sanctuary in their massive old convent on Grand Avenue, and they were inviting Marin County churches to a series of monthly meetings in hopes that some congregations in this bastion of American liberalism might be persuaded to do likewise.

I drove to San Rafael from my home in Mill Valley on the appointed evening. Sister Bernadette Wombacher greeted me and introduced me to the eight or ten others who had assembled. Four months later, we organized ourselves, adopted the overlong moniker we have been known by ever since — the Marin Interfaith Task Force on Central America — and thereby added our little tuft to the grassroots movement that was then springing up, unbeknownst to us, all across the land. Sister Bernadette put us all together. Suzanne Bristol, a member of the Community Congregational Church in Tiburon, and I did most of the organizing and for our efforts were elected co-chairs of MITF, the acronym by which we soon came to identify ourselves.

This grassroots movement, which sprang up in communities from Burlington, Vermont, to Southern California, came to be known as the Central America solidarity movement. Bubbling up independently in church parish halls and community peace centers in the early 1980s, rivulets of the solidarity movement eventually flowed into streams of coordinated action — nationwide networks of emergency telephone trees that jangled the alert when life was threatened, or taken, in El Salvador, Guatemala, and Nicaragua; regional coordinating bodies of sister cities and sister parishes; and periodic conferences where solidarity workers could learn from each other's experiences in Central America.

Though most of the U.S. solidarity organizations were action oriented, always seeking some undertaking that might save a few lives or reduce by some fraction the financial and logistical support given by our government to the Central American regimes that laid waste to their peoples, all of them eventually learned that their primary tasks were those of watching and listening. The struggle of the Salvadoran people is by definition a Salvadoran struggle, with its own risks, its own suffering, its own tactics, its own political and personal imperatives. For our solidarity movement to be of any use, we first had to learn that we went to Central America to help, not to lead. The essential discipline of solidarity is discernment — learning how to put ourselves at the service of others in ways that are useful to them, how to stand with them in their struggles for liberation. Theirs are the lives at risk, not ours.

Not all of the Americans who mobilized on behalf of the poor of El Salvador were religious by any means, but those who were returned to their congregations and denominations in the United States speaking of the spiritual awakening they had undergone in the company of campesinos whose relatives had been killed, tortured, or disappeared and who forgave us for our trespasses, and our country for its trespasses, nevertheless.

Given the savagery of the repression in El Salvador — the systematic slaughter of whole villages, the dismemberment of victims' bodies, the extreme nature of the torture visited on men and women alike, the practice of dumping bodies where the torn and burned flesh would be witnessed by family members and friends, the complete impunity of the perpetrators — this campesino forgiveness staggered the imagination and the spirit alike. How could these humble citizens extend the hand of friendship to people like me whose tax dollars made it all possible? How indeed? There is no answer — only the forgiveness itself, and the shame and humility that come with it. And then the understanding that we have nothing to teach these people and everything to learn from them.

In El Salvador, death squads were the instruments the government and the ruling elite used to crush their political adversaries and oppose the teachings of liberation theology. From 1978 to 1990, the death squads and army of El Salvador killed and disappeared at least 50,000 civilians, including El Salvador's famous archbishop Oscar Arnulfo Romero. On March 23, 1980, at a time when the death squads were slaughtering thousands every month, Romero addressed the members of the Salvadoran Armed Forces with these words during his nationally broadcast radio homily from the National Cathedral: "In the name of God, then, and in the name of this suffering people whose cries raise daily more loudly to heaven, I plead with you, I beg you, I order you, in the name of God: stop this repression!" On the following day, an assassin shot and killed Oscar Romero while he was celebrating Mass in the little chapel on the grounds of the hospital where he lived.

By the time Romero was killed, scores of popular organizations had sprung up in El Salvador to protest human rights abuses and to press for changes in the social order. For their organizing efforts, the members of these popular organizations often paid with their lives. Among these organizations was the Nongovernmental Human Rights Commission of El Salvador. The commission had been formed in 1978 with Oscar Romero's blessing when he realized that no one was documenting and reporting the massive human rights violations taking place in his country.

Eight Salvadoran citizens — lawyers, law students, a doctor — began documenting these abuses. They established their headquarters — at first in the office of one of their founders, Dr. Mendez, and later on the patio at the archbishop's office complex — and set about counting and photographing the dead, interviewing relatives, taking testimonies from people who had been tortured or raped, and reporting their findings to the United Nations Commission on Human Rights at its annual meetings in Geneva. On the basis of this testimony, and that given by other human rights monitoring organizations, the United Nations listed El Salvador among the half-dozen worst human rights violators in the world. For their efforts, the members of the Human Rights Commission of El Salvador were themselves assassinated, one by one, until seven of their early members had been eliminated. By the time I first visited El Salvador in March 1987, leadership of the commission had passed to Herbert Anaya, who had joined in 1979.

While the Human Rights Commission of El Salvador and its sister organizations stood up to Salvadoran oppression, U.S. citizens began to respond in whatever ways they could. Congregations sponsored certain of their members on long-term trips to El Salvador to shadow specific priests or human rights workers on their daily rounds. This work, called accompaniment, was undertaken in the belief that the security forces of El Salvador would not strike in the presence of an eyewitness from the United States, the country whose administration and populace seemed willing to tolerate Salvadoran deaths on a scale mathematically proportional with the Holocaust but unwilling to tolerate even a handful of dead Americans. The only time during the 1980s when U.S. aid to El Salvador was suspended was when four U.S. churchwomen were raped and killed in December 1980. Even so, funding resumed only a few weeks after Jean Donovan, Maura Clarke, Dorothy Kazel, and Ita Ford died. Apparently, the message conveyed to the Salvadoran security forces was, Kill anyone you want, but don't kill a gringo. People who provided accompaniment were safe, and in most cases, so were those they accompanied.

Other U.S. citizens visited El Salvador and returned home to organize solidarity organizations in their towns and churches, organizations that pressured Congress to end military aid to El Salvador, published newsletters about what was happening there, established sister relationships with Salvadoran churches and communities, and welcomed refugees into their homes.

During 1985 and early 1986, MITF did the types of things so many other solidarity organizations were then doing — we sponsored events around Marin County, conducted meetings in people's living rooms, and expanded both in coverage and circulation the newsletter that Suzanne Bristol had begun publishing from her church. Then, in the spring of 1986, Jesús Campos, one of the Salvadoran nationals who represented the Human Rights Commission of El Salvador in the United States, showed up. The next thing we knew, we were commuting to El Salvador.

The pages that follow contain the story of that long and varied journey. It was a terrible ordeal and an incalculable blessing. It shoved into our faces atrocities that our hearts begged to deny, yet it also introduced us to people whose love and courage enabled them to stand up against something truly inhuman, and to find in that stance their deepest humanity.

It was my great privilege to get to know a handful of these Salvadorans who dared oppose their government during this period of terror and resistance. The stories that follow are their stories and the stories of some North Americans who stood with them. But they are my stories, too.

That afternoon in Berkeley was one of those turning points in my life that I didn't recognize as such until long after. Rounding that first corner — one of many — led me to new friendships and unexpected commitments, and it cost me some old friendships along the way. But the truly significant corner came in March 1987 with my first trip to El Salvador. Jesús Campos was responsible for that.

_1_
JESÚS

When I asked Jesús Campos why his parents had named him Jesús, he told me there were three reasons: he was born on Christmas Eve, 1952; his father was named Jesús; and his maternal grandfather was also named Jesús. Then he told me the story of his maternal grandparents — Jesús Guandique, the son of a Salvadoran coffee baron, and Rosa López, one of the Guandique family maids with whom the privileged young heir had his way. From this maternal grandfather, who died young in a riding accident, Jesús believes he inherited two of his characteristics — intelligence and a propensity for alcoholism.

Jesús was born in a San Salvador *mesón*, a dwelling that might be described as a dirt-floored tenement without running water in the United States. The third of four children, Jesús was from childhood the *manzana* of his mother's eye. He remembers being taken as a child to the spacious San Salvador house of the Guandiques. His mother, the illegitimate daughter of Jesús Guandique and Rosa López, wanted this son of hers who was growing up in a San Salvador barrio to know the family from whom he came.

The first time Jesús visited his great aunt in what seemed to him a vast palace, he made the mistake of playing with some toys belonging to his second cousin, whom he had never met, that were lying about on the floor. When they returned home that day, his mother beat him for the transgression. Her aunt had drawn her aside as they left the house to vent her disapproval: young

Jesús might have germs. On subsequent visits he was instructed to sit on the sofa and stay put. Jesús internalized this childhood lesson so deeply that to this day he always finds a place to sit when visiting someone's home, and he always feels a great reluctance to get up and move about the room.

So Jesús grew up on the social margin of a marginalized land, but always with the expectation, imparted to him by his determined mother, that he would succeed in life, that he would shine in school, start a career, and elevate himself from his modest circumstances. Prompted by these maternal aspirations, Jesús did indeed excel in school and enrolled in the National University of El Salvador. As a student he stayed clear of politics, reserving his passion for San Salvador's Alianza soccer team, whose games he never missed, and for the exciting social life available at the university to one as engaging and outgoing as he. In 1973 he met Amalia, a shy and lovely fellow student. They started dating, then moved in together and started a family before eventually marrying on Christmas Eve in 1981. During the 1970s, he supported himself as a teacher as he prepared to enter law school, then took a variety of jobs in the courts while earning his law degree.

By the late 1970s Jesús was becoming involved in politics, albeit indirectly. "I was a supporter, sympathizer, and friend of many FMLN (Farabundo Martí National Liberation Front) people," he says. "I had a good friend in the Popular Liberation Forces. They used my house from time to time for meetings. I added my grain of sand, but I was not affiliated."

The guerrilla fighting forces of El Salvador appropriated for their collective name that of Farabundo Martí, the popular leader of the last peasant revolt in El Salvador. The Martí-led uprising of the 1930s resulted in what Salvadorans refer to as La Matanza, the Massacre, a monthlong bloodbath that left 30,000 dead.

The FMLN of the 1980s commanded between 7,000 and 15,000 troops, both men and women, their forces swelling and shrinking irregularly due to combat mortalities and new enlistments. The FMLN emerged in the late 1970s when a short-lived, progressive, democratically elected junta composed of reform-minded young army officers and popular politicians enjoyed a brief period of ascendancy in El Salvador. When the army toppled that junta in a 1979 coup and rolled back the land reforms it had instituted, many of its followers headed for the hills to save their lives — and to restore their political agenda by force of arms.

El Salvador in the late 1970s was an unstable powder keg primed with briefly held — and quickly dashed — aspirations. Second only to Haiti's poor in measures of human misery — infant mortality, poverty, illiteracy, scarcity of medical care, and starvation — El Salvador's vast underclass had stooped along under the yoke of the so-called *catorce familias* (the fourteen families) since the late 1800s. Beginning in the 1860s, peasants had been evicted from their ancestral farming lands in broad-bottomed river valleys by European businessmen who saw the profit potential of those lands if planted in cotton and sugarcane. Hired thugs — the lineal ancestors of the security forces of the 1970s and 1980s — drove the peasants off the land, then drove them back onto it as chattel laborers. Through force of arms, El Salvador's oligarchy employed the campesinos in their cash crop economy through the decades that followed, and when they chafed or resisted, as they did under Farabundo Martí in the 1930s, the oligarchs had them slaughtered.

Suddenly, in the late 1970s, hope was sparked by the reform junta and fanned both by the great spiritual movement of liberation theology then sweeping Latin America and by the young political radicals constellated around the National University. When the army moved against the junta and its adherents, and when the paramilitary security forces began to hunt down priests, catechists, labor organizers, journalists, and archbishops, the battle was joined.

As the counterpoint of insurrection and reprisal inexorably gathered momentum in the last two years of the 1970s, Jesús found work as an assistant to the attorney general in the eastern part of the country, a commonplace assignment for law students in El Salvador, where the shortage of lawyers willing to take rural postings leaves ample opportunities for qualified students. The grandness of the title is misleading; his job consisted of prosecuting people accused of common crimes — drunkenness, fighting, murder, theft. He commuted by bus between San Salvador, where he continued his legal studies at the university, and his various postings in Ciudad Barrios, San Francisco Gotera, and San Miguel.

In May 1980, a friend helped him obtain a promotion to justice of the peace in La Unión, a charming port town on the Gulf of Fonseca. He worked there until November, considered a transfer to the small city of Zacatecoluca, but decided instead on a transfer to the western city of Santa Ana, El Salvador's second largest urban area. For Jesús, that passed-up opportunity to go to

Zacatecoluca was a near miss. Had he taken that job, it would have been his responsibility to "recognize" the bodies of the four U.S. churchwomen — Jean Donovan, Maura Clarke, Dorothy Kazel, and Ita Ford — whom soldiers raped, murdered, and buried near Zacatecoluca on December 2, 1980. When a murder is committed in El Salvador, it is the responsibility of the local justice of the peace to examine the scene of the crime and identify the deceased. This function is known as recognition, and Jesús figures that had he been the one to recognize the bodies of the *religiosas Norteamericanas,* he would have suffered the same fate as the justice of the peace who did and subsequently turned up dead.

Instead, Jesús was initiated into the reality of the death squads on his first day in Santa Ana. "On my very first day in Santa Ana, there was a massacre of twelve people. I went out to conduct the recognition, and there they were, lying on the ground. A brother identified to me two of his brothers. The odor of human death was in the air, and the buzzards were standing around. Later I ushered a mother and her daughter into the morgue where the bodies had been taken. The daughter went inside, then came back and said to her mother, 'Yes, Mother, it is him.' The mother said to me, 'Fifteen minutes ago I was in the cemetery crying over another son. And another three months ago. This is my last. I have no tears left to cry.' That was my initiation."

Two months later, in January 1981, the FMLN conducted its first offensive, striking military installations across the country, including the garrison at Santa Ana, where the army's soldiers joined the uprising, then torched their own barracks. The next day, Jesús boarded his bus in San Salvador unawares and took the long ride out to his district office in Santa Ana. The bus left him off at an unusual spot, far from the customary place, so he began to trudge toward the city, briefcase in hand. As he reached the outskirts of town, he saw a line of soldiers ahead of him. When he approached, several of them turned on him with their weapons, then commanded him to halt and raise his hands. They thought he was a subversive. When he protested that he was the justice of the peace on his way to work, they refused to believe him and would not examine the identifying documents in his briefcase. Jesús attributes this refusal to their fear and to the likelihood of their illiteracy. Fortunately, an officer came along, opened Jesús's briefcase, convinced himself that Jesús was who he said he was, then provided an apology and an escort for him as he made his way into town. In the days following the offensive, the military exacted revenge on the civilian population of Santa Ana. Jesús recognized ninety-seven corpses before the week was out.

Jesús acknowledges his three-year stint in Santa Ana, during which he recognized more than 1,000 corpses, as the turning point in his life. "You don't know what it is like to pick up a human head. I have seen horrors — eyes hanging down by the mouth, faces divided in two, machete chop marks in human flesh. Once, when I was still new on the job, I had to go out to recognize a corpse. The body was lying out in the bushes, but it had been decapitated and we could not find the head. My assistant was with me, so we went off in different directions, looking for the head. When I found it, I picked it up in my hands, and I began to think of what his last moments had been like. Maybe he was defiant, saying, 'Go ahead. Kill me.' Or maybe he begged for his life. I stroked his hair as I stood there, and I began to talk to him. I said, 'God, little brother, how you did suffer yesterday.' Then my assistant called to me, '¡Bachiller! ¿Qué pasa?' The sound of his voice woke me up. I had been talking unconsciously, like a robot. After three years of that, it almost became routine."

I asked Jesús once if he was certain that all of the hundreds of bodies that he identified were death squad victims, wondering if combat casualties or victims of common crimes might have been among the dead. "Yes," he replied, "I suppose that is possible, but essentially all of them were victims of the death squads. The death squads were such a pervasive reality that they entered the folklore of El Salvador. Everyone knew what was happening, but it was not a reality that people talked about directly or openly. It was as if they had to distance themselves through some kind of humor. So people took the initials of the death squads — E.M., which stand for *escuadrones de la muerte* — and gave them another meaning. They spoke instead of the *escuela de música* [music school]. They escaped with jokes. When they heard gunfire, they would say it is band music, the band is rehearsing."

Diligent young Jesús actually tried to prosecute the soldiers and death squad members he knew were responsible for the killings, but the authorities completely ignored him. When he sent subpoenas to the army, demanding that they produce a particular soldier, the answer always came back, "He has been transferred to Chalatenango."

"That's when I began to feel that I needed to do something. Here I was, receiving good pay for my work, and witnessing all of this suffering.

That's when I began to look for something to do. So I went to a friend who I knew was in some way connected to the FMLN, and I told him, 'I can't fight, but I want to do something.' He told me that he had an idea for me, that he would set up a meeting with someone for me.

"My friend sent me to meet a man — he didn't say the name — at a cafeteria in San Salvador. This man would be sitting in a certain place, wearing a certain necktie, reading a certain magazine, and drinking a Coke. He told me to carry a certain periodical with me — *Selecciones* — and also to order a Coke. If any detail of the arrangements deviated in the least, I was told not to make the contact. I went into the cafeteria at the appointed time, and there was Pedro Flores sitting in the designated place, wearing the designated tie, and reading the designated magazine. But he wasn't drinking a Coke. He was drinking a grape drink called Uva. I knew Pedro because he was such a popular figure at the university, but he didn't know me. I had been told to observe every detail of my instructions, so I didn't know what to do since he was drinking an Uva instead of a Coke. So I went to the counter and ordered a Coke for myself, but the clerk said, 'I'm sorry. We're out of Coke.' So then I knew. In a loud voice I told the clerk, 'Well, then, I'll have an Uva instead.' That's how I met Pedro Flores. We became close friends."

Pedro Flores, who had earned his reputation as a prominent student radical, directed Jesús to yet another contact who in turn introduced Jesús to the Nongovernmental Human Rights Commission of El Salvador, an independent human rights monitoring organization established in 1978 with the blessing of San Salvador's archbishop, Oscar Romero. By the time Jesús stumbled into the Human Rights Commission's orbit, seven of their eight founding members had been assassinated and their offices bombed on three occasions. The commission's work — documenting assassinations, disappearances, tortures, and massacres; taking testimonies from survivors and family members of victims; publishing their findings wherever they could — apparently offended some elements of Salvadoran society. At the commission, Jesús was given collaborative status and asked to provide documentation about what was happening in Santa Ana. From then on, Jesús's bus rides back to San Salvador from his departmental posting became anxious occasions. His specific task was to duplicate prints of the photographs he took when recognizing corpses, then carry those prints, along with data about the victims and their circumstances of death, to his conduit in San Salvador. Jesús began this work in 1981 and continued it until he fled El Salvador in 1983.

In addition to his clandestine duties for the commission, his law studies, and his work as justice of the peace, Jesús began teaching undergraduate classes in the history of political science and the history of political doctrines at the university. By now he was married and the father of three — Marta, his daughter, and Jesús Jr. and Guillermo, his twin sons. How he managed such a full and hectic life is beyond me, but he did. It was his teaching at the university that finally drew to him the attention of the death squads.

Pedro Flores, now Jesús's fast friend, also taught at the university, and the two of them spoke boldly — perhaps rashly — in their classes. Jesús took the opportunity provided by the lectern to draw unflattering parallels between fascism, the writings of Niccoló Machiavelli, and the current situation in El Salvador. Pedro preached a similar doctrine to his students. It was a heady time for both of them. Because the army had taken over the university's main campus off the Boulevard de los Héroes, teachers conducted their classes in rented space here and there around San Salvador. Militant opposition to the forces of repression was the order of the day among university students, so Jesús and Pedro ladled out their criticism of the lawlessness that Jesús witnessed every week in Santa Ana. Perhaps assuming that their classes were free from the *orejas* (ears) that had by then penetrated many areas of Salvadoran life, they said what they thought and described what they saw.

On Tuesday, September 9, 1983, Pedro left the law school building to meet his wife downtown. He was captured along the way by elements of the Anticommunist Salvadoran Army — a typical death squad designation — and was never seen again. The next day, Hugo Carrillo, head of the School of International Relations, was captured in front of his family. He, too, was never seen again. A week later, Jesús found a sheet of paper in the typewriter at his office, on which someone had typed an inelegant message: "That Campos. You stop teaching your subversive lessons and leave the University, or suffer the consequences."

The writing was on the typing paper, so to speak, and everyone — his family, his friends, his students — told Jesús to waste no time getting out of the country. But he had no money, no idea where he might flee. Fear dominated him, and he lay awake at night waiting for the knock at his door and plotting a route by which he could scamper to safety over the neighborhood rooftops. He found himself thinking of his life and his family in the past tense: "Amalia was a wonderful wife. I was glad to see the births of my children." He operated on autopilot, even taught his class several times more, and waited for the blow to fall.

Then his conduit to the Human Rights Commission — the man Pedro Flores had introduced him to after their first meeting at the cafeteria — bumped into Jesús at the Mr. Donut outlet in the Metro Centro shopping center. He spotted Jesús through the window, and a look of astonishment swept over his face as he signalled Jesús to join him outside. "What are you doing here? Why are you still in the country?" When Jesús explained that he didn't know what to do, that he had no money for his family or for transportation abroad, his conduit was incredulous. "You've been saying those things in your classes at the U, and you haven't made any plans for getting out of the country?"

The conduit gave Jesús $200, told him to get a passport as quickly as he could, to stop using public transportation or his car, and to use taxis exclusively for getting around town. During the next several days, members of the commission helped Jesús obtain his passport and his Mexican visa, arranged for some living money for Amalia and the kids, and sent him on his way to the commission's office in Mexico City. He left El Salvador on October 17, 1983, not knowing when he would next see his family, not knowing if he would ever be able to return. In Mexico City, he met members of the Human Rights Commission who were working there in exile: Herbert Anaya, Miguel Angel Montenegro, Reynaldo Blanco, and Dr. Roberto Lara Velado, who had assumed the presidency of the commission after the assassination of its first great leader, Marianella Garcia Villas.

Jesús also met a U.S. priest from Iowa named Mike Colonese. Mike had lived for seventeen years in El Salvador before being expelled by the government in the late 1970s, and he had come to know the members of the commission in Mexico City. Mike proposed that Jesús go to Iowa to become the commission's representative in the United States. He called an old friend in Des Moines, a Methodist minister named Chet Guinn, to suggest that Chet arrange sponsorship for Jesús through the Des Moines Area Urban Mission Council, which Chet staffed. Chet replied, "Who could say no to Jesús?" and promised to make the arrangements.

Jesús flew to Los Angeles on December 15, 1983, bearing a letter from Dr. Lara authorizing him to represent the Human Rights Commission in the United States. He spent a month there at the office of El Rescate — a Salvadoran legal advocacy agency — then flew on to Des Moines on January 11, 1984. Chet Guinn met Jesús at the airport, introduced him to clergypeople all around Iowa, and made arrangements for Jesús to speak to church and civic groups at every opportunity. In halting English, Jesús began to convey to the people of America's heartland that their government was funding a terror machine to the south.

Jesús made his rounds to churches all over the state, learning how to drive in ice and snow as he did so, trying to accustom his tropical blood to a Midwestern winter. But he was preoccupied always with Amalia, Marta, and the twins. He had to get them out, and with Chet's help he devised a plan. The first order of business was to accumulate enough money for airfares, bribes, and phony Mexican visas. Chet took care of that, raising $3,000 from the people and churches in his Iowa network. Jesús called Amalia in El Salvador and, in a coded message, informed her that the money was being transferred to their San Salvador bank account. Then it was up to Amalia — gentle, smiling Amalia — to get herself and her children to Matamoros, Mexico, just across the Rio Grande from Brownsville, Texas.

Neighbors told Amalia that forged Mexican visas could be obtained outside the Mexican Embassy. So there she went, taking her place at the end of the block-long line of people looking for some way out of El Salvador, and waited to see what would happen. Sure enough, by 10 A.M. a woman approached her and offered to arrange the visas. Not knowing what else to do, Amalia agreed. The woman returned late that afternoon, forged visas in hand, and sold them to Amalia for $350. Amalia then began to sell their household possessions a few at a time. The plan was for her and the children to enter Mexico on fifteen-day tourist visas, so they had to look like tourists, not refugees scurrying to sanctuary with heaps of personal items, when they arrived in Mexico City.

Meanwhile, Chet and Jesús worked the phones with the underground network in Mexico that helped Salvadoran refugees make the long passage through their country to the Rio Grande. When Amalia escorted the children off the plane in Mexico City on March 17, 1984, she was met by a man who identified himself as Marcello. Marcello drove them to a safe house in Cuernavaca, where they waited for ten days while the rest of the plans jelled. Amalia nearly went nuts with anxiety as she waited for word about her next move. Finally, on March 27, she and the children boarded a plane for Matamoros while Jesús and Chet drove from Iowa to Brownsville.

In Brownsville, Chet made prearranged contact with a nun who worked clandestinely with the U.S. side of the refugee network. She drove Chet and Jesús to a fast-food restaurant and introduced them to a man named Harry. Harry would drive into Mexico with Chet, meet Amalia at the church where she would be waiting with the children, and take them to the bank of the river. They would have to rely on coyotes — men who made their living conducting refugees into the United States — to wade them across. Jesús gave Harry a letter for Amalia, by which she would know that he was to be trusted, and began his long wait.

Harry drove Chet across the border, through the twisting alleys of Matamoros, to the church where Amalia waited. He told Chet to stay in the van while he went in to meet Amalia, explaining that he would not bring them out until after dark. When night fell, the family crept out and joined Chet in the van. Harry drove them to an embankment two blocks from the river and told Amalia that she and the children would have to proceed on foot from there. The coyotes would meet them at the water's edge. At this point, Amalia was filled with fear. Marta was eight years old, the twins four. Would the current be too deep for them? Would they have to swim across? What if the coyotes weren't there to meet them? There was nothing to do but go on.

Amalia hustled the children out of the van in the darkness, and they began to make their way down to the river's edge while Chet and Harry sped back through the border crossing to meet them on the other side. As if Amalia didn't already have enough to worry about, thieves approached and ordered her to disrobe so they could search her for money. The coyotes, however, saw what was happening, ran to her rescue, and chased the thieves away before demanding their $40 fee. Then they helped her carry the children into the United States and waited with her on the other side until the van arrived.

It was time to take Amalia and the children to meet Jesús. Harry told Chet to call ahead and tell Jesús to meet them in the parking lot outside a certain supermarket. Chet later described their reunion in an article about the Campos family published in the *Des Moines Register:* "When Jesús got about thirty feet from the van, he fell to his knees, opened his arms, and yelled,

'Come to Papa' in Spanish. His family went scrambling out towards him. They were huddled there in the parking lot, kissing, hugging, crying. We all had tears streaming down our cheeks. That reunion made the trip for us — it made the danger, the anxiety, the fear worth it."

They were together. They were safe. They were deeply thankful for that and for the intervention of Chet Guinn and the underground network. But their lives were shattered. The brilliant young lawyer from El Salvador whose efforts had fulfilled his mother's ardent wishes was stranded and penniless in a foreign land, dependent on the goodwill of strangers for his income and for his family's well-being.

In all, Jesús spent six months in Des Moines before taking a position teaching Spanish at the University of Iowa in Iowa City. During this period, his contact with the commission offices in Mexico City and San Salvador gradually diminished, causing commission members to wonder whether Jesús was moving out on his own. Herein lay the seed of future problems.

After his teaching assignment concluded in Iowa City, Jesús drove the family out in March 1985 to Los Angeles, where he assumed the position of paralegal at El Rescate, the legal services agency where he had spent his first month in the United States. At the end of that year, he flew back to El Salvador to work in the Human Rights Commission office for two months. By then, the various commission members were once again concentrating their efforts on their San Salvador headquarters. Having dispersed to Mexico City and elsewhere in the early 1980s when seven of their members were assassinated, they felt that the time had come to risk returning. They simply could not represent the victims of human rights abuses in El Salvador from a safe perch abroad.

Having been on the periphery of the commission until then, first as a collaborative member in El Salvador and then as a representative of the commission in the United States, Jesús now had the opportunity to return to the maelstrom as a core member. The commission leadership had a specific task in mind for Jésus: to replace Joaquín Cáceres, head of the commission's press section, who had been captured by the Treasury Police in San Salvador's downtown shopping area a month earlier, on November 8, 1985. After beating and torturing Joaquín, the Treasury Police sent him to the political prisoners' section at Mariona Prison. No one knew when Joaquín might be released, so the commission decided that Jesús should return permanently to El Salvador to replace him.

Jesús flew back to Los Angeles in February 1986 and began the tour that was to be his last assignment before returning home. The purpose of the tour was to drum up support among U.S. solidarity organizations for congressional pressure to have Joaquín released from Mariona. He planned to return to El Salvador in July.

In March 1986, Jesús came to the San Francisco Bay Area and met with members of the Marin Interfaith Task Force on Central America at the Dominican convent in San Rafael. By then, I had met dozens of Salvadorans, but Jesús was the first who planned to return to El Salvador. I simply couldn't imagine taking that risk, had I found myself in his circumstances.

Sister Bernadette Wombacher, our hostess for the luncheon with Jesús, invited her Spanish tutor, Kate Bancroft, to join us for the meeting in case Jesús needed help with translating. He called on Kate from time to time for assistance with a word or phrase. Jesús described the work of the Human Rights Commission of El Salvador, handed around a little brochure that detailed the circumstances of Joaquín's capture and detention, and solicited our support of the congressional campaign to have Joaquín freed. When we probed him about his own work here in the United States, he disclosed his plans to return to El Salvador in four months.

We were shocked to hear that, but probably not as shocked as Jesús was when Kate Bancroft offered to accompany him on his trip home. He was clearly delighted at the prospect. He knew, as we all did, that in those days many Spanish-fluent North Americans provided accompaniment to Salvadoran priests, catechists, unionists, and political organizers on the premise that the Salvadoran security forces would not risk an attack that might strike a gringo — a premise that held true throughout the 1980s.

Once he had recovered from his surprise, Jésus joined the rest of us in considering the implications of Kate's sudden offer. What had been planned as a brief luncheon meeting stretched into the afternoon as we began to ponder the practicalities. Would Kate's presence really insulate him from attack? How would we maintain contact with Jesús and Kate in El Salvador? Where would they live? Would it be okay for Kate to accompany Jesús when he went to work at the commission's office? Where would we get the money for Kate's airfare and living expenses?

We settled the details, invited Jesús to return to Marin in June, exchanged phone numbers, and sent him off to conclude his "Free Joaquín

Cáceres" tour. Ten days before his scheduled return to Marin, he called with frightening news. Four additional members of the commission had been captured in San Salvador — Herbert Anaya on May 26, then Reynaldo Blanco, Miguel Angel Montenegro, and Rafael Terezón three days later. When Jesús drove up to Marin from Los Angeles on June 5, all he knew was that the four men were in the custody of the Treasury Police, the most feared and hated of El Salvador's security forces. Jesús was badly shaken, and so were we.

The minute he arrived, we sat down to take stock of the situation. Clearly, this terrible turn of events called his plans — and Kate's — into question. If Jesús were to return as intended, of what use could he be? The uncaptured members of the commission had all gone into hiding. What would be the point of his returning to El Salvador only to choose between going underground or into the hands of the Treasury Police? We scheduled a meeting for the following morning to make some decisions.

Jesús's wife, Amalia, had accompanied him from Los Angeles. It had taken Jesús, one of the world's slowest drivers, most of the night to make the long drive up and find my house, where they would spend the next few nights. Then we had spent the morning of June 5 grilling him about these recent developments in El Salvador. After lunch, he excused himself and said that he needed some quiet time with Amalia. They ducked into my office and closed the door. When I peeked in a while later, Jesús was stretched out full length on the floor, asleep, with his head on Amalia's lap. Even as he slept, I could see terrible strain etched on his face and reflected in his wife's face as well. What should he do? Return to El Salvador and to whatever awaited him there? Stay in the United States when his colleagues in El Salvador might need him more than ever? Amalia stroked his tortured face, then looked up at me and smiled. Whatever it was I had to say would wait. I pulled the door closed and thanked God that I had never had to face a decision like the one Jesús faced.

When we gathered the following morning, we all impressed on Jesús the need for him to at least delay his plans to go back to El Salvador. To return now, with the entire commission either in custody or in hiding, seemed futile, if not suicidal. As he had all but wrapped up his affairs at El Rescate, we wondered if he might be willing to move to Marin, join the Interfaith Task Force, and help us expand Kate Bancroft's offer of accompaniment into a formal project through which he would recruit a steady stream of volunteers to assist the commission however possible. By lunchtime the outlines of the project had fallen into place. We agreed to begin formal recruitment of volunteers, to solicit funding from the National Council of Churches, and to undertake formation of an advisory board whose members we could call upon to sound the alarm if any of the recruited volunteers should come in harm's way.

In the end, Jesús agreed to assume leadership of the project, and Kate decided to go to El Salvador without him. Assuming that we could pull things together before she departed in July, she could tell the commission of our intention to initiate an accompaniment project on their behalf, should they so desire. After our morning of planning, Jesús departed with Amalia for the long drive back to Los Angeles.

At the end of June, he packed his family and all their possessions into their car and a U-Haul trailer and drove them to Marin. As soon as the family was settled in, we started work on the Accompaniment Project for the Human Rights Commission of El Salvador.

We had to find some money, and we had to build an organization. A week after Jesús and his family moved to Marin, he joined Suzanne Bristol and me on a plane to New York to seek funding and advisory board members. I had knocked together a budget for the Accompaniment Project, not knowing that I was about to throw a monkey wrench into Jesús's relationship with the commission. We knew the airfare between the United States and El Salvador, and Jesús had advised us about living expenses for the volunteers. I made best guesses for office expenses, phone bills, and postage. Then I had to decide on a reasonable annual salary for the project coordinator, Jesús Campos. I settled on $18,000, an extremely modest income for a family of five in Marin County, but a princely sum by Salvadoran standards. We sent along a copy of the project proposal, including the budget, with Kate when she flew to El Salvador in July.

This may have been a tactless blunder, or it may have been unavoidable; I'll never know. Maybe we moved too fast. Maybe we should have waited until Kate met with the commission before working out the details of the project. But we didn't want to send Kate to El Salvador with the offer of an accompaniment project unless we knew we could deliver. To do that, we needed promises of financial support, and to secure such promises, we needed to present potential funders with a budget. In addition, we felt we should disclose all of our actions to the commission. So we moved ahead, assuming that when Jesús approved each step, he did so with the voice of the commission.

In New York, we received positive signals from the National Council of Churches, the United Church of Christ, and the Funding Exchange. By the time we returned to Marin, we felt confident enough about funding to give Kate the green light. If the men in Mariona Prison wanted long-term accompaniment for the commission, we told her, offer it. Kate took off for El Salvador in early July. But when she presented the project budget to the five commission members she met in Mariona and they saw an $18,000 salary typed in next to Jesús's name, it looked to them like Jesús was feathering his own nest instead of knocking himself out on their behalf.

Jesús had found a small apartment for his family in the Canal, one of Marin County's few concentrations of low-cost rental housing. A twenty-block area of San Rafael that butts up against a canal running out to San Francisco Bay, it was the place of residence for most of the 4,000 Central American refugees then living in the county. Much to his surprise, as soon as Jesús moved to the Canal, he began to bump into people he knew from home, and he began to realize the perilous circumstances in which most of these refugees lived.

Jesús, who had obtained an entry visa from the U.S. Embassy in Mexico City, had entered the United States legally and lived here legally ever since on the strength of the H-1 visa extension granted by the Immigration and Naturalization Service. Most of the Canal's residents, however, had entered as Amalia and the kids had — by slipping across the 2,000-mile-long Mexican border. Having entered illegally, they were subject to deportation if they fell into the hands of the authorities. They were broke to start with. Lacking green cards, they could seek no legal employment. So they lived several families to an apartment, slept in cars or in the bushes, and sought employment by standing on street corners waiting for contractors, landscape gardeners, or homeowners to troll by looking for cheap labor.

Around the time Jesús got settled in at the Canal, Kate returned from El Salvador, bringing both good news and bad. The commission members in Mariona Prison had all survived episodes of torture, were in good spirits, and had accepted our offer of accompaniment. But they no longer wanted Jesús to represent them or to be involved in the Accompaniment Project in any way. The news devastated him. He felt betrayed and abandoned and angry.

We were devastated, too. We had constructed the whole Accompaniment Project around Jesús, feeling that only he understood the complexities of El Salvador — and the commission — sufficiently to manage the work we had before us. We asked Kate why they had made this decision. Didn't they understand how vital it was for Jesús to administer the project? All they had told her was that Jesús was acting too independently. We speculated for hours. Did they really want Jesús back in El Salvador? Were they angered at his budgeted salary? Did they have any idea what it cost to live in Marin County? We finally decided to appeal the decision by flying Kate back to San Salvador, but the incarcerated members of the commission stood firm. Kate returned from her second trip with their reiterated instructions. We would have to run the project without Jesús.

I doubt that Jesús will ever face a worse time in his life than that period in 1983 when he had to flee his country, his family, and his future, but I'll bet that the second half of 1986 runs a close second. It was terribly stressful for him, and for me. I had given Jesús my word that if he moved his family up from L.A., his anticipated work directing the Accompaniment Project would pay him a living wage. But these plans had now evaporated.

Jesús began earning a little money on the side giving Spanish lessons, and Amalia got some housecleaning jobs in Kentfield. Several churches in Marin pledged modest monthly amounts toward the family's support. Then Jesús came up with the idea of establishing a self-help project for the refugees living in the Canal. If we could whomp up a project like that, with Jesús as the executive director, we would accomplish three goals: providing badly needed services to those refugees, generating income for Jesús, and solving his residency problem.

The H-1 visa that Jesús had obtained while teaching Spanish at the University of Iowa was about to expire, and of course the rest of Jesús's family was without documentation of any kind. He was terribly preoccupied with the possibility of deportation back to El Salvador. We called on Marc van der Hout, outgoing president of the National Lawyers Guild, whose offices in San Francisco handled asylum cases for Salvadoran refugees. Marc offered his services to the Campos family for next to nothing. Jesús and I commuted into the city on a regular basis that fall for discussions with Marc. If anyone knew how to secure residency status, Marc did, but there were options to consider, strategies to weigh, documents by the cubic foot to be obtained and filed, all with no guarantee of success.

After one of these sessions in Marc's office, Jesús and I bought sandwiches at a deli and walked across the street to eat them at a picnic table in Dolores Park. Jesús needed to talk about being rejected by the Human Rights Commission of El Salvador. Knowing that we at the task force were developing a relationship with the commission (by then we had recruited several volunteers to succeed Kate Bancroft in accompanying commission members), he had been constrained from disclosing his feelings to me, but the time had come to unload.

"Who are these guys to reject me, to judge me?" he said, fighting back tears. "They have no idea what it is like here in the United States, trying to support my wife and kids, being broke, having no family to turn to. I have served the commission loyally, but I have to provide for my wife and kids, too."

His precarious situation put him under punishing emotional strain, which made the commission's rejection even more unbearable. But there was nothing to do except carry on as best he could. With financial support from the Marin Community Foundation, Jesús started the CARE (Central American Refugee) Project a few months later in a small office provided by Canal Ministries, a project of the Marin County Episcopalian Churches. He organized festivals at Pickleweed Park Community Center on Salvadoran holidays, at which gaily dressed young women danced with booted swains under the watchful eyes of their mothers while San Rafael Police Department cruisers idled through the parking lot looking for beer drinkers. He organized a Latin *futbol* league, indulging his long-dormant youthful passion, and Amalia earned pin money selling her delicious *pupusas* on the sidelines. He collected small mountains of used furniture and toys from various churches and distributed them to indigent families. He organized sympathetic gringos to protest before the San Rafael City Council against the occasional roundups of refugee day laborers who congregated in front of the 7-Eleven waiting to be hired by employers driving pickup trucks. He accompanied sick and injured Salvadoran nationals to the hospital, translating between them and the doctors and nurses. He began to contemplate his family's future.

Over a decade has now passed since Jesús settled his family in the Canal. Somewhere along the way, all of the members of the Campos family obtained residency status. After several years, the CARE Project ran out of funding and saw its functions taken over by larger, better established agencies.

But by then, San Rafael High School had hired Jesús as a staff counselor, recognizing the need for someone to relate to the hundreds of refugee youths in attendance there. Jesús started taking classes at Dominican College, working toward a degree in education and a California State Teaching Credential. In the fall of 1992, credential in hand, Jesús landed a job teaching Spanish and English-as-a-second-language at the high school, where his innate teaching skills shone. In the spring of 1993, Jesús was recognized at a ceremony in Sacramento as one of fifteen California Teacher Honorees among the state's 227,000 educators.

Marta graduated from San Rafael High School in 1993, moved back to San Salvador to live with her aunt's family while she pursued a degree at the National University, and met a young man whom she married in the summer of 1994. She got a job at TACA Airlines, supported her husband while he continued with his studies, then moved back with him in the spring of 1996 to her parents' home in San Rafael. She now works at a travel agency in San Francisco.

Jesús Jr. and Guillermo, now nineteen and taller than I am, graduated as straight-A students at San Rafael High School in 1997. Jesús represented his school at Boys State, an organization that invites top high school juniors to a week of leadership training at Sacramento State University; Guillermo put his size to good advantage as a lineman on the football team.

With the war well over and something approaching normalcy reestablished in El Salvador, the whole family has flown home a few times for vacations, family reunions, and Marta's wedding. The twins, thoroughly Americanized, loathe these forays into the primitive land of their birth, a land of inferior television and music where the moisture-laden tropical heat saps their energy. But their mother, who has somehow managed to learn only scant phrases of English in all her years in Northern California, lives for these trips. When Amalia steps off the plane in San Salvador, a confident matron replaces the bashful woman who cleans the homes of the rich in Marin County.

Jesús loves these trips, too. And he loves to drive me around in his country, where every passing sight prompts an anecdote: "Down that street is the house where I first courted Amalia" or "That little statue, just there, marks the place where a friend of mine was killed in an automobile accident" or "This very table is where I was sitting when the guy from the commission spotted me through the window."

For ten years, Jesús has been my primary interpreter of the complexities of Salvadoran life, my window into the human costs exacted from those who dared to resist the forces of Salvadoran oppression. Our friendship has developed under trying circumstances. For the first five years of Jesús's residency in Marin, he had to rely on me for so many things — scrounging up church donations for him to augment the pittances he and Amalia earned tutoring Spanish and cleaning houses, guiding him in constructing the CARE Project and securing foundation funding for it, introducing him to Marc van der Hout, interpreting to him the requirements of institutional funders, counseling him when the strains of his tenuous new life in Marin robbed him of sleep and drove him to the brink of madness and despair, and lending him money from time to time. His nickname for me is *Jefe* (Boss); by calling me that, he made light of the excruciating burden of his dependency on me, a dependency that has now passed. More than anything, I believe, he hated asking for money. However, as I have so often found since I became involved in Jesús's benighted country, the real benefit of our relationship has not flowed from me to him, but from him to me. Jesús has been one of the people who have shown me what the human spirit can endure and what the human heart can bear.

The time may come, as Amalia ardently hopes, when she and Jesús will return to El Salvador for good, maybe to retire. Should that day come, surely the twins will stay behind in what is for them the only homeland they know. Like generations of American immigrants before them and generations yet to come, Jesús and Amalia have learned to live bifurcated lives. On the business cards that Jesús has had printed for himself, these words appear in bold letters across the top: "¡El Salvador, Qué Lindo El Salvador!" El Salvador, beautiful El Salvador.

_ 2 _

KATE

We met Kate Bancroft and Jesús Campos on the same day in March 1986. Kate speaks fluent Spanish, having learned it as a child in Peru while her father served a two-year stint with the U.S. diplomatic corps. On the day we met her, Kate happened to be at the Dominican convent giving Sister Bernadette her weekly Spanish tutorial, so Bernadette asked her to sit in on our meeting with Jesús in case he needed help with translating.

The six or eight of us available for a midday meeting assembled around the small conference table where Bernadette had first gathered us in the fall of 1984. Jesús introduced himself, described the campaign to free Joaquín Cáceres from Mariona Prison, and solicited our support of that campaign. We told him we were all for it and would do what we could.

We then began to discuss with Jesús his own situation as a representative of the Human Rights Commission in the United States and to ask him about his future plans. When Jesús said he was about to return to El Salvador to continue his work with the commission, Suzanne and I simultaneously wondered whether Jesús would like someone to accompany him. One of us voiced the thought, to which Jesús replied with delighted astonishment, "Yes, I would like that very much. But where will you find someone who is willing to do such a thing?" The red-haired woman sitting at Bernadette's elbow spoke up in her quiet voice. "I speak Spanish," she said. "I could accompany you." Vintage Kate, as we would come to know in the months and years that followed.

Raised in a Quaker family that routinely discussed politics at the dinner table, Kate as an adolescent had marched with her parents in demonstrations against the Vietnam War and had developed a lifelong skepticism toward the mass media and the pronouncements of her government. As a young adult, she spent the better part of a decade outside the United States traveling and working in Europe, North Africa, and the Middle East, picking up French, German, and a smattering of Arabic along the way. By her mid-twenties, Kate knew that she could move easily and comfortably in almost any situation, any culture.

In 1985, Kate's aunt, a volunteer with Peace Brigades International, recommended that Kate spend three weeks in Guatemala accompanying members of the Grupo Apoyo Mutual (Mutual Support Group). Kate happened to be reading Rigoberta Menchu's autobiography when the call came from Peace Brigades, and she said to herself, "How could I say no?" In Guatemala she lived in a dirt-floored, tin-roofed house from which one daughter had already been disappeared. Because a second daughter was being followed by the authorities, Peace Brigades wanted the family to have constant accompaniment and so recruited Kate at short notice, on the strength of her aunt's recommendation, to fill the gap between regular volunteers.

Kate had been short on funds at the time (not an unusual circumstance) and called her father back East to solicit a loan. After she described the situation to him, he responded as a father who knows his daughter well. "Don't go. The Guatemalan Army is capable of absolutely anything," he said. "How much do you need?"

We knew none of this as we sat around the table at the Dominican convent that day, only that this unassuming woman whom Bernadette liked and trusted was offering to accompany Jesús to the place from which, three years earlier, he had fled for his life. As I look back on that day, it seems almost bizarre that we so readily accepted this stranger's offer. Sister Bernadette's endorsement helped, of course, and Kate's spontaneous offer to drop everything and go spoke volumes about her, but our ready acceptance, and Jesús's, had more to do with the way Kate presented herself than anything else. We may have perceived her offer as rash and risky, but her demeanor suggested that she considered it no big deal. We achieved consensus in a matter of minutes, then turned our attention to settling the details.

Jesús planned to return to El Salvador in July. First he had to finish his "Free Joaquín Cáceres" tour and return to Los Angeles to wrap up his work at El Rescate while Kate arranged a leave of absence from her usual responsibilities. The rest of us would have to raise money for Kate's airfare and living expenses. We all exchanged phone numbers before parting company.

Plans progressed apace until the last week of May, when word came from El Salvador that four additional members of the Human Rights Commission — Herbert Anaya, Miguel Angel Montenegro, Reynaldo Blanco, and Rafael Terezón — had been captured. Joaquín Cáceres had been taken into custody the previous November. When Jesús decided to delay his return, Kate had a new decision to make: should she go to El Salvador alone?

Kate felt that her status as a gringa would protect her, a conclusion with which the rest of us reluctantly agreed. The commission surely needed whatever assistance we could provide just then, and Jesús figured that Kate might be able to help by going to the commission's office on a regular basis to greet and accompany any of the commission staffers who were still at large and might return to work. When he heard a week later that the four men had been remanded to Mariona Prison, Jesús suggested that Kate might be able to visit them there as well.

Kate scheduled her departure for early July. When Jesús returned to Marin in June, the two of them set some time aside to discuss the contacts she could make in El Salvador. Suzanne Bristol placed a call to Emmanuel Baptist Church in San Salvador, where she had done an accompaniment stint in 1984, to ask if they could provide housing for Kate. We arranged for Kate to keep in touch by telephone. The rest was up to her.

The night before Kate's departure, a score of us assembled at Community Congregational Church to wish her Godspeed and safe journey. I was filled with admiration and fear for her, but as she told me years later, she was totally relaxed about the whole venture. "I just knew that nothing would happen to me." As for the rest of us, I'm sure that others were wondering, as I was, whether something drastic might befall her, whether we would ever see Kate again. We stood in a circle, holding hands, and shared blessings and words of good luck. Then Kate drove home for a good night's sleep before heading to the airport the following morning.

Edgar Palacios of Emmanuel Baptist Church met Kate at the airport in El Salvador and provided her with lodging. The next day, following Jesús's suggestion, Kate went to the office of the COMADRES (Committee of Mothers and Relatives of the Politically Imprisoned, Disappeared, and Murdered of El Salvador — Monsignor Oscar Arnulfo Romero) to solicit their advice on how to get into Mariona Prison. The COMADRES, commonly known as the Mothers of the Disappeared, had made a name for themselves on the streets of San Salvador by regularly protesting in characteristic black dresses and white head-scarves the deaths and disappearances of their sons and daughters, and they had at one time shared office space with the Human Rights Commission. They knew the members of the commission, knew how things worked in El Salvador, and, Jesús hoped, would show Kate what to do.

Kate hung out at the COMADRES office for several days, doing some translating for them, until eventually one of them said, "This woman is going to Mariona today. Go with her." So Kate tagged along.

In those days the political prisoners at Mariona were housed separately from the common criminals — the thieves, rapists, and murderers. Nevertheless, prison officials maintained the implausible fiction that no such thing as a political prisoner existed in El Salvador. To get into Mariona, visitors went along with the fiction. Kate's COMADRES chaperone gave her the name of a common prisoner, which Kate dutifully recorded on the sign-in sheet at the prison gate. Kate then stashed her purse in one of the cubbyholes provided and passed through the gate into the large exercise yard that separated the two prison populations. The cell complex to the left housed the common prisoners, but Kate turned the other way and entered the cell block on the right, enquiring after the members of the Human Rights Commission.

When Joaquín Cáceres came into the reception area to greet her, Kate explained her errand. Jesús Campos had sent her to Mariona to see whether she could be of assistance. To her surprise, Joaquín informed Kate that two other *Norteamericanos*, both lawyers, had preceded her to Mariona that day on similar missions: Lisa Brodyaga from Texas and Bill Van Wyck from Washington, D.C. Both were inside at that moment, conversing with the others. Lisa and Bill came out into the receiving room; after speaking with the three of them for a few minutes, Kate took her leave, promising to return the following week.

She returned every Sunday and soon became friends with the five prisoners, and with their family members as well. Her calm, humorous approachability, her no-big-deal attitude, had the same effect on the men in

Mariona as it had had on us. And as they came to trust Kate, and to understand that she represented an organization that was willing to provide long-term accompaniment to the commission, they began to ask her to do little jobs for them. Their first request was for the commission's seal and a supply of letterhead. They had work to do, messages to send.

By then, two other members of the Human Rights Commission had resumed their duties at the commission's office in the neighborhood called Urbanización La Esperanza, a few blocks from the U.S. Embassy. Kate spent her days there with Pablo Martinez and Cecilia Pérez, conveying the messages she carried from the imprisoned men. Once Kate had delivered the letterhead and seal, the prisoners began corresponding with outside organizations and preparing paid advertisements denouncing human rights abuses for distribution to the Salvadoran media. For this latter task, they needed a typewriter. Kate conveyed their request to Cecilia, who somehow had one smuggled in. As the men prepared their ads and announcements, they directed Kate to deliver them. "Take this one to *El Mundo* and this one to the Catholic radio station."

Kate soon found that she could pass as a Salvadoran. She modified her Spanish to include Salvadoran colloquialisms and a Salvadoran accent. She discovered that some native Salvadorans have her skin color and ruddy hair. She adopted the clothing styles she saw around her. She fit in. She felt at home.

By the time Kate's first stint in El Salvador drew to an end, she had won the trust of the men in Mariona, and they had won her lasting allegiance and affection. With Herbert and Reynaldo she had become, as she puts it, good buddies.

Reflecting back on all the volunteers MITF sent to El Salvador, Joaquín Cáceres remembers Kate more vividly than any of the others. "She is very affectionate," he says. "The fact of her affection was like an opportunity to tell about your problems. When she asks, 'How are you?' you can tell her. She was always there, with all of us. We came to trust her quickly in Mariona. Her relationship was mostly with Herbert and Reynaldo, but once I saw their trust in her, and her way of treating us, it wasn't difficult for me to trust her, too."

Of all the people we sent to El Salvador, Kate was closest to the commission members. As I later said from time to time, we at MITF spent the next five years following Kate Bancroft's heart around El Salvador.

The men in Mariona gave Kate one last chore before she flew back to Marin. They had drawn up a work plan for the office, which they gave to her during her last visit, asking her to assemble the staff who had not yet returned and instructing her to deliver the work plan to them. By the time Kate caught her plane, the Human Rights Commission of El Salvador was back at work and already planning the enormous task that lay ahead — the preparation, inside Mariona Prison, of their report, *Torture in El Salvador*. Having discovered 430 other political prisoners in Mariona, all but four of whom had suffered torture at the hands of their captors, the five men decided to resume the work of the commission right where they were by gathering and publishing the testimonies of their co-tenants.

By the time we greeted Kate in Marin, we had initiated plans to develop her first mission into the work that would define MITF for the next five years: the Accompaniment Project for the Human Rights Commission of El Salvador. It took a while, however, to recruit other volunteers. While we waited, putting word out over the nationwide solidarity network that we were seeking volunteers to accompany the commission, Kate was our mainstay, which was fine with her. There was nowhere she would rather be than with her new friends in El Salvador, nothing she would rather do than help them in their work. During the weeks of her first sojourn in El Salvador, Kate's motivation had switched from her belief in a cause to her friendship for the commission members. She flew south at every opportunity. Between July 1986 and October 1987, Kate made six trips to El Salvador.

By the time Kate made her second trip in late September 1986, the men inside Mariona were hard at work interviewing every other political prisoner as preparation for writing *Torture in El Salvador*. Having made friends with Herbert Anaya on her first visit, Kate now extended that friendship to Herbert's wife, Mirna, and their five children. The oldest Anaya child, Rosa, had lost her right arm at age five when a car driven by a drunk driver jumped a San Salvador sidewalk and struck her. Once a year, Rosa flew to Shriners Hospital in Houston, Texas, for adjustment of her prosthesis. Kate suggested to Mirna that next time, Rosa might go to the Shriners Hospital in San Francisco and stay with Kate at her apartment in San Geronimo Valley. Mirna liked the idea and arranged the change of venue with the Shriners. Rosa spent January 1987 with Kate in San Geronimo Valley, making friends there with children her age. Rosa's connection with San Geronimo families paid dividends months later when her brothers and sisters came with her to seek sanctuary there.

Kate made her fourth trip in March 1987, just after Herbert, Reynaldo, and Rafael were released from Mariona. Miguel had been freed in November and Joaquín in December, so Kate was reunited with all of them at their office in Urbanización La Esperanza. The Human Rights Commission of El Salvador was up and running again, and Kate slipped into the role that would define the work of all volunteers who followed. Labor groups, church groups, and human rights groups corresponded with the commission from the United States and Europe, and Kate translated the letters back and forth. When solidarity delegations came to visit the commission, as they did every few days, Kate interpreted for them when they met with Herbert and the others. She ran errands and accompanied the members when they had business away from the office. She showed the ropes to Patrick Hughes, a lawyer from Michigan whom we had recruited as an acccompanier. Together, she and Patrick rented a small house with funds MITF provided, the first of many "volunteer" houses. She deepened her relationships with the members of the commission and their families.

This laid wonderful groundwork for what followed. Having relied thus far on Kate to be our link to the commission, we decided that the time had come to formalize arrangements. Suzanne Bristol and I flew down at the end of the month for a series of meetings with the commission. We wanted to meet the members ourselves, hammer out the details of MITF's Accompaniment Project, and make it official. I was somewhat fearful about going, but I was excited at the prospect of finally meeting these men about whom I had now heard so much. I hardly knew what to expect.

Thank goodness Suzanne went with me. She had been there before and spoke a little Spanish. When we deplaned from our overnight flight into the steamy, crowded airport, she guided me through customs, identified the uniforms of the ubiquitous armed personnel, led me through baggage claim, and flagged a cab at the curb out front. As I immediately discovered, March is El Salvador's hottest month. By the time we reached our hotel, I had soaked through my shirt and needed a shower and nap. While I collapsed, Suzanne called the commission office to confirm our appointment the following morning.

That evening, we found an open-air restaurant across the street and enjoyed some delicious chicken in the cool night air. When I returned to my room, I couldn't sleep. Helicopters and distant thumps (mortars? bombs?) kept me awake. My room was hot. I decided to turn on the light to read, but the electricity was off, so I lay in the dark and imagined dreadful things.

The next day warmed up before breakfast. I took a cold shower when I crawled out of my wrinkled bed but dampened my shirt before we finished eating. We caught a taxi and directed the cabbie to a roundabout in the neighborhood of the commission's office. We paid him and got out. The tropical heat bore down, wilting us as we blundered through the neighborhood, following Kate's handwritten, confusing directions as best we could. In those days, one simply did not ask people on the street how to find the commission, nor did one take a cab directly to their door. Because the security forces maintained constant surveillance — employing taxi drivers, street vendors, and others — one paid off the cabbie blocks away and proceeded on foot.

Finally, we stopped before a building that matched Kate's description: heavy metal front door to the left, equally heavy metal garage door to the right. In the middle of the garage door was the steel-covered entry with a peep slot at eye level and a buzzer button alongside. After we buzzed, someone peered out at us through the slot, then swung open the door and admitted us to the waiting room that had been converted from a garage. We shuffled in and greeted the eight or ten campesinos who waited there to give testimonies.

An interior window opened into the waiting area. I peeped in and saw Kate talking to someone. When I called to her, she came out through the kitchen to usher us in and show us around. It all seemed a little chaotic — and very hot — to me. In the far room, two women (Cecilia and another typist) attended to the people who had come in to make their *denuncias* — campesinos, mostly, who took their turns in the chairs by the typists' desks to tell their stories of beatings and bombings and rapes and tortures and death. I made seven trips to El Salvador before peace came in January 1992 and never once saw the chairs by the typists' desks sitting empty. Cecilia once told me that when she started that work, she would sit weeping over her typewriter day in and day out until eventually she got used to it. The poor of El Salvador knew how to find the commission, despite the secret location of the office. By bus and on foot they came, from every corner of the country, to record what had happened to them and their families and their friends in this one place where people listened.

Kate showed us the offices of the press section, the administrative section, and the international relations section — gritty rooms in need of paint with jumbles of documents and newspapers in the corners and on the desks. She introduced us to the two organizations upstairs that sublet space from the commission and to the young refugees who used a storage room at the back of the garage for the first headquarters of their fledgling organization — CRIPDES, the Christian Committee for the Displaced of El Salvador. A shy elderly woman with wrinkled brown skin and a gap-toothed smile prepared tortillas and vegetable broth in the kitchen. Several people stood in line behind a young man on the single telephone, waiting their turns. Finally, Kate brought us back to the central reception area, the walls of which were covered with photographs of slain commission members and charts of human rights abuses, and introduced us to the men who had recently published *Torture in El Salvador* from inside Mariona Prison.

We spent the balance of the morning chatting with Kate and getting acquainted with Patrick Hughes, our new volunteer, whom we knew only through his letter of application and phone calls. The members of the commission would sit down with us after lunch for our first official meeting. Over several long afternoons in the week to come, Patrick and Kate translated for us as we sat for hours in meetings with Herbert, Reynaldo, Joaquín, Miguel, and Rafael.

It took me a while to get used to the style of work there, to get over wondering how anything ever got done in the stifling heat, in this casual atmosphere where grimy children wandered into meetings to crawl into someone's lap and where everyone stopped to chat with everyone else on the way from one room to another. It was a different reality, and a strange one. Every trip outside the office had to be elaborately planned to ensure that a gringo would be available to drive the car, that someone knew where you were going and when you were expected to return.

Kate and Patrick patiently taught us the ropes and made conversation possible for me, the gringo without Spanish. Kate especially knew how to read between the lines of what was being said, how to read the emotional content of the words she translated back and forth. When we broke at midafternoon from our first long session with the commission members, Kate leaned over toward Suzanne and me to whisper that things were going well. "The vibes are good," she said. "I think this is going to work out."

Suzanne and I were gratified to hear that but wondered whether the vibes would remain good when we broached a topic we had discussed at great length before coming to El Salvador — whether the commission was affiliated with the FMLN or any of its constituent political organizations. We had a great deal to work out in those initial meetings — finances, security arrangements, recruiting procedures and requirements, orientation of volunteers, publicity — but all of these arrangements were contingent upon first confirming that for both our organizations, the project was a go. On our side, we needed to know whether the Human Rights Commission was the impartial monitoring organization it claimed to be or the partisan organ of the guerrilla fighters that the U.S. Embassy claimed it to be.

I had given the whole matter a great deal of thought. It seemed to me that there were essentially three possibilities. The first was that the members of the commission had no political affiliation of any kind, that they were all motivated in their work by the carnage that swept their country. The second possibility was that the commission members did have political affiliations, or at least political leanings, but that whatever these might be, they stopped somewhere short of an organizational connection with the guerrillas. Commission members might well know various members of the armed resistance — in a country as small as El Salvador, it was all but certain that they did — without in any way being under their control. The commission and the guerrillas might share aspirations for a more just society without coordinating the pursuit of those aspirations. The third possibility was that the FMLN and the commission were in fact closely linked, that the FMLN called the shots at the commission, and that they did indeed coordinate their different activities in pursuit of the same goal. Within these three general possibilities, of course, any number of permutations might exist.

Having determined to ask the commission members about their connection, if any, to the FMLN, we then had to decide under what circumstances we would work with them. We also had to wonder whether they would be completely candid with two gringos fresh off the plane from California. If they *were* connected with the FMLN, would they tell us so? And did we have any right to expect them to? In a country like El Salvador, where barbaric social and political inequalities are enforced by any means necessary, including the wholesale slaughter of innocents, did the moral imperative to resist outweigh any niceties about whether to resist with a rifle, with political organizing, or with documentation of human rights abuses? Should the day ever dawn in the United States when dissident clergypeople and labor organizers are dragged from their homes in the night and decapitated, might not I feel compelled to resist with force of arms, or to abet those who do?

The Salvadoran popular organizations went to great lengths to disavow any imputed connections with the guerrillas, and the commission, as an organization claiming opposition to human rights abuses committed by any parties to the Salvadoran conflict, had greater reason than most to insist on their nonpartisanship, greater motivation to deny any connections with the FMLN they might indeed have.

When we raised the question during our second day of meetings, they answered with great care. They told us that as Salvadoran citizens, they reserved the right to hold whatever political philosophy suited each of them and even reserved the right to sympathize with the political ideals espoused by any faction of the guerrilla fighting forces. They further claimed that their individual political leanings did not compromise the work of the commission so long as they held those leanings subservient to their organizational commitment to accurately report any and all human rights abuses and so long as they had no organizational affiliation with the FMLN. They then told us that the commission was not part of the FMLN, that the commission did not take orders from the FMLN, and that the commission opposed activities or policies of the FMLN whenever those activities or policies violated the United Nations' 1948 Universal Declaration of Human Rights, on which they based their work.

I believed them. For one thing, I confess, I was inclined to do so. In my eyes, their courage, their suffering, and their cause all represented ideals that I could only hope to emulate, should I ever find myself in a situation as desperate and dangerous as theirs. For another, the Human Rights Commission of El Salvador had long ago earned affiliate status with the United Nations Commission on Human Rights and had for the better part of a decade been invited to present documentation before the U.N. commission at its annual meeting in Geneva. Evidently, the United Nations considered the Nongovernmental Human Rights Commission of El Salvador a legitimate organization. Finally, anyone who troubled themselves to read the monthly reports published by the Human Rights Commission could see in an instant that they did report violations committed by the guerrillas and in fact had a category exclusively devoted to such violations.

Whatever their politics might or might not have been, the commission members had staked their lives on the issue of human rights, and on that territory MITF was more than prepared to walk with them. So walk with them we did.

Kate steered us through this delicate conversation with discretion and care and was relieved when we concluded it as we did. I have no doubt that her affection and regard for the members of the commission was such that she would have continued to accompany them and assist them even if MITF had decided to bail out. With the issue laid to rest, we devoted the balance of our sessions to more mundane details.

Kate and Patrick invited Suzanne and me to dinner one evening at their rented house just off Avenida San Antonio Abad. During the meal, they described what it was like to live under constant surveillance, to leave all the decisions about their movements and activities to the commission, and to learn the disciplines of unquestioning service. Kate chafed under these restrictions less than Patrick — less, in fact, than anyone we ever sent to El Salvador. She would have been hard pressed to come up with anything she would rather be doing with her life than hanging out at the commission's office, getting to know its members, and helping them in any way she could.

Kate understood perfectly that North Americans had to take their cues from the commission in all things, had to trust that the commission members' instincts had been honed by years of working under precarious and threatening circumstances. North Americans, even the wisest and best-intentioned, were prone to security blunders and to thinking that their judgment was as good as the Salvadorans', which, of course, it wasn't. When I continued in a taxi a conversation that had started on the sidewalk or asked people about their travel plans or mentioned in a public place the names of popular organizations, Kate would catch my eye or poke me. She knew that members of the commission spotted surveillance cars that followed us as we drove about the city, cars that I never noticed until they were pointed out to me.

Our meetings with the five men were often interrupted by someone coming in to consult about an errand that needed running. These interruptions would sometimes stretch to half an hour as the commission members considered who should go, which car should be taken, what other errands could be run while they were out, when they were expected back, and so on. When I began to chafe, Kate would tell me to cool it, reminding me that these guys had just been released from long imprisonments during which they had had the crap beat out of them; arranging their movements, though time-consuming, was crucial.

Among the many attributes of Kate's that endeared her to the commission members were her simple trust in them and her patience. Kate had an opportunity to exercise her instinctive deference on her next trip to El Salvador — her fifth — in September 1987. Journalist Mary Jo McConaghy contacted Kate to ask if she might tag along when Kate next went to El Salvador, then write a story about her and the commission. When Kate discussed this proposal with Suzanne and me, we thought it was a terrific idea. It would give the commission some much-needed international exposure, and it would also publicize our project on their behalf and perhaps help us in our recruiting.

Kate shared our enthusiasm but knew she could not give Mary Jo permission to publish until the commission saw her finished story. Only if Mary Jo accepted those terms would Kate allow her to tag along. With some understandable reluctance, Mary Jo agreed. She accompanied the accompanier to El Salvador and returned with Kate to the United States to write her story, hoping to secure the commission's permission to print it. Before Mary Jo finished her work, Kate was called back to El Salvador.

On the morning of October 26, 1987, Kate awoke suddenly at 4:30 in the morning, jolted into consciousness by something she could not identify. She looked at her clock, wondered sleepily what had woken her, then rolled over and slept again. When she woke at the normal time, she went jogging, then returned home. Her telephone rang a few minutes later. It was Suzanne. Suzanne had just heard something over the radio about a Salvadoran human rights worker who had been killed that morning while taking his children to school. Suzanne hadn't heard the name of the victim. "Does Herbert have school-age children?" Suzanne asked.

Remembering that she had been jolted from sleep earlier that morning, Kate told Suzanne that she would call her back in a few minutes, then dialed the number for the commission's office in San Salvador. Pablo answered. After identifying herself, Kate asked, "¿A Herbert no le pasó nada, verdad?" Pablo replied, "Como no. Lo mataron." Nothing has happened to Herbert, has it? Yes, it has. They killed him.

With Pablo's words, Kate's usually placid demeanor instantly vanished and was replaced by a wild and inconsolable grief. "No, no, no," she cried into the phone. "It can't be." As she wept and searched for words, Pablo tried to calm her, then handed the receiver to Reynaldo, who confirmed that Herbert had been killed by unknown assailants that morning at 6:30 — 4:30 Pacific Standard Time — when he took his children to school. He gave Kate the remaining details, then asked her, "When are you coming?" She told Reynaldo she would be there as soon as she could.

Kate called Suzanne back, confirmed the worst, then drove her stepdaughter to school, turning left through a red light as she did so. By the time Kate returned, Suzanne had phoned me with the news and suggested we call a press conference in San Francisco that afternoon. When I called Kate, she was still on the edge of hysteria, wild with grief, all but incomprehensible. Between sobs she told me that she had to get to El Salvador right away, whatever it took. The commission needed her help, and she didn't want to miss Herbert's funeral. When I asked whether she would be able to attend the press conference, she said she probably would; it would likely take a few days to obtain a visa from the Salvadoran Consulate in San Francisco.

Later that morning, while Suzanne and I made arrangements for the early afternoon press conference, Kate called the consulate to request an emergency visa so she could attend a friend's funeral in El Salvador. The official said, "You want to go to Herbert Anaya's funeral, don't you? We won't be able to issue you a visa."

When we assembled in the city for the press conference, Kate told us that her visa request had been denied. Desperate to get to El Salvador, she was stymied. Later that evening Kate joined the noisy all-night vigil outside the Salvadoran Consulate, unaware that Suzanne had thought of a potential way for her to get to El Salvador.

Suzanne had heard of a man named Ely Bergmann who served as a Salvadoran consular official in San Antonio, Texas. The word in the solidarity movement was that Ely would issue a visa to anyone at a moment's notice. Suzanne called a friend, Suzy Prenger, who worked at CRISPAZ (Christians for Peace in El Salvador) in San Antonio, and Suzy confirmed that the Ely Bergmann stories were true. On Wednesday morning, Suzanne drove to San Francisco, found Kate among the demonstrators in front of the consulate, and said, "I think we have a solution." But time was running out. Herbert's funeral was scheduled for Friday.

Kate gave Suzanne her passport, which Suzanne sent by Federal Express to Suzy Prenger while Kate rushed home to make airline reservations and last-minute arrangements. As the calls flew back and forth between Texas and the Bay Area on Wednesday evening and Thursday morning, it became clear that there was not enough time to get Kate's passport stamped and back to her before flight time Thursday night. One last possibility remained: perhaps Suzy Prenger could Fed Ex the passport to the airline ticket office at Los Angeles International Airport, where Kate had an hour-long layover. Suzy would see what she could do.

Just before Kate left home, Suzanne gave her something to take along: prints of the photo Suzanne had taken of Herbert at the commission office the preceding March. Jan Bauman — MITF's unofficial photographer — had printed a score of five-by-sevens, as well as an eight-by-twelve. Kate took the photos and headed for SFO, praying that her passport would be waiting for her in Los Angeles.

Kate had done a lot of praying in that desperate two-day stretch, most of it to Herbert. Frantic to get to El Salvador in time for his funeral, she prayed to him for a solution as she drove from one place to another. "Help me, Herbert. Help me find a way." Then, as she tells it, she heard his voice saying, "That body is not me." Still later, she sensed Herbert's presence. With it came a feeling of total calm that replaced her desperation. She felt at peace. Later on, she discovered she is not the only person to have had postdeath experiences of Herbert, nor is she the only one to have had inexplicable experiences with him during his life.

Kate hopped the shuttle to Los Angeles, then hurried to the TACA Airlines ticket counter. There it was. Suzanne and Suzy Prenger and Ely Bergmann had managed to get her passport there on time. Kate boarded the midnight flight for El Salvador, arrived there Friday morning, and grabbed a cab outside the arrivals terminal. The cabbie drove her straight to the church in the center of San Salvador where people had gathered for Herbert's funeral.

Kate had hidden the large picture of Herbert among other papers and had stuffed the smaller ones inside her waistband, knowing that she would have been denied entry by customs officials at the airport if they were found. Now, as she nudged her way through the thousands of people jamming the church for Herbert's funeral, she fished out the photos. There, near the front, at the side of Herbert's coffin, sat Mirna and the children. Kate edged and shouldered her way up to them, then touched Mirna on the shoulder. Mirna and the kids threw their arms around her. Then, when Kate gave her the pictures of Herbert, Mirna burst into tears.

The children clustered near. "Why are you crying, Mama?" they asked. "Because I am so happy to see Kate," she answered. As happy as she was to see Kate, it was not the only reason she wept. The grief and strain that Mirna experienced at Herbert's death and in the days that followed would have disabled a lesser person, but she had somehow kept herself together, made all the decisions about the funeral and the cemetery and the press releases, overcome the archbishop's reluctance to hold the funeral on church property, and managed to look after her children, at least until Kate handed her that wonderful picture that captured Herbert as he had been, humorous and proud and fierce and gentle all at once, and utterly indomitable. Her tears were tears of happiness to know that Kate had come to be at her side, and tears of grief to have lost her man and all that he was.

Those prints were widely distributed. I have seen Suzanne's image of Herbert in publications and on posters and banners all over El Salvador and throughout the North American solidarity network. The big print now hangs in a prominent place on the wall of the commission's new offices in San Salvador.

Kate stayed with Mirna and the kids as they moved from one place to another during the next three weeks, never sleeping in one house any longer than necessary, trying to evade the armed men who kept Mirna under surveillance in the days immediately following Herbert's death. On the day after the Anaya family boarded a plane for Canada, where they lived for the next seven months, Kate returned to Marin.

After Herbert's death, Kate did not return to El Salvador for several years, but her ties with Mirna and the children became ever stronger. When Mirna was recruited by CODEHUCA (the umbrella human rights organization for Central America) to become their general secretary in May 1988, she was eager to take the job and to resume the work that had defined both Herbert's life and her own. But she needed someone to care for her children while she made a previously planned tour of the United States and then while she preceded the children to Costa Rica, where CODEHUCA had its offices.

Mirna called Kate from Toronto to ask if Kate might be able to find families who would house the children for a while. Kate allowed that she might. And so it was that on her way to San José to assume her duties at CO-DEHUCA, Mirna deposited Rosa, Neto, Gloria, Rafa, and Edith in the care of Kate's friends in the San Geronimo Valley.

When peace returned to El Salvador, Mirna and her children moved back, hopefully for good. Mirna resumed her work at the commission and took a position at the National University, serving as general secretary.

Those five children lost a father in October 1987, but they gained a network of extended family in Marin and elsewhere — people who have made room for them in their lives and in their hearts. And no one more than Kate. She is almost their second mother. She has been there when they needed her, just as she has been for Mirna. Whenever the Anaya kids came to live in Marin, as they did on three occasions, they lived with various families. But on the weekends, the five of them often spent the night in Kate's tiny apartment, talking the night away before falling asleep in a heap on the bed.

Everyone should have a friend like Kate Bancroft — someone utterly nonjudgmental whose good humor invites disclosure, someone who has put her life together in such a way that she can pick up and go on short notice when needed, someone whose interest in people far outstrips her interest in money and possessions. Kate keeps her luxuriant red hair cropped to about two inches and giggles when you run your fingers through it. Her easy demeanor and comfortable ego make her a great traveling companion. She relates to people of all ages, and her varied life experiences make for fascinating listening. She hugs easily and tells you she loves you when you do a good thing. She bears no grudges that I know of.

Mainly, though, Kate uses her innate radar to seek out people struggling for justice, then provides them with steadfast companionship. Best of all, her help does not feel like help, but like friendship and interest. Kate knows everybody's secrets because everybody trusts her. We simply couldn't have chosen a better person to bring our task force together with the Human Rights Commission of El Salvador. But we didn't choose Kate; she fell into our laps. In the trusting space that she created, MITF and the commission linked arms. I like to think that something very good came of that.

_ 3 _

HERBERT

I knew Herbert Anaya only briefly. But of all of the people I met in El Salvador, Herbert made the most lasting and powerful impression on me. Even now, a decade after the time we spent together in March 1987, when I look at Herbert's poster on my wall and read there the words inscribed on his tombstone, I miss him.

I happened to meet Herbert when he was at the pinnacle of his brief career as leader of the Human Rights Commission of El Salvador. At the time, he was undoubtedly the best-known opposition figure in the country, in whose person the aspirations of the Salvadoran popular movement were concentrated. He and four other members of the Human Rights Commission had just been released from the political section at Mariona Prison, where they had published their 160-page report, *Torture in El Salvador*, a perfectly audacious undertaking that had won them international acclaim and the amazed admiration of their countrymen and -women. Against the repressive Salvadoran security forces he then flung his bouyant personality, his bravura, and his defiance, as if to say, Kill me if you like, or torture me again, but know that you cannot cow me or silence me or make me afraid. From his perch at the Human Rights Commission, Herbert spent the last seven months of his life proclaiming for all to see and hear that his government ruled its people with terror, torture, and assassination. I happened to meet him just as he rang up the curtain on this final act of his life. It was truly something to behold.

Herbert's outrageously forthright condemnation of human rights abuses endeared him to the oppressed of his country — the majority of the population. He was released from Mariona, along with fifty-two other humanitarian workers, as part of a prisoner exchange between the Salvadoran government and the FMLN arranged by El Salvador's Catholic Church and the International Red Cross. Back at the commission's office Herbert authored the paid advertisements that the commission placed in the *Diario El Mundo* on a regular basis. He wrote the ads longhand, as if he were merely transferring to paper the messages he had already formed in his mind. Between February and October 1987, these paid ads were virtually the only coherent attacks against the government that appeared in the national press. He spent much of the money donated to the commission on those ads and always said that the opposition voice had to be made available to those Salvadorans too frightened to appear at rallies or visit the offices of organizations promoting respect for human rights.

When Herbert called a press conference on behalf of the commission, every newspaper, every radio station, every television station showed up. Even the foreign reporters would appear. He drew attention because of what he was willing to say and because of how he said it; he was the voice of the Salvadoran conscience, and an entertaining voice at that. His assassination sealed his status among the Salvadorans as a hero and a martyr.

Herbert was a charmer, and an impish one. Without his charm and persistence, he would never have won Mirna. Herbert and Mirna met when they both arrived early for the first session of Political Doctrine II at the National University in the spring semester of 1974. Both were twenty. Both shared a zeal for the political activism of the day. They soon found themselves engaged in common activities and organizations: the Society of Scholarship Students, where Mirna was the only woman, and a left-wing student front, where they marched together for university autonomy from the military and for more university support of the popular movement. They studied together, discussed politics, and became close friends. But Mirna's resolute commitment to the popular movement precluded romantic involvements. She wanted to dedicate herself to the work, unencumbered by a boyfriend in facing the risks that work entailed. Herbert bided his time.

In the summer of 1975, the National Guard took over the university's Santa Ana campus and busted up the floats and banners that students had prepared for a demonstration. In response, the students at the main campus in San Salvador planned a protest march, despite a warning from General Romero (the head of the armed forces) that they would face "the ultimate consequences" if they proceeded into the streets. Perhaps goaded by Romero's threat, 1,500 students turned out and marched noisily through the streets of the capital, straight into the ambush that awaited them in front of the maternity hospital. While surveillance aircraft circled overhead, army troops and riot police sealed off the street with tanks, then opened fire on the demonstrators, killing nine. One girl was crushed to death against a wall by a tank.

During the melee that ensued, many were injured, including Mirna, who climbed up on a bridge to quarterback the frantic students to safety, then broke her knee when she jumped down to elude the approaching riot police. Two friends lugged her to the hospital, where the doctors encased her leg in plaster and sent her home. Four days later, Herbert showed up to bring her the latest news — that the savage response to the student's peaceful, if raucous, demonstration had galvanized the country. During the August holidays, he returned often to keep her up-to-date.

When classes resumed in September, Herbert and Mirna joined the United Front of Revolutionary Students Salvador Allende (FUERSA) and campaigned for FUERSA in the upcoming student election. When FUERSA won the election and gained control of the Student Association, the pace of their work intensified as they advocated widening the focus of the Student Association beyond campus issues to broader social issues and the popular movement.

On her way to take a sheaf of paid advertisements to the newspapers one day, Mirna slipped in a puddle and reinjured her knee. This time the doctors operated to set the badly dislocated kneecap, and Mirna's second rehabilitation promised to take even longer than the first. She needed a great deal of help getting around, and Herbert was the one to provide it — along with selections of the poetry he liked to write. With this, their relationship finally shifted to romance, but at no sacrifice to Mirna's activism.

In a country and a culture where women are expected to accommodate the wishes of men, Mirna was a formidable exception. As was true for so many in El Salvador's popular organizations, Mirna's activism on behalf of the people was her defining characteristic. She was not about to subjugate her essence to any macho man. So Herbert proposed a political accommodation, explaining that they could do their social work better *juntos*. Of the two, Herbert was the more idealistic, spiritual, poetic, and flaky. Mirna was the more realistic and pragmatic. Herbert proposed that they combine their attributes in the struggle.

By Mirna's account, Herbert became more practical when their relationship progressed beyond friendship, although it took a while for Mirna to convince her father of that. On the night Mirna took Herbert home to introduce him to the family, he stayed up late drinking with her dad and passed out on the floor.

Herbert was often careless of his appearance and took puckish pleasure in tweaking people's sensibilities with his outlandish behavior. During the months he spent at Mariona Prison, he sometimes went around in his underwear, thereby offending the leaders of the Political Prisoners Association, who would ask him to set a better example. But he couldn't be troubled and told them, "We are all familiar with one another. Why bother?"

Joaquín Cáceres tells how Herbert would often walk around the commission's office with his shirt unbuttoned and his pants undone, almost falling down. And he liked to leave his underpants hanging up in the bathroom, where visitors would see them. Several of our volunteers have told me of his habit of initiating conversations by sprawling out full length on the desk where they were sitting, propping up his head with his palm, and yakking the hours away. No subject was beyond his interest, and the more intimate, the better. With his charm, humor, and familiarity, he had a facility for getting people to open up about their beliefs, their romances, and especially their dreams.

During that period in the late 1970s when the Salvadoran situation was becoming so desperate, Herbert needed all of his infectious good spirits as he simultaneously courted Mirna and deepened his commitment to the poor of El Salvador. As law students, both Herbert and Mirna sought clerical work in the courts; they needed the legal experience and they needed the income. Captures, tortures, and disappearances were becoming commonplace, and when people sought redress in the courts, Herbert and Mirna witnessed firsthand the complete corruption of the legal system. Mirna remembers the case of one young girl who was arrested for carrying a hymnal in which the arresting officers discovered a photograph of Oscar Romero.

In the midst of this frightening time, Herbert and Mirna began their life together and started their family. Their first child, Rosa, was born in 1976. Neto followed in 1977, then Gloria in 1979, Rafa in 1980, and Edith in 1982. In 1980, Oscar Romero offered to marry them. Romero had been Mirna's priest in the barrio where she grew up, and he was still her friend despite the childhood pranks she used to pull on him. When her devout mother would send her and her brother to catechism class a half hour early, they used the extra time to mess up his papers or clamber over the roof and up the belfry. Before he could marry them, however, Romero was assassinated. Herbert and Mirna finally wed in 1985.

Eventually, Herbert's outrage at the injustices he witnessed daily in court and on campus prompted him to join the Human Rights Commission in 1979, just when Mirna was pregnant with Rafa and repression against the commission was about to begin in earnest. In 1980, two commission members — María Magdalena Enríquez and Ramón Valladares Pérez — were assassinated, the commission's offices were bombed on March 2 and again on September 9, and the government began distributing propaganda accusing the commission of being part of the international Communist conspiracy. Despite this increasing pressure, the commission continued to denounce human rights abuses by giving press interviews, purchasing advertisements in the newspapers when they couldn't persuade anyone to interview them, and preparing briefs for and giving testimonies to international human rights monitoring organizations, especially the United Nations Commission on Human Rights. In those days only the Human Rights Commission of El Salvador and Socorro Jurídico (Legal Aid) were doing this kind of work, so joining the commission was regarded as almost suicidal. Mirna was afraid for him.

During 1980, the killings, threats, and bombings forced the commission to move its offices twice and led many of its members to flee to Costa Rica, Nicaragua, and Mexico. The commission began the year with fourteen members working in San Salvador and ended it with six, including Herbert, who worked in the legal department taking testimonies. In February 1981, Archbishop Rivera y Damas offered them space at his office complex. They moved into a one-room office, which they shared with the COMADRES and Socorro Jurídico. For the next three years, they made do in that cramped space, happy to have a place where people could safely come to give their testimonies. They cooked meals in a shack out back and gave their press conferences under the mango tree in the courtyard.

Herbert began taking a more public role, participating in the courtyard press conferences, providing human rights information to diplomats, and petitioning the various security forces for the release of prisoners. In 1982, he worked out of the commission's Mexico City office for six months and continued to travel there periodically once he returned to El Salvador that November.

Between 1981 and 1983, the security forces killed five additional members of the commission, including the commission's president, Marianella Garcia Villas, in March 1983. Mirna's fears for Herbert were well founded, but he kept out of harm's way while continuing his work. In late 1984 Herbert went on tour in the eastern part of the country, absenting himself from the city for a year. During this time, he documented human rights violations out in the campo, where the FMLN engaged the army, whose military operations included bombing of villages, crop burnings, and dislocation of the peasantry. How much contact Herbert may have had with the guerrillas during this period, I have never determined. But it is probably safe to assume that he couldn't have spent that much time in and around Morazán Department without significant contact with the ERP (Revolutionary Force of the People), the arm of the FMLN that controlled northern Morazán. The ERP's political tendencies coincided with Herbert's own.

When he returned to San Salvador in 1985, he found conditions there extremely difficult. The commission had moved out of the archbishop's complex and rented offices of their own a few blocks away. Surveillance was intense. On November 8, the National Police captured Joaquín Cáceres, ratcheting up the pressure on the commission even further. By the time the Treasury Police captured Herbert in May 1986, he had emerged as the commission's leader and spokesperson.

Herbert and three other members of the Human Rights Commission — Reynaldo Blanco, Miguel Angel Montenegro, Rafael Terezón — were picked up off the streets of San Salvador on May 26 and May 29, 1986, by armed men in civilian clothing. This was the standard method of capture by Salvadoran security forces and indicated their efficiency in surveilling those members of the popular organizations whom they considered subversive. Some captures were made at night by men who stormed into victims' houses;

some were made in neighborhoods near where the victims worked; others were made in broad daylight in stores or restaurants or on the street. Armed men, usually dressed in civilian clothing or partial uniforms, would approach their targets and, without producing a warrant or announcing their intentions, wrestle them into a waiting vehicle, often a Jeep Cherokee with polarized windows.

Sometimes the bodies of those captured would be found several days later at the side of the road or in a body dump or in the parking lot of the Camino Real Hotel, where members of the international press maintained their offices. Sometimes the victims would never be seen again, alive or dead; they would be disappeared, leaving family members and colleagues in a limbo of despairing uncertainty for months and sometimes years. Rarely, as happened with Herbert and the three others, those captured would surface in one of the political prisons.

Herbert was shopping in the Mejicanos district of San Salvador shortly after 5:00 P.M. on May 26 when they came for him. As he stepped out of a store, a blue, double-cabin pickup truck with tinted windows pulled to the curb in front of him. Three men dressed in civilian clothing got out of the truck with pistols drawn, forced him into the back cab, handcuffed him, blindfolded him, and threw him to the floor. They removed his documents, examined them, and said, "This is the one."

After driving for fifteen minutes or so, the truck arrived at a prearranged location, stopped, and blew its horn. Herbert heard an iron gate being opened. Once inside, he was taken from the truck and led up a flight of stairs into a room that he remembered as very hot. Peeking through his imperfectly tied blindfold, he could see that his captors wore camouflage uniforms without insignia. When he asked where he was, they told him he would never know. They also assured him that he would not be tortured or killed. One of them said, "We don't kill people here anymore; that was before."

For the next thirteen days, operating in shifts, his captors accused him of collaborating with the armed guerrillas, tried to extract confessions from him, threatened him with the capture of his family, and told him that they had captured other members of the commission and that those others had abandoned him.

Meanwhile, Mirna and others urgently tried to locate Herbert. They soon found out, thanks to one of those strange coincidences that strained family ties and political loyalties so often during the Salvadoran conflict. Mirna's sister was married to a member of the Treasury Police. Ten hours after Herbert's capture, Mirna's brother-in-law sent word through his wife of Herbert's whereabouts. Mirna immediately filed a writ of habeus corpus, then alerted the archbishop's human rights office (Tutela Legal), Bishop Rosa y Chavez, and the International Red Cross, all of whom contacted the authorities to insist on his safekeeping. The Red Cross sent a representative to visit Herbert at his place of detention.

At the beginning, Herbert was forced to do exercises — push-ups and sit-ups — and compelled to stand with his arms over his head or out to the side for hours at a time. Except for brief periods, they kept him handcuffed and blindfolded. Herbert lost track of time, and the separation between day and night, during the first several days. He was not permitted to sleep. When the interrogators tired, new interrogators replaced them. Nor was he fed. He began to feel ill and to doze on his feet. When they caught him dozing, they would make a loud noise to jolt him awake.

The days he spent standing caused his feet to swell and turn red. A woman whom they identified as a doctor was called in to examine his feet. She gave the captors some pills and told them to administer regular doses. After his release, when thinking about the hallucinations that had gripped him as the days passed by, Herbert came to believe that the pills he swallowed brought them on.

Later, after their repeated demands for his cooperation had failed, the beatings began. They pulled a cloth over his head, covering the blindfold and the rest of his face, and then one of the interrogators silently approached him, delivering a hard blow to his forehead before beginning the questioning again. He beat Herbert on the face and on the head. Someone else slapped him a number of times on the ears, with hands cupped. They beat him until he felt that his whole body was on fire. Then they would lay off for a while before resuming their torture. At times, an interrogator would grab his throat and apply pressure until he was on the verge of unconsciousness.

Herbert did not know where he was being held, but he assumed that it was one of two places — the Depository or the Treasury Police headquarters — because he could hear the whistles and rumbling of trains passing nearby. Those two locations are the only security force installations near railroad tracks. When he told his interrogators that he knew they were keeping him in one of those two places, they said he was wrong, that he was crazy. Having already lost track of time in the hot room always illuminated by two lightbulbs, he did indeed begin to fear for his sanity. In the declaration he later prepared, Herbert described his mental state as the days of interrogation, beatings, sleeplessness, and hunger wore on.

"I held on to the idea that I was not crazy, that I was all right, that I could withstand these trials. I saw human forms on the walls, with lances and helmets, as in medieval times, and I said, 'They are all with me.' Mainly this happened when I took the pills. Moreover, since I have always sweated excessively, I needed water with great urgency. I began to talk with the interrogators about a great number of things; about why we were right, about the crimes they had committed. They had told me that they had captured all the members of the Human Rights Commission there, and that they were all collaborating . . . . Once, an official came in and said that a couple of old women had been captured, and that they were even burning the files in our office. They told me, 'That's what we are going to do to you; you'll see the little surprise that we have in store for you.'

"I told them that I could not collaborate, that there was something inside me that would not let me do this, and that they were wrong about everything of which they accused me. I told them that it was a moral point that would not let me do this, that I was well aware of the consequences, that the worst they could do to me was to kill me, and that this was not a problem because if they killed me, it would be my body, and my soul would continue to work for justice."

But by June 9 Herbert had reached the end of his endurance and signed the papers they put before him without permitting him to read the contents. Then they asked when he had joined the commission. "I told them that I had joined in late 1979, that I had done so out of my own convictions, because I had always been moved by a personal motivation to defend the persecuted among the people. They insisted that I was in the commission by the order of the ERP [the Revolutionary Force of the People, one of the constituent bodies of the FMLN]. I told them that this was not the case, and if they said it was so — and they said they knew everything — then why were they interrogating me? They told me that it was in order that I would say it was so myself. I agreed to everything they said so they would leave me in peace. They calmed down a little, and allowed me to eat. They brought me food and water, and took me to the bathroom."

By coercing Herbert to sign this "confession," the Treasury Police accomplished their apparent goal — verification of their assertion that Herbert (and by extension, the commission) was not an independent human rights monitor, but rather a surreptitious arm of the guerrilla fighting forces. Shortly after Herbert signed the paper, he was driven to the outskirts of San Salvador and incarcerated in the political section of the prison at Mariona, the prison whose cruelly ironic official name — La Esperanza — is the Spanish word for hope.

Once inside Mariona, Herbert was reunited with Reynaldo, Miguel Angel, and Rafael, all three of whom had been interrogated in a similar fashion. There, the four of them were brought together with Joaquín Cáceres, who had already been in Mariona for six months. Once the five members of the commission were reunited inside Mariona, they embarked on a remarkable undertaking. Of the 430 other men serving with them in the political section at Mariona in May 1986 (female political prisoners were incarcerated in the women's prison at Ilopango, near the military air base), all but four had suffered torture upon capture. So the members of the commission set about interviewing each and every one of them, meticulously charting and documenting the specific kinds of torture to which each had been subjected. The result was a 160-page report entitled *Torture in El Salvador*, a detailed portrait of terror published from inside Mariona Prison in September 1986.

Of those interviewed, 138 were laborers, 100 were soldiers, 86 were factory workers, and 46 were farmers; the rest were office workers, technicians, teachers, students, and other professionals. The longest-serving prisoners had been in Mariona since January 1983. Only four of those interviewed had escaped torture; of the rest, the vast majority had been subjected to many of the forty forms of torture depicted in the report by pen-and-ink drawings. Among these were application of "the hood" (the infamous *capucha*), which is made of cloth or rubber and filled with a caustic powder such as lime, then inverted over the head and tied around the neck, causing facial burns and asphyxiation; application of "the airplane," in which a person's hands (or thumbs) and feet are tied together behind the back and the victim is suspended by the hands from the ceiling, causing intense pain and dislocation of different body parts; application of electric shocks to different parts of the body — for example, the ears, chest, tongue, penis, anus, neck, and feet — causing burns; and application of "the bucket," in which the victim is forced to remain standing while a bucket is suspended from a string tied around the genitals and then filled with water. Sleep deprivation, cigarette burns, immersion in water, blows to the testicles, denial of food, removal of clothing, application of drugs, and rape were also used.

The list and the pen-and-ink drawings, which seem to go on and on, are followed by charts that name each of the 434 men and list the tortures to which they were subjected. Each man signed (or thumbprinted, if he was illiterate) his line on the chart. The report concludes with extensive first-person accounts of tortures suffered by eight of the prisoners at Mariona.

When *Torture in El Salvador* was smuggled from Mariona, translated into English, and distributed in North America and Europe by the Marin Interfaith Task Force in late 1986, the response was minimal. *Sojourners* ran an article, as did *The Nation* and several European publications, but in the end, the story of the torture in Mariona Prison, and of the commission's courageous reporting of that torture, made the list of the ten most underreported news stories of 1986. People in the United States didn't seem to care about what Herbert and the others had done, but the people of El Salvador did, and when they were released from Mariona on February 15, 1987, an enthusiastic crowd greeted them outside the gates.

Having recruited Kate Bancroft — and later a Texas lawyer named Lisa Brodyaga, who actually smuggled the torture report from Mariona and translated it into English — we at MITF soon made plans to fly to El Salvador to meet Herbert and the others. Although the public at large knew nothing of our efforts on the commission's behalf, people around the United States who were aware of what was happening in El Salvador knew to contact us if they wanted to help in some way. Feeling reasonably confident that we could recruit a steady stream of accompaniment volunteers for the commission, Suzanne Bristol and I boarded a night flight for El Salvador on March 23, 1987.

My recollections of that first visit to the commission are in some aspects indistinct, in other aspects as vivid as if they happened yesterday. I do not recall the moment I met Herbert, but in the days and nights that followed our first handshake, he made a growing impression on me that distinguished him from the other commission members. I do recall the oppressive heat and humidity; in the room where all of us gathered, an oscillating fan distributed the steamy air evenly among us until the electricity went off, as it often did, in midafternoon. I do recall the respectful knot of shabbily dressed campesino men and women who had made their way to the commission's office to give their testimonies about missing or murdered relatives, about beatings and tortures they had suffered, about bombing and strafing attacks on their rural communities. During the few days of our first visit, one young man removed his shirt for us, exposing the welts and bruises of his beating.

Most vividly of all, I recall the charts and pictures that covered the walls, and the photo albums that rested silently on a shelf in the room where we held our meetings. The charts listed by month and by year the numbers of dead and disappeared, as recorded by the commission and by Socorro Jurídico and Tutela Legal, the other human rights monitoring organizations then operating in El Salvador. The grand total by March 1987 exceeded 50,000. Out of a population of 5,000,000. The pictures showed the seven early members of the Human Rights Commission who had been assassinated by the security forces, Marianella Garcia Villas most prominent among them.

On that first of my many visits to the commission's office, the photo albums held a morbid attraction for me, an attraction I was able to resist for most of the day. Albums like these — notebook-sized, with images of yellow daisies or wistful lovers on the cover — are available in any stationery store. But Suzanne and Kate had told me what was *in* those albums, and I was reluctant to look. Finally, though, late in the afternoon, I found myself alone in that back room. Everyone had stepped out on one errand or another. So I walked over to the shelf, picked up an album, and began paging through it, confronting the reality of El Salvador as graphically as I could without driving out to the body dumps myself. By the dozens, by the scores, by the hundreds, I saw page after page after page of disfigured corpses — mostly men, some women; some fully dressed, some naked, some partially clothed; some riddled with bullets, some knife-carved, some showing the welts and burn marks of violent tortures and beatings. Here was the grisly human residue of a paramilitary machine run amok, a paramilitary machine to which my government was then providing training, logistical support, and approximately $500 million a year, making the Salvadoran government — the government responsible for the photographs before me — the third-highest per capita recipient of U.S. foreign aid.

In those silent moments before someone wandered back into the room, I was stunned into emotional numbness. The rage and the shame and the tears would come later. If those moments did anything for me, they changed forever my ability to delude myself that my country of birth — the country that I will love to my dying day — was somehow less needful of judgment and repentance than any other country, in any other time or place.

Most of our time at the commission's office was spent in meetings that stretched through the humid mornings and steamy afternoons. Kate Bancroft alternated as translator with Patrick Hughes, our third volunteer, a lawyer who had heard of our connection with the commission from Lisa Brodyaga. What we didn't know as we sat with Herbert, Reynaldo, Miguel Angel, Joaquín, and Rafael was that they had recently contemplated going into exile — one to Mexico, another to Canada, another to Europe. Before leaving Mariona, they had wondered if they might be able to better disseminate information about human rights abuses while alive in distant places than while dead in El Salvador. At that point, none of them expected to be around for very long.

In the end, however, they decided that their place was in El Salvador, come what may. Having made this decision, they were especially glad to receive our offer of long-term accompaniment. Apparently, they felt that if they had reliable international accompaniment, that if the U.S. Embassy knew that U.S. citizens would always be with them in their office, in the field, and at the safe houses where they ate and slept, and if thereby the Salvadoran Treasury Police and National Guard knew that violence directed against commission members might also strike Americans, then the chances of their being recaptured or killed, or of having their offices bombed again, would be somewhat diminished. What we didn't know, Suzanne and I, as we sat and talked with them was that they were trying to assess whether they could rely on us to keep the volunteers coming. And beyond that, whether they could trust us to be who we said we were.

Just as we had had to ask ourselves whether the commission maintained the kind of organizational connections with the FMLN that would compromise their independence, so they had to ask themselves whether MITF might be something other than the grassroots solidarity organization we claimed to be. Specifically, they wondered whether we might be a CIA concoction designed to penetrate the Salvadoran popular movement. Or, if we were not actually a CIA front, might we inadvertently recruit a volunteer the CIA sent our way? This was no theoretical issue for them, believing as they did that Luz Janeth Alfaro, the former commission member who had turned against them and publicly accused them of being an FMLN front, had been induced to betray the popular movement by the CIA when she visited the United States and Europe in 1986. Were the benefits of accompaniment worth the risks of allowing unknown gringos among them on an ongoing basis? Opinions varied, but Herbert felt that we could be trusted, and eventually his viewpoint prevailed. He had his reservations about foreigners, but he trusted his instincts about people, and he had a great curiosity about the world beyond El Salvador that only foreigners could satisfy.

Patrick Hughes remembers his first meeting with Herbert, on the day after Herbert was released from Mariona. The commission office was jammed with others who had been released from Mariona at the same time. Large sheets of fabric were doing double duty as blankets at night and protest banners by day. Reporters, human rights monitors, and victims of human rights abuses waiting to tell their stories jostled through the kitchen at mealtimes. Herbert watched Patrick interact with a few people, then approached him and asked his reaction to what he was seeing. Patrick chatted with him, thinking Herbert to be a reporter covering the story of the prisoner exchange, only to discover later on who it was that had quizzed him so avidly about his take on the day's events. Over time, Herbert learned that Patrick listened nightly to the BBC on his shortwave radio and made a point of grilling him about the latest on the Iran-Contra scandal, South Africa, Palestine, the Philippines, the stock market dive of October 1987 — anything that might remotely relate liberation struggles around the globe to his work in El Salvador.

In the end, because they had decided to stay and continue their work, Herbert and the others agreed to take a chance on us, even though they had no way of knowing whether the benefits of accepting volunteers would outweigh the potential security risks — inadvertent or otherwise — that they posed or whether we would be able to deliver the volunteers we had promised. Happily, we were able to make good on our assurances. Over the years, we recruited twenty-eight volunteers, providing all-but-continuous accompaniment from July 1986 until May 1991. Of that accomplishment I am as proud as I am of anything in my life. But their decision to stay in El Salvador ultimately cost Herbert his life.

We had been told that Herbert was president of the Human Rights Commission, but he never used that title, nor did any of the others. They had made a collective decision to no longer identify a particular person as their leader, fearing that anyone so designated was more likely to be targeted for further violence. Herbert was therefore careful not to dominate our discussions. But nothing could have been clearer than that he was their leader, in spirit if not in title, as we sat in a circle of chairs, discussing the potential for an official MITF accompaniment project on their behalf. For one thing, Herbert was the most humorous of them, always ready with a joke, always flashing his wide smile when someone else shot off the funny line. For another, it was always he who initiated Spanish-only discussions among the five of them when a consensus was required before giving a response. Finally, although he was careful not to assume the prerogatives of leadership, they were extended to him. The others looked in his direction when it was time to close discussion and agree on a particular point, and they waited for him to break the silences that interrupted the conversation from time to time.

Herbert was bold and spirited and resiliently good humored. He was damned if he was going to let the thugs who had captured, tortured, and incarcerated him quash his ebullience. On the last day of our meetings, after we had covenanted with each another to undertake this project that Suzanne and I had flown down to propose, she and I suggested we all go out to dinner and enjoy some beer and *pupusas*. Several commission members felt that going out in public for dinner was too risky, but not Herbert. He phoned Mirna and asked her to meet us at the end of the day, then engaged the others in a lengthy discussion about which *pupuseria* in town offered the best fare. When Mirna came by to pick us up, we all squeezed into her Volkswagen and drove across town to an open-air place where we ate and drank and talked for hours. Some may have regarded Herbert's decision to enjoy an evening of discussion in a public restaurant as an act of bravado — and Herbert was surely capable of bravado — but to me it seemed simply that his spirit resisted containment, that what some may have perceived as bravado made others love him — and look up to him — all the more.

At one point during our stay, the commission members had invited us to accompany them on a march through the city to commemorate the funeral of Oscar Romero, the archbishop who had been shot while saying Mass on March 24, 1980, and buried several days later at the cathedral in the city center. When we met them at a small park a mile from their offices, hundreds of others were already assembling, among them members of the COMA-DRES (Mothers of the Disappeared), dressed as always for such occasions in black and carrying posters bearing the names of their disappeared loved ones. The mood of the crowd was tense and nervous as the marchers awaited the signal to begin walking toward the cathedral, and a number of people approached the commission members and spoke with them in quiet tones.

Groups were starting out simultaneously from four or five other points in the city. Once the marching began, the mood of the crowd lightened. At the front of the procession, marchers carried huge banners painted with the likeness of Archbishop Romero. Others, a bit farther back, carried an enlarged version of the picture of Marianella Garcia Villas that I had seen earlier on the wall of the commission's office. During another march I participated in several years later in San Salvador, Herbert's picture accompanied Romero's and Marianella's.

From time to time throughout the several hours it took us to snake through the streets to the plaza before the cathedral, people would step off the curb to shake Herbert's hand or walk with him for a few paces. The wary look he had about him at the assembly place was soon replaced with his characteristic broad smile. He clearly loved the attention. And when, as we reached the downtown district, a camera crew from one of the television stations spotted Herbert, he gladly permitted them a walking interview. The reporter strolled at his side with a microphone while the cameraman backpedalled before them.

Herbert gave another interview, this time on the government-run television station, in September of that year, an interview in which he debated with Reynaldo López Nuila, head of the National Police. In their heated exchange, broadcast live, Herbert denounced López to his face for the military's repression and its lies. Patrick Hughes, who was watching on television at a house nearby with some friends, remembers Herbert's articulate anger and his prediction that the death squads would be brought to justice in times to come. Patrick's companions were amazed by what they saw. "This has never happened in El Salvador before," said one. "Oh, Jesus, how can he do it?" asked another. Afterward, Patrick and Mirna picked Herbert up outside the television station and sped away from the Cherokees that pulled out to follow them.

Some believe that the relish with which Herbert lit into López is likely what got him killed. Mirna Anaya disputes this assessment, as do the surviving commission members. According to Mirna, it was clear from the time Herbert left Mariona that his days were numbered. Agents of the security forces frequently followed Herbert; his children would often see cars with polarized windows when Herbert picked them up at school. Plainclothes police tailed him when he went to Ilopango Prison with Patrick to interview the women inmates who had suffered torture. Herbert's father was picked up on May 2, and he later reported that his interrogation consisted entirely of questions about his son. Herbert narrowly avoided a kidnapping attempt near his apartment later that month. When Mirna's brother-in-law, who worked for the Treasury Police and had tipped Mirna off as to Herbert's whereabouts when he was captured in 1986, was transferred from his job at Treasury Police Headquarters to a position that isolated him from command decisions, Mirna's heart sank. She could think of no reason for his transfer other than the desire of his superiors to keep him in the dark about their plans for Herbert.

On the morning of October 26, 1987, Herbert walked from his apartment to warm up his car, which was parked in the lot beside the building. He was about to take his five children to school. As he opened the car door, three men in civilian clothing stepped up behind him and drew their silencer-equipped pistols. They shot Herbert repeatedly, until he fell to the asphalt and died in a pool of his own blood.

Eleven-year-old Rosa, Herbert's eldest daughter, heard the stifled reports as she emerged from the building. She crept down the sidewalk a few paces, stooping to look beneath his car. She saw her father's body lying there, then ran back upstairs while neighbors gathered up her younger siblings as they stepped out into the morning unawares. When the children and neighbors rushed frantically back into the apartment, Mirna ran out to see what had happened, confronted her husband's corpse, determined that Herbert was not breathing, and ran back inside to call the commission.

Even now, Mirna continues to press for a full investigation of Herbert's death. Events that preceded and followed it suggest to her that the highest members of the Salvadoran military — and by extension the U.S. advisors who oversaw them and, presumably, were privy to all their deeds — were responsible. Among the indicators of Salvadoran high command complicity, Mirna includes a radio broadcast made two months before Herbert's assassination, in which Colonel Reynaldo Golcher, head of the Treasury Police, asserted that Herbert was a guerrilla commander. Such public statements by members of the security forces often served as death warrants.

Mirna takes the sophistication of the cover-up as another indicator. Several weeks after Herbert was killed, the Treasury Police captured a young man named Jorge Alberto Miranda Arévalo, held him incommunicado for four days, then held a press conference in which Miranda, emaciated and with his eyes swollen almost shut, testified that he had participated in Herbert's assassination at the instruction of the FMLN high command. According to this scenario, Herbert had opposed the FMLN's plans to bring the war to the streets of San Salvador, and they had settled the dispute by killing him, a fabrication distinguished only by the plausibility of its premise — that Herbert Anaya did not operate at the behest of the FMLN. Miranda subsequently recanted his testimony, saying that it had been tortured out of him. In most death squad killings, the authors make no attempt at deflection. But Herbert had a great presence in El Salvador — a presence he had earned with his complete willingness to confront the perpetrators of terror and death — and his killers therefore laid careful plans to confound the investigation that international and popular movement pressures demanded.

When Herbert was killed, his death served only to galvanize others into more courageous action, among them Celia Medrano, who joined the commission shortly thereafter. Celia had come to know Herbert in early 1986 when, as a leader of Christian Youth for Peace, she had invited Herbert to make several presentations on human rights to her group. Celia had studied journalism at the National University and worked there at the Office of Communications, covering (and leading) strikes and demonstrations. Herbert tried to recruit Celia for the commission's press department, but she resisted his overtures despite becoming his friend. She didn't understand the significance of human rights work at the time and felt that directly attacking injustice through street demonstrations was more efficacious than denouncing injustice from behind a desk. She knew the commission was a target of repression and didn't see much sense in working at an office where the security forces could find you at any time.

Celia weathered Herbert's inducements and his ire until he died. Then, when Reynaldo Blanco sought her out and repeated Herbert's entreaty, she came to work at the commission in Herbert's name. Of Herbert's impact on her she says, "Herbert's life redefined a lot of people, even people who only saw him on TV. His sacrifice was worth it, reaching a lot of people, transmitting a message of courage, raising consciousness. It is amazing how a public declaration can change people."

Herbert's death blew a gigantic hole in the collective psyche of the commission, especially among those with whom he had been incarcerated at Mariona. Six years after Herbert's murder, Joaquín Cáceres wept when he remembered the death of his friend. "For me, it was an irreplaceable loss. He represented, for me, something no other person had. After his death, we went on, but it affected us a lot. There was a huge empty space, but the work, the demand from the people, made us go on. We couldn't abandon the work he started. He was a good *compañero*, a friend, a brother. I still miss him a lot. I was sorry that I was not there when they killed him. I was on a trip to Canada at the time and could not return for his funeral because it was necessary to stay there and denounce what had happened to him. Because I never saw him dead, it was as if he was still around somewhere and would come back. They decided to kill him because he was a person who could face any risk, because he denounced the government and the armed forces, because he was so courageous. He had a great strength."

Of all those who were commission members at the time, the one who misses Herbert the most, I think, is his best friend, Reynaldo Blanco. When Reynaldo met Herbert at the commission's Mexico City office in 1983, the two soon found that they complemented each other. Reynaldo was tall and studious, Herbert stocky and impulsive. Reynaldo describes Herbert as a very active guy, a decision maker who didn't always think things through and whose decisions were sometimes good, sometimes bad. Reynaldo found that his patience tempered Herbert's impulsiveness, and Herbert's decisiveness prevented Reynaldo from being too passive. Together, they discovered the balance between them.

Their complementary natures drew them together, but it was their common interests that deepened their friendship. Reynaldo laughs now when he recalls these common interests, which made them seem like madmen in the eyes of their colleagues. Herbert and Reynaldo shared a mutually perverse sense of humor, a reciprocal fascination with dreams, and a common belief in the supernatural. I think that their perverse humor helped them deal with the realities of being prominent members of the commission. One day at the office, they happened to be looking at the wall where pictures of the corpses were hanging. Reynaldo said to Herbert, "That's what you'll look like." To which Herbert replied, "Yeah, with flies crawling all over me and my blood outside me."

Their dreams provided a constant source of conversation and disclosure. One time when they were in Mariona together, Herbert came to Reynaldo to discuss a dream he had had the previous night. They were driving together in a car, Herbert at the wheel, Reynaldo alongside. It was a car owned by the commission, and they were happy that for once, the commission had a car. They looked behind them as they drove along and saw that a hearse was following them with an empty coffin. This they interpreted to mean that death would be following them when they left Mariona and that one of them would come to occupy that coffin.

After its members were released from Mariona, the commission rented a house in the northern part of the city where members could live together with their accompaniers. One night while sleeping there, Reynaldo heard the voice of his brother, who had died of cancer in 1978, in Herbert's snoring. His brother told him to "check out Alexander," another brother still living. In the morning Reynaldo called his mother, who told him that Alexander was in some financial trouble and that his telephone and water had been disconnected. When Reynaldo related all of this to Herbert, Herbert assured him that such things were real and that Reynaldo should be alert for them, a suggestion Reynaldo has followed many times since Herbert's death — particularly on those occasions when Herbert has seemed to manifest himself, often to warn Reynaldo of impending danger.

Shortly after Herbert died, Reynaldo and Cecilia, the commission's typist, were staying with Mirna and the kids. He and Ceci talked late into the night, finally going to bed at around 4:00 A.M. They found places for themselves on the floor among the slumbering children. As they dozed off, Ceci complained to Reynaldo that he was standing on her foot. Reynaldo replied, "That's impossible, Ceci! I'm lying down over here, halfway under a cot." They settled themselves, but soon Reynaldo heard a voice speaking to him through the sound of ten-year-old Neto's snores. The snoring voice said, "Reynaldo, be careful. They're going to kill you." Reynaldo said nothing, wondering if his mind or his ears might be playing tricks on him, but then Ceci said, "Do you hear that? Your name. Someone telling you to be careful, that they're going to kill you."

As their common interests strengthened the bond between the two men, many of Herbert's singular characteristics endeared him to Reynaldo, among them his zaniness, his sensitivity to the poor, and his disregard for possessions and money. According to Reynaldo, Herbert died with thirty centavos in his pocket. To those who observed the commission members after Herbert's death, it seemed that of all of them, Reynaldo suffered most deeply over the loss of this man, of whom he says, "We looked at each other as one person, as different aspects of the same man."

In January 1992, four years and three months after Herbert died, I took my wife, Lori, and my children, Kate and Tucker, to El Salvador for the first time. The peace accords that ended El Salvador's civil war had been signed in Mexico and the cease-fire was about to begin. We spent several days at the beach with Mirna and her children — Rosa, Gloria, Neto, Rafa, and Edith — enjoying with them their first extended family vacation in years. After our sojourn at the edge of the Pacific, we drove back together to San Salvador.

Mirna and Lori rode in one pickup truck with all the girls, and I followed them in another pickup with the three boys — two sons of Mirna's and Herbert's, and one son of Lori's and mine. As we drove into the suburbs of San Salvador, Neto and Rafa told of the terrible day their father died. Before they knew what was happening on that suddenly confused and frightful morning, Mirna had bundled all of them off to school. They knew that something awful had happened to Herbert, but they were not sure of his death until Mirna came for them at school later that day.

As they were telling me this story that no child should ever have to tell, Neto noticed the neighborhood through which we were traveling and said to me, "This is near where my father is buried." Sure enough, a few moments later Mirna pulled to the curb, and we all got out to pay our respects.

As we walked in a group through the iron gates of the cemetery, one of the workers recognized Mirna and ushered us excitedly up the hillside. Mirna pointed out the words that had been painted by the crowds on the sides of some of the larger whitewashed mausoleums back in October 1987, words that celebrated Herbert's life and mourned his death. The cemetery worker scurried off when we reached Herbert's grave, then reappeared a moment later with a bucket of water that he sluiced over the limestone marker, cleaning away the dust and the accumulated twigs with his palm. When he stepped back, we formed a circle and held hands all around. I translated for Lori and Kate and Tucker the inscription, words spoken by Herbert a few weeks before they killed him: "The agony of not working for justice is stronger than the certain possibility of my death; this latter is but one instant, the other is one's whole life." Then I said a prayer and Mirna spoke to Herbert for a few moments before we dropped hands and straggled back down the hill and into the trucks.

I have a picture of Herbert and me standing together in the door of the commission's office, and I will always treasure it. But the best picture of Herbert is the one that Suzanne took a moment later when I had stepped out of view, the one Kate took to Mirna at Herbert's funeral. Herbert stands there in the doorway with his arms folded across his chest, smiling his irrepressible smile. On the day Suzanne snapped that picture, he had already stood up to the worst that the security forces could dish out, and he already knew that he would continue the work that defined his life. Like so many others in the Salvadoran popular organizations, Herbert's vitality and presence seemed to reflect his acceptance of death, if death was what the struggle required. In many ways, it seemed he lived beyond it.

The Christian concept of resurrection has become a living reality for me through my experience of Herbert's life and death and through my experience of him in the years that followed. He is alive for me now and is deeply integrated into my being. Like Oscar Romero, he lives on as well in the people of El Salvador. To Herbert I am indebted for my heartfelt experience each time I break the back of a Communion loaf. To Herbert I am indebted for that part of me that relates to the resurrection of Christ as a lived experience instead of as a concept. Herbert's spirit prevailed during his life, and he knew that it would prevail in his death.

_ 4 _
THE (OMMISSION

Three of the members of the Human Rights Commission of El Salvador — Joaquín Cáceres, Miguel Angel Montenegro, and Celia Medrano — joined the Salvadoran struggle — and ultimately the commission — due to an event that none of them witnessed: the El Despertar Massacre of January 1979.

By the late 1970s, liberation theology was springing up and taking root in rural communities and urban barrios all across El Salvador. Through Bible study, literacy classes, and social analysis, Catholic priests and catechists taught the poor of El Salvador the principles that Latin American bishops had promulgated at conferences in Medellín, Colombia, and Puebla, Mexico: that God makes no distinction between rich and poor; that the instruments of social control by which a wealthy few subjugate an impoverished populace are unjust; that the people have every right to peacefully demand medical care, living wages, and freedom from military domination; and that God intends freedom and joy for people in this life as well as the next.

In their final statement at the Medellín Conference of 1968, the Latin American bishops summarized in a few sentences the systematic nature of social oppression in the region — oppression amounting to institutionalized violence — and the need to establish social justice as a prerequisite for peace:

[The Christian] believes in the value of peace for the achievement of justice, he also believes that justice is a necessary condition for peace. And he is not unaware that in many places in Latin America there is a situation of injustice that must be recognized as institutionalized violence, because the existing structures violate people's basic rights: a situation which calls for far-reaching, daring, urgent and profoundly innovative change.

This Christian movement swept through the neighborhoods of El Salvador like wildfire, articulating as it did the visceral experience of economic, social, and personal oppression that defined the lives of most Salvadorans and raising as it did their aspirations. Christian base communities, as they are called, sprang up in rural *cantóns* and urban barrios, and in them for the first time people studied the Bible in their own language. In the story of the Israelite liberation from Egyptian slavery, in the diatribes directed by Old Testament prophets against the economic elites of their day, and in the words of Jesus of Nazareth, these communities of the faithful discovered parallels to their own situation in El Salvador.

Organizing soon followed consciousness-raising. So the authorities moved against the liberation theology movement with a vengeance, coincidentally converting Archbishop Oscar Romero to adherence when they assassinated his friend Rutilio Grande, a young priest who preached and organized in the town of Aquilares.

One of the Christian base centers quickly targeted by the military was the El Despertar Retreat Center, located in the San Antonio Abad neighborhood of San Salvador where Joaquín and Miguel Angel had grown up. The First Infantry Brigade and the National Guard rolled their tanks into the retreat center one Sunday morning in January 1979. They crushed its leader, Father Octavio Ortíz, beneath the treads of a tank, killed four youths, and carried the rest off to National Police Headquarters. In the months that followed, the forces of repression cruised the streets of San Antonio Abad, rounding up those who participated in Christian base activities for interrogation, torture, assassination, and disappearance.

Joaquín Cáceres's mother was a leader in the El Despertar community. When she heard that her name and that of one of her daughters were included on the security force list, she moved the family to another neighborhood but continued her advocacy. At about this time, Joaquín's mother heard that the Human Rights Commission needed someone to help with office work and suggested to Joaquín that he apply. He was seventeen when the commission's secretary hired him to collect newspaper clippings, run errands, clean up around the office, and help with correspondence.

During the early 1980s, the repression was at its most ferocious, and Joaquín witnessed it on two fronts: at work and among his family. Within four years of his hiring on April 1, 1979, seven commission members were assassinated, and their offices were bombed twice. On March 2, 1980, a bomb exploded in the garage. None of the four people in the building suffered injury, but the bomb destroyed the photo lab, office furniture, files, and records. On September 3 of that year, someone piled three bodies by the front door, then detonated a bomb on top of the corpses, blowing out the door and the windows. Some commission members interpreted the three bodies to mean that three commission members would die, and two soon did. On October 3, the First Brigade captured María Magdalena Enriquez when she stopped at a store on her way home from work. Her body — shot four times in the face and possibly raped — was recovered from a shallow grave the next day and identified by another member of the commission, Ramón Valladares Pérez. Members of the National Guard approached Valladares at the exhumation and demanded to see his identification. Three weeks later, Valladares stopped for a beer after work. Afterward, as he drove home at 10:00 P.M., a vehicle pulled up next to him. The occupants of that vehicle forced him from his car and shot him to death.

As the violence unleashed against the commission, and El Salvador's populace, mounted, Joaquín began to understand the importance of the commission's work. He knew from his experiences in San Antonio Abad that he wanted to contribute in whatever way possible to the resistance. In the commission's work of denouncing massacres and killings, he found a way to do that. Among his duties was delivering press and radio releases the commission had prepared. His route to the offices of the media would sometimes take him past the sites of slayings; occasionally, he was compelled to step over the very corpses his papers documented.

Things were little better at home. On December 19, 1980, the National Guard conducted one of its periodic sweeps of San Antonio Abad. Juan José, Joaquín's sixteen-year-old brother, worked for the Green Cross, the Salvadoran equivalent of the Red Cross. As he returned from work, Juan saw the Guardia's truck, talked his way through the military checkpoint, and sprinted home to warn his mother and sisters. After walking them out to a bus stop, Juan headed back to intercept other family members as they came home. He made the mistake of assuming he could pass through the checkpoint again. This time, one of the soldiers said, "Oh, you're with the Green Cross? Everyone in the Green Cross is a subversive." They put him on a truck with other youths and took them away. Three weeks later, the family learned he was being held by the Treasury Police. He was released from the prison at Santa Tecla six months later and left the country.

Before Juan's release, their father was captured twice — in April by the National Police and in June by the Treasury Police — and suffered beatings both times. The Treasury Police held him, and many others, in the basement. At night, guards with flashlights would take people away and kill them. Joaquín's father may have been saved from this fate by the intervention of a relative who happened to be a National Guardsman. This relative took him to a psychiatric hospital from which he was released two weeks later, a changed and terrified man. In the remaining nights of his life, Joaquín's father woke up screaming many times. He died before the year was out.

I spoke with Joaquín once about what it was like to have family members on both sides of the conflict. Most of his immediate family worked in one way or another with the popular organizations, but he had a cousin in the First Infantry Brigade of the Salvadoran Army and another in the National Police. By a strange coincidence, the cousin in the First Infantry Brigade was assigned to Mariona Prison during Joaquín's incarceration and visited him there. When he asked Joaquín whether he would keep working when he got out, Joaquín replied, "Of course."

It was common in an extended family to have members on both sides of the conflict. In most cases, they found a way to temporarily bury the hatchet at holidays and other family gatherings. In Joaquín's family, when arguments sprang up, they were conducted outside. The underlying family covenant was expressed this way: "Don't do anything to me, and I won't do anything to you." In other families, however, people fingered their own relatives for death, even their brothers and sisters. Joaquín explains this by saying that the military managed to fill these people with hate. He has maintained his family relations with everybody. Of those who joined the military or the security forces he says, "They needed the income."

With his trimmed mustache and pressed clothes, Joaquín is cleanly handsome and possesses a winning way. His expressions shift quickly from bright smile to studious composure. Joaquín is the type of guy parents hope their daughters will bring home. Of his early years with the commission Joaquín says, "I became aware that I might be murdered. I felt a certain powerlessness — what could I do? So I gave myself strength, and so did my family. Anything can happen to you, but it is necessary to be there. My mom told me, 'You are doing something very important there. Even though you are afraid, we are with you.' Part of this was my faith, but more came from the experience of injustice. It became impossible to keep our hands folded. My family is very strong. We won't accept injustice. We keep on moving forward. This is a Salvadoran characteristic. We maintained our strength as a family group."

Miguel Angel Montenegro, one of the commission members captured in May 1986, had similar roots in the Salvadoran conflict, similar support from his family, and similar involvement in the Christian base organizing that grew out of the El Despertar Retreat Center in San Antonio Abad. In fact, when Miguel Angel and Joaquín first met in Mexico City in 1983, they recognized each other from their days in that neighborhood.

Miguel Angel is burly and often a bit rumpled. He leaves the upper part of his shirt unbuttoned, and as he speaks in his animated and voluble fashion, you can see against his chest the small cross that dangles from a slender chain. "I come from a campesino family in the area of the San Salvador Volcano. All of my family — my grandfather, parents, aunts and uncles, brothers, cousins — worked in the Christian communities. My interest was in youth work, and that's where I developed my knowledge of realities, around age fourteen or fifteen, from Padre Guillermo and Padre Rogelio Poncell. I worked in the area around El Despertar with my family. When the repression started after the massacre at El Despertar, all of us who were involved in the development of the Christian communities were accused of being Communists. When that repression began, many people withdrew from the work.

"I remember the massacre of Padre Octavio and all of them. The repression weighed on my family. In early 1980, my grandfather was captured, along with my father, my sister, and four uncles, by the First Infantry Brigade. They were all tortured there and accused of subversive attitudes but were released later through the intervention of Monseñor Romero and the Red Cross.

"Later, three of my cousins were disappeared. My sister was captured and sent to the National Guard, then freed. They captured another of my cousins. He was found murdered near the Psychiatric Hospital at Soyapango.

"Before that, I was detained by three men in civilian clothes who said I belonged to the 'talk givers.' That was the name they gave to those of us involved in the Christian communities. They put me against a wall and put the point of a machine gun against my back. They had another young guy with me, and a crowd gathered. My mother cried out, 'Don't hurt them,' and the other people cried out, too. So the pressure made them let me go. But the other guy, they took him two blocks away and killed him.

"Then, in the fall of 1981, the Guardia began to give out pencils to the children in the neighborhood with my initials written on them. They gave out pencils with the names of my sisters and my cousins, too. Also on the pencils were the letters E.M., which stand for *escuadrón de la muerte* (death squad). So my sister left the country in October of 1981, and then I left, too. This was when the murders and tortures and disappearances were happening.

"I followed my sister to Mexico, where she had started working in the Mexico City office of the commission. At the end of 1981 I met Marianella Garcia Villas, and she invited me to join the commission, too. Most of the members of the commission worked there then, and Marianella involved me and explained everything to me. I joined in October of 1982. Because of all that I had seen, I put my fear to one side.

"In 1983 the United Nations High Commission for Refugees asked us to compile information on the effects of the chemicals being used by the Salvadoran Army [principally phosphorus bombs, fragments from which burned people and buildings alike], so Marianella went to El Salvador to do that work. One day they called us in Mexico and told us that she was killed. It was unbelievable to me that she was dead. After seeing how she dedicated herself to the work, I came to feel more committed. So I came back to El Salvador with Reynaldo and others in 1984 to do the First Congress on Human Rights, then returned here to work directly in January of 1985."

Celia Medrano joined the struggle years later, but she, too, came from a group that had its roots in the El Despertar Massacre. Many Salvadoran organizations include the names of people or places in their titles. Celia's group — The Christian Youth for Peace, Martyrs of El Despertar (or JCP for short)

— was no exception. She helped found the JCP in January 1986, believing that true Christian behavior followed the example of Padre Octavio Ortíz, that is, awakening to the injustices of life, then striving to rectify those injustices on behalf of God's people. Two of Padre Octavio's nephews were JCP members, as were others who had been among the children at the El Despertar Retreat Center when the Guardia tanks rolled through the gates in January 1979.

Among the commission members I came to know best, only one has no connection to the Christian base communities of San Antonio Abad: Reynaldo Blanco. But Reynaldo differs from the other commission leaders in more ways than this. For one thing, Reynaldo is tall — as tall as I am at six foot two. When I look at group photos I have taken at the commission, I am reminded of the club photos in my own high school yearbook. Reynaldo and I stick out from the line, a head taller than our friends. For another thing, Reynaldo comes from a middle-class background and was headed for a career in government when his heart derailed him.

He is studious, moderate, and deliberate, but despite these sober characteristics, he maintains a winning vulnerability and openness. Reynaldo is a good listener, and he is a softy. When I asked Reynaldo where his convictions came from, he described himself as follows.

"From when I was small, I always had this feeling toward the poor. We were middle class, and when my mother gave us money for candy or movies, I would save it and give it to the man who came through our neighborhood on the weekends begging. Then he told others, and other beggars would come, too. So I began to collect clothes and money from my friends. We understood that we were helping the poor, but we didn't understand the fundamental social problems of oppression, marginalization, exploitation, and violations of human rights. Only later did I understand the importance of sharing that feeling I had with others. I alone could not do anything. This is what led me to my early work in the public and agricultural sectors. And the older I got, the more I realized that this attitude has risks in this country.

"During the period just before I left the country in 1982, I was working for the Ministry of Labor in a program called Labor Law Compliance. I liked this work, in which it was my job to take the side of the workers and represent them in their grievances against employers. But I was unusual in this because the other workers in this program sold themselves to the employers.

"I was also on the Executive Council of State Employees. Many of the council members were assassinated. The pressure [not to organize] came from those who wanted to prevent public employees from organizing. This was during the time when there was a general state of killings and disappearances. After they captured and disappeared a woman who was a co-worker of mine, armed men came one day looking for me at home when I wasn't there. That's when I decided it was time to go to Mexico. I left El Salvador in September of 1982.

"I already knew Marianella Garcia Villas, and I considered the commission to be a humanitarian organization where I could channel my concerns about needy people. I wanted to continue the work I had been doing, so I went to the commission and asked to join. In those days, that office in Mexico City was an international resonance box for what was happening in El Salvador. There was a team still in El Salvador collecting information, but the leadership was in Mexico. Marianella was president and Dr. Mendez was the vice president. We transmitted information internationally and made trips to Europe. Marianella did most of the traveling. Most of us used aliases to protect our families at home from reprisals. There in Mexico is where I met Herbert sometime in 1983."

Reynaldo referred to the Mexico City office as a resonance box because in those days it was from there that the commission communicated its findings to international human rights organizations, to the OAS, and to the United Nations. In 1984, Reynaldo briefly returned to El Salvador with other commission members to hold the First Congress on Human Rights. Then, in early 1986, he began preparing to return to El Salvador for good. "It was a certainty for me. I knew that from the minute I returned, something would happen to me — that they would kill me or disappear me or jail me. But I always had this conviction to struggle for human rights, and my wife and daughters were safe in Mexico, so I readied myself."

Reynaldo prepared daily by squeezing into a closet among the clothes hanging there, assuming an uncomfortable position in the stifling darkness and resisting the desire to sit down for as long as he could. When he told me this anecdote, I had to laugh at the image of large Reynaldo scrunched in among his wife's dresses, and I asked him incredulously if he was practicing to be tortured.

He smiled and laughed when he answered. "Yes, it helped me when I was at the Treasury Police, where they kept me standing for three days. It located me in that reality, but with the difference of the blows and threats they gave me. The torture was more a mental and ideological thing than a physical thing, so my practicing helped me."

Reynaldo returned to El Salvador on May 14, 1986. They captured him fifteen days later.

"In the moment when they captured me, in those moments of pressure and anguish, my body didn't tremble. I was tranquil. I was on the street, and I saw a friend of mine across the way. I was about to wave to him when someone held a pistol to my head. His hand was trembling, and he told me to get into the vehicle. So I didn't wave to my friend, just made a little gesture that said, 'Oh, well.' Then they put me in the vehicle, a Toyota Hi-Ace, told me to look at no one, beat me, and took my wallet and glasses."

Herbert had been captured three days earlier. Joaquín had been captured the previous November. Miguel Angel was captured along with Reynaldo, near the offices of the commission. Rafael Terezón was captured that same day. With the capture of these five men, the security forces gutted the leadership of the commission. Except for the commission's treasurer, Oscar Hernandez, they had all of the commission's department heads in custody.

In the days following their capture, all five men suffered physical and psychological torture before being taken to Mariona. They were choked to the point of asphyxiation and beaten on face and body with clenched fists. They were hit on the testicles and about the ears. They were thrown to the floor with hands cuffed behind their backs, then lifted by their arms until they felt like their shoulders were being pulled from their sockets. They were kept standing for days on end and deprived of sleep as threats were hurled against their families. The motive for interrogation was always the same — to get them to "confess" that the Human Rights Commission of El Salvador was a compromised organization, a front for the FMLN. One by one, they inked their signatures on blank pieces of paper that were laid before them and then affixed to their "confessions."

By the middle of June, they were reunited in Mariona. Crowded in with them were more than 400 other political prisoners. It didn't take them long to figure out what to do next. As Miguel Angel puts it, "The situation itself in Mariona made it the thing to do. Everyone having been tortured was the motivation. The torture report was an impressive piece of work. It gave us prestige. People knew we did our work even from prison."

Reynaldo recalls that they started working on the torture report in August, having already resumed their work for the commission by placing paid ads in the newspapers. When I remarked to Reynaldo that this work inside Mariona was like waving a red flag at a bull, he replied, "We had been waving the red flag since 1978."

As bad as life was in Mariona — the heat, the crowded conditions, the total lack of privacy, the lousy food — amazingly enough, the positive aspects of their time there together seem to have outweighed the negative. For starters, they five men were alive. Miguel Angel remembers it this way.

"As for me, I was brutally tortured — psychologically and physically — to break me. The physical is less harmful than the psychological. You are in a dark place. You are isolated. You have lots to think about. My mom came to visit me at the Treasury Police, and I told her that I had resigned myself to die. But then, when you are freed from that place of torture, you come alive again, after thirteen days of resisting torture and pressure. You know that others have died or never come out of there, so you feel free. Then, in Mariona, you leave the terror for a more passive terror. The other prisoners support you with great unity and strength."

Beyond the joy of being alive and free from torture, the men in Mariona experienced an ironic sort of safety. The very fact of their incarceration protected them from further torture or death. If anything were to happen to an inmate there, all of the prisoners would know who had done it, and so would the outside world. There was no need to plan every move to avoid capture, no need to watch the rearview mirror, to remember unknown faces encountered along the street. They were on the other side already. They could relax. Everyone else jammed in there with them had run the same risks, suffered the same consequences. They were safe.

And they had their work to do. Even as they conducted the interviews on which the torture report is based, they knew they were doing something audacious and truly worthy. This gave them great pride. But the most redeeming aspect of their life together in Mariona was the solidarity they shared, the feeling of brotherhood beyond brotherhood, the certainty of shared commitment, shared risks, shared experiences.

Joaquín describes that feeling of solidarity: "To be in Mariona was the best experience of my life — to be alive with so many people, having shared their experiences, having shared their work for the people, having been tortured. The feeling that each of us had. The solidarity work. Living there like brothers. We faced our problems together — the pressure, the threats, cutting off of the water, the terrible food, the mistreatment of our families. It created a solidarity in each of us. You don't forget that. To be able to experience that, it won't happen again. I would like to live like that again, with other people again, but in different circumstances."

When the authorities finally released them from Mariona, their experience of freedom was tainted by their sense of renewed vulnerability, which Miguel Angel describes this way: "Then you get out, and it's a psychotic situation. When I got out, they said they'd kill me unless I left the country. They often said that. María Julia Hernandez of Tutela Legal came to get me out, but when I went home, I felt unprotected. The open doors. People coming in and out. It preys on your mind. They can come for you at any time, so I was worried, and I wanted to leave the country. The temptation was great, especially because you worry about your loved ones. But then you think, 'If I leave, I'll save my life, but what about the others? What about those who stay?' "

Of the five men who worked together in Mariona, only Rafael Terezón left the commission. I met him on my first trip to El Salvador, then never saw him again. The others all considered leaving, even going so far as to choose their countries of self-imposed exile, but ultimately they stayed. Before they left Mariona, they had agreed to leave the decision to each individual.

Joaquín told me, "We have always been conscious of the fact that at any moment we could lose our lives. But we never felt so close to death that we didn't want to be with the commission. The threats, the persecution — it gave us strength and pride to work for the commission. What they tried to do against us showed us that the commission did a lot for the Salvadoran people. Had we not, they wouldn't have done anything to us. Sometimes we have joked with each other, when months have gone by without an attack, 'We must not be doing enough.' "

In my view, the commission did indeed do enough: enough before the five of them were captured, enough during the months in Mariona, and enough to have made them who they were and are. As I got to know them both during and after the Accompaniment Project years, they lodged themselves permanently in my consciousness.

During the five-year period that MITF recruited volunteers to accompany the Human Rights Commission, I made six trips to El Salvador. As the director of MITF, it was part of my job to stay in close communication with the commission, and the only way to do so was to meet face-to-face. We tried to get together every six months and nearly succeeded, what with my six trips to El Salvador, one meeting in Mexico City, and one meeting with Oscar Hernandez in Marin. But we always knew that we could not realistically expect to coordinate our affairs smoothly when we met so infrequently. The problem of maintaining close communication proved the most daunting of the whole Accompaniment Project.

We could discuss nothing of substance over the phone — no names, no dates, nothing to indicate that such a thing as the Accompaniment Project even existed — and we therefore devised simple codes for certain subjects. For example, when the commission needed exact arrival dates and times for volunteers so that someone could meet them at the airport as they cleared customs, we conveyed this information with the help of a key sheet at each end of the line. If I said, "That woman from Massachusetts is coming at 6:00 A.M. on September 25," they knew I meant that Lisa Sheehy was arriving at 6:00 A.M. on May 8. Volunteers hand carried letters back and forth — as did other friends in the solidarity movement — and we debriefed them at length over the phone when they returned to the United States, but we knew we could hardly expect to keep abreast of developments short of shuttling someone back and forth every few weeks, and there was no way we could afford that.

We got together as often as we could and prayed that the plans we improvised would suffice. We would sit around a conference table in the commission's office for hours at a stretch evaluating the volunteers, discussing ways in which the commission might improve volunteer supervision and training, coordinating projects that we undertook from time to time as part of our work together, planning message routes and message codes, assessing the current situation in El Salvador, and wrangling over finances.

The pressures and dangers of the work we were doing with the commission ensured that there would be strains and misunderstandings, all compounded by the different cultural assumptions we brought with us. It was difficult, for example, for some of our volunteers to understand the need for elaborate security precautions. To them, the commission's office seemed like any other office, with people coming and going all the time, telephones ringing, and the staff gabbing and laughing in the hallways. They simply were not attuned to the surveillance agents that kept the commission under watch, had not yet learned to scan the rearview mirror for cars that followed them as they drove about the city on errands. So they balked at the restrictions and chafed at the endless hours spent preparing for what seemed like simple tasks.

I experienced my share of cultural differences as well. My work in the United States had taught me to go about business in a straightforward manner. At meetings it is my practice to lay out a problem that needs to be solved, consider the options, reach a conclusion, and then move on. Whenever I headed to El Salvador to meet with the commission, I would draw up a list of discussion points on the plane, then present those points when we began our meetings, expecting we would get right to the issues. But this is not how things are done in El Salvador, where important subjects are approached indirectly and the interpersonal components of a discussion often outweigh the subject at hand. They found me blunt; I found them oblique. It took a couple years for us to get used to each other.

Far and away the biggest mystery for me had to do with the commission's collective demeanor. The first few times I visited them, I always came away wondering how they could be so doggone cheerful. Here they were, working every day in an office whose walls were plastered with the faces of their fallen comrades, with photos of body dumps, with charts of statistics documenting the voracious activity of the very security forces whose operatives lurked across the street. At any time, a dozen frightened people might be waiting out in the garage, barefoot and exhausted, to denounce the mistreatment they had suffered. When the members of the commission ventured out on an errand, you could almost see the hairs on the backs of their necks rise as they hesitated at the door, looking slowly right and left before stepping into the disclosing sunlight. At least half of them had been detained at one time or another and had suffered the disorienting terror that such mistreatment is intended to inflict.

Yet life in the commission's office was buoyant and cheerful. The young staff joked and laughed and flirted. Graciela always made a point of snapping my suspenders and dazzling me with her perfect smile. Celia brought her baby to work so everyone could crowd around to coo and snuggle. When someone's birthday came up, they passed the hat, then smuggled in a cake slathered with pastel icing and spun sugar; at lunchtime or at the end of the day, we would scrunch together on the sofas in the central hallway to balance paper plates on our knees and tell embarrassing stories about the birthday boy or girl.

I had expected an atmosphere sizzling with tension. I had expected to see the strain of their work tooled into their faces. I had expected depression and heaviness. Instead, I witnessed high spirits and good humor. How could this be? Were all of them in advanced states of denial? Did their solidarity and their affection for one another shield them from the horrors that they witnessed daily? Had all of them confronted the great likelihood of their deaths and moved beyond mortal fear to some rare psychic realm? Had each experienced an epiphany — or a lifetime of epiphanies — that filled him or her with resolve and courage?

I pondered this at great length, especially after I had my own modest epiphany on the way to San Francisco International Airport on May 31, 1988, as I headed south for my second visit to the commission. In those days, other North Americans may have gone to El Salvador with light hearts, but I did not. I was scared. On my first trip, Suzanne had gone with me, had told me what to do and say at the security checkpoint in El Salvador's airport, had identified by their insignia the affiliations of the omnipresent young men in uniform who stood on corners and in doorways with their forefingers curled around the triggers of automatic weapons, had warned me off when I was about to say the inappropriate thing in the inappropriate place. She had slept in the adjacent room at the hotel, and I had taken comfort in knowing she was nearby when I jolted awake in the humid nights at the sound of not-too-distant gunfire or mortar thuds or rooftop-skimming helicopters. She had laughed with me, and at herself for having had the same thoughts, when I shared my morbid fantasies about death squad operatives hammering on my door in the dark hours of the morning.

Now I was headed for El Salvador on my own, representing an organization that had for more than a year been affiliated with the notorious (in the eyes of the Salvadoran government) Human Rights Commission. Since that first trip fourteen months earlier, we had broadcast far and wide our compact with the commission and had written long stories about its members and about our volunteers in the MITF newsletter. And Herbert had been killed. Did Salvadoran military intelligence know who we were, know who I was? Would I be turned back at the airport security checkpoint? Would I be taken into one of the side rooms for interrogation or God knows what else? These thoughts whistled through my brain as I kissed Lori and the kids goodbye and headed for the airport.

My car radio happened to be tuned to National Public Radio when I flicked it on to catch the news. Sure enough, a story about El Salvador came over the airwaves. In those days, José Napoleón Duarte was the president of El Salvador and a great favorite of the Reagan administration. On one occasion, he had even kissed the American flag at a ceremony in Washington. Duarte was suffering from stomach cancer, though, and everyone knew that his days were numbered. The words coming over my car radio stated that moments ago Duarte had boarded a jet for the States, where his friends in Washington had arranged treatment for him at Walter Reed Army Hospital. When the newscast ended, a commentator — Daniel Schorr, I think it was — analyzed the story. The situation in El Salvador was fragile and perilous, he intoned, and only Duarte's presence had been holding things together. With him out of the country, San Salvador was about to become Beirut. Fierce factional fighting could break out on its streets at any time. Within days, San Salvador could be a free-fire zone.

Great. You can be sure that I asked myself in those moments what was the responsible thing to do. If San Salvador was really about to lurch into generalized street violence, did it make sense just now to fly in and risk widowing Lori and orphaning Kate and Tucker? On the other hand, having recruited others to live with the commission day in and day out, how could I stay safe at home just when the going got rough? Did Daniel Schorr really know what he was talking about? Only a moment passed before I pressed my foot down on the accelerator and continued to SFO.

As it turned out, that commentator was wrong. No street battles raged in El Salvador, and I returned home in one piece. But that moment in the car changed me. It deepened my commitment, lessened my tolerance, drew a line that I would never retreat across. I had pushed past my momentary fear and decided the risk was worth taking; whether that risk was real or imagined was beside the point. If that moment alone had changed me, I wondered what a whole lifetime of far graver experiences might have done to the members of the commission. I wondered whether a series of such experiences might explain their customary cheerfulness, their simple willingness to carry on.

Precisely what it was that made their office such a wonderful place to be, I'll never know. Something different for each of them, I suppose. There is something about oppression that seems to bring out the best in people — in some people, anyhow. And the members of the Human Rights Commission of El Salvador proved the truth of that to me. Not many could have done what they did. They have the primary virtue of hard experience, experience that changed them for the better, made them see life differently; the rest of us are left only with the secondary virtue of admiration.

When I interviewed him in July 1993, Miguel Angel told me, "You start to see things clearly. If they kill me, they kill me. Things change. You realize that you have to hang on to reality. I'm still alive. You come to a moment when you just get used to it, when you get linked to the work. Then you celebrate each day and the *compañeros* when you meet them in the morning. You feel happy. You feel that the work must be done. You get calluses. You get strong. I remember going to the Treasury Police headquarters for a release of prisoners and meeting my torturer there. He said to me, 'You're a terrorist.' So I told him, 'Well, you're a torturer.' When you go out to the garrisons, to the *cuarteles*, you get strong."

And Reynaldo told me about saying goodbye to his daughters when he left them in Mexico to return to El Salvador. "I told my daughters, 'If I die, you'll see me in heaven, in the spiritual life.' My eight-year-old said, 'Look, Dad, who is going to come and get us when we get there? No one will know us.' So I told her, 'I'm going to be paying attention and waiting for you.' She said 'Okay,' but her eyes were filled with tears. It was the first time I told her that we must all die someday.

"So, we were all prepared to face that reality."

_5_

THE VOLUNTEERS

Of the twenty-eight volunteers who served in the Accompaniment Project for the Human Rights Commission of El Salvador, Jack Hammond was the only one ever taken into custody by Salvadoran authorities. They probably wish they had never run into him. Others experienced close calls — they witnessed gunfire, were tailed, or ran for cover during the November 1989 offensive — but only Jack looked down the muzzle of a gun and spent time behind bars.

Jack's experience in El Salvador had other unique aspects, most of them attributable to Jack. At forty-six, Jack was one of our oldest volunteers (I would guess the mean age to have been around thirty). A professor of sociology at Hunter College in New York City, Jack had written extensively about Central America over the years, had traveled there on a number of occasions to conduct his research, and was familiar with the scene and perfectly fluent in Spanish — this in contrast to other volunteers, whose experience of Latin America was slight and whose Spanish skills were marginal. Jack is tall, sports a bushy beard that flows to his breastbone, and speaks in stentorian tones virtually all the time. If I were a casting director looking for someone to play the part of Moses, Jack would be at the top of my list. When I conducted Jack's evaluation session with commission members, their only complaint was with his booming voice. Extremely inquisitive by nature, Jack quickly assesses any situation and places his stamp on it. One of the last things anyone would call him is shy.

When Jack arrived in San Salvador shortly after Christmas 1988 to begin his assignment, he immediately asked the commission members what he should do if he were ever captured. They advised him, "Hay que ganarles la moral." This expression begs literal translation but means something like, "You must beat them morally. If they see that you are afraid, they'll give you the works. If you're not, they'll back off." Few could have applied this advice better than Jack, a natural master of indignant outrage.

On Saturday, January 7, 1989, a young man named Lisandro appeared at the commission's office. Lisandro had come in from Usulután Department when a friend tipped him off that the army was looking for him. He wanted to tell the commission about his situation and alert them to the general situation in his hometown, Puerto Caballos. Thirty-five people from Puerto Caballos had been captured during 1988, and five people had been killed, including an eight-year-old boy on his way to school. Planes had bombed the community four times in December.

After listening to the young man's story, the commission decided to investigate. The task fell to Celia Medrano, who headed to Usulután on Monday morning. She asked Jack to accompany her. When they arrived in the town of La Ringlera at 4:00 in the afternoon, the peasants there advised them not to proceed to Puerto Caballos, where a military operation was currently underway. Celia asked someone to go to Puerto Caballos to collect witnesses who would be willing to provide testimonies. As people straggled in, Celia interviewed them while Jack recorded the conversations on video. A father broke down and wept as he described how a soldier killed his sixteen-year-old son. A wife described how the soldiers left her tortured husband on the doorstep to die. Others described captures and interrogations. Jack and Celia worked into the evening, then resumed their interviews on Tuesday morning, until someone ran in to tell them that soldiers were approaching.

Celia tried to convince the soldiers that she and Jack were tourists on their way to the beach, but when they didn't buy her story, she explained that she and Jack were there to take testimonies for the Human Rights Commission. While the sergeant radioed Sixth Infantry Brigade Headquarters for instructions, Jack and Celia took advantage of a few moments alone to pop the videocassette out of the camera and hide it. If that cassette fell into the hands of the soldiers, they would know who had come forward with testimonies.

While headquarters sent a helicopter out for Celia, one of the villagers slipped away to the nearest town with a telephone and alerted the commission in San Salvador. The soldiers kept Jack under guard in La Ringlera overnight, then escorted him into Usulután on Wednesday, where he was reunited with Celia at the Sixth Brigade stockade. They had not mistreated her.

Lisa Magarrell, the other volunteer then on duty at the commission, called me late Tuesday afternoon to tell me Jack and Celia had been captured in Usulután. It was time to activate our emergency procedures for the first time. Lisa gave me the particulars, then I placed calls to the emergency contacts Jack had provided on his application form — his father in Texas and two friends in New York City. Next, I called the Chicago number for the Christian Urgent Action Network for El Salvador (CUANES), a nationwide telephone network. Whenever an emergency arises in El Salvador, CUANES alerts solidarity organizations from coast to coast and provides them with specific response instructions — where to call, what to say. When each organization in turn alerts its local members, CUANES can light up any switchboard in El Salvador in a matter of hours. I phoned Suzanne, and we split the remaining calls, contacting the U.S. Embassy in San Salvador, the offices of Jack's congressman and senators, Marin County congresswoman Barbara Boxer, the members of our advisory board, and MITF's urgent action telephone tree.

When offices in El Salvador opened for business on Wednesday morning, calls began pouring in to the embassy, to the Salvadoran Army chief of staff, and to the Sixth Infantry Brigade. Celia told me later that the officer who interrogated her there was thoroughly exasperated at constantly being called away to answer the phone. The calls poured in to MITF, too. Lisa Magarrell kept me posted as things unfolded there. Jack's father called half a dozen times. Jack's friends in New York had spread the word among Jack's colleagues, many of whom called to find out what they should do. At midday, the chancellor of the City University of New York phoned. Hunter College, where Jack taught, was one of his campuses. He pledged to call the Estado Mayor (the Salvadoran high command headquarters) in San Salvador every hour on the hour until Jack and Celia were released.

Meanwhile, in El Salvador, Joaquín and Miguel Angel drove out on Wednesday morning to the Sixth Infantry stockade in Usulután. As they motored along the coastal highway, a convoy of military vehicles passed them, heading in the opposite direction. When Joaquín and Miguel Angel noticed Jack and Celia's car in the middle, they made a U-turn, caught up, and pulled alongside the car, which Jack was driving. While the military escort looked on, Jack pulled to the side of the road so Celia could tell Miguel Angel and Joaquín where they were headed: Salvadoran high command headquarters — the Estado Mayor — in the capital city. When the convoy resumed its journey, the two commission members found a pay phone and relayed this news to the office.

The one amusing aspect of the whole affair happened when Lisa Magarrell relayed this news, in turn, to me. I immediately called the Estado Mayor to enquire after the safety and well-being of two people imprisoned there — Celia Medrano and Jack Hammond. The guy who answered the phone said, "Well, we don't have anyone here by those names." When I insisted, he left the line for a minute, then came back and said, "You're right. They are here. They just came in. How did you know they were here?"

That afternoon, the authorities separated them, sending Jack to the Treasury Police and Celia to the National Police. As Jack said later, "At 7:00 P.M. I was put in a genuine jail cell. When the door shut, the situation hit me hard." When they began interrogating Jack later that evening, he gave them hell. "I'm a U.S. citizen. I'm here on a legal visa. I'm working with the Human Rights Commission. You have no right to keep me here. I want to see the ambassador. I don't have to answer these questions." They did not physically mistreat him, either that night or when they interrogated him the following morning, and they were probably glad to see the last of him when an embassy official escorted him out on Thursday morning.

The National Police treated Celia less gently, cuffing her around and throwing her against the wall as they accused her of being a Communist and demanded the names of her contacts in the FMLN. Because she did not represent the FMLN, she had no answers. For Celia, the urgent action network extended all the way to Europe. Various European diplomats asked the Spanish ambassador to look out for her, and he stirred up a good strong fuss until they released Celia at 3:00 P.M. on Thursday. Joaquín was waiting for her outside, but she shouldered past his embrace. "I was so tense, so much not wanting to cry, that I pushed Joaquín away. If I felt the warmth of my *compañero's* hug, I would have cried. And I did not want to cry there."

Jack spent the next few days trying to have his visa, which had expired while he was in custody, extended so he could complete his assignment. But the Immigration Service denied him, not surprisingly, and Jack headed back to New York the following Tuesday. Just before Jack left for the airport, one of the men from Puerto Caballos showed up in the office carrying a big pot of *cuajada* (curd). It was delicious, and embedded inside it, carefully sealed in a plastic bag, was the videocassette.

During the years we administered the Accompaniment Project, security concerned us most deeply, and for all the obvious reasons. The project's whole premise — placing volunteers beside people who were likely targets of violent repression in hopes that their presence would keep violence at bay — made it a scary undertaking. Other solidarity groups and churches had pioneered accompaniment in El Salvador without ever losing anyone. No North Americans that we knew of had been targeted for attack since the four churchwomen died in 1980. But still, we never knew when a bomb might go off or when the security forces might simply decide "The hell with it" and blow somebody away. So we took every step we could think of to protect the volunteers.

When people expressed interest in an assignment with the commission, we spelled out the dangers in great detail over the telephone before sending an application packet. In it, we included a waiver form detailing the risks and indemnifying MITF from liability in case of injury or death, and we insisted that they sign it before we would begin processing the application. On the application form itself, prospects had to provide the names of emergency contacts, as well as the names and phone numbers of their congressional representatives. For each candidate, we conducted at least three telephone reference checks before scheduling the final face-to-face interview. We interviewed West Coast applicants here in Marin; advisory board members and project alums who had returned from their assignments in El Salvador interviewed people from other parts of the country. Perhaps a third of the volunteers came our way via the recommendations of returned alums.

When we recruited our advisory board, we asked only two things of its members: that they allow us to use their names on our letterhead and that they stand ready to make the necessary calls to influential people should the commission or any of our volunteers come under attack. Whenever I went to El Salvador, I made it a point to visit with people who might be quick sources of information if we should ever lose contact with the commission — if someone cut their phone line or bombed their building, for instance.

When Suzanne and I first went to El Salvador in March 1987, we visited the U.S. Embassy to let officials know that U.S. citizens would be at the commission for the indefinite future. We had two reasons for paying this visit. First, we could think of no surer way to put Salvadoran authorities on notice about the presence of North Americans. Second, we fully expected the embassy to respond appropriately in the event of an emergency, as they did in Jack's case. Our dealings with the embassy perfectly represented the deep ironies of life in El Salvador: we expected help from the very entity that funded the violence we aimed to deter.

When volunteers were about to leave for El Salvador, we used simple substitution codes to notify the commission by telephone of their exact arrival times. When the volunteers were safely on board, the commission would call back to let us know that the package had arrived safely.

Two apparently contradictory mandates guided our actions throughout: do everything in plain sight and disclose nothing. Regarding the project itself, we told everyone of its existence. The more people who knew that North Americans accompanied the commission, the better. Regarding any details of the project, we told no one. The fewer people who knew the identities and travel plans of the volunteers, the better.

We tried to maintain at least two volunteers on duty at all times so that one could stay in the office while the others accompanied commission members into the field. In addition, we expected the old-timers to show the rookies the ropes. It was up to the commission to provide a detailed orientation and security briefing to newly arrived volunteers, but when all was said and done, we all knew that volunteer safety could not be guaranteed. When the volunteers went to El Salvador, they took their chances, and they knew it. I admired every one of them.

During the first eight months of the project, the volunteers maintained their own residence. But after the men came out of Mariona, this changed. At that point, the commission rented a large house, and most members moved in there with Lisa Brodyaga and Lisa Magarrell. Joaquín once referred to this house as a second jail, and because conditions there were crowded, not everyone moved in. Two months later, the commission rented a house directly across the street from their office and moved the safe house there. They stayed there most nights but sometimes ventured home for a night with their families.

During my second trip to El Salvador, Lisa Magarrell and I drove Miguel Angel out to his remote home near the volcano so he could spend an evening with his wife, Ester, and their kids. He wanted to introduce me to their newborn twins. As we drove into his neighborhood, Miguel became incredibly tense and alert, scanning every parked car we passed and looking over his shoulder constantly. When Lisa finally parked the car, Miguel Angel got out and walked along the street a few paces to speak with a man who suddenly stepped from the shadows.

Lisa explained that the whole neighborhood was like a cul-de-sac, with only one way in or out, and Miguel Angel wanted to be certain that no one was parked there waiting for him, that no one was preparing to block off our escape route, and that we were leading no one to his doorstep. The man he was quietly speaking with was his father, who had come out to wait for us.

We left the car and walked up a narrow dirt path into the forest. As we picked our way through the gathering darkness, Lisa told me of another time she had escorted Miguel home. As they walked up this very path, someone had stepped out of the bushes up ahead and fired a couple of shots at them before dashing off through the underbrush. On yet another occasion when Lisa had chauffeured Miguel home for a night with his family, a car had followed Lisa as she drove back through the city alone.

When we reached his cinderblock home, Miguel Angel introduced me to Ester, to several cousins, and to his children, for whom he had brought a bag of sweets and toys. When Miguel went into the other room to speak with Ester, I watched the five-year-old slip a Hershey bar out of the bag, unwrap it with extreme care, lick it once from bottom to top, then rewrap it and place it in the bag.

When Miguel and I went into the yard to look around, I noticed a gigantic mango tree arching over the house and mentioned to him that I loved mangoes. Later, as we all sat around in the living room, gabbing and admiring the twins, there was a sudden loud bang, then several more in quick succession. I just about leaped from my chair. Every instinct screamed at me to find cover, but I contained myself as I observed everyone else continuing the conversation unruffled. A few moments later, one of the young cousins stepped through the door with a shirtload of mangoes. He had climbed the mango tree and dropped a number of them onto the corrugated roof after Miquel had told him that the gringo liked mangoes. Everyone was accustomed to the sound of ricocheting mangoes but me.

When I next visited the commission in January 1989, they invited me to stay at the safe house across from their office on Pasaje #1 instead of at a hotel, as I had done on previous trips. It was a big old place, originally built as a combination doctor's office and residence, and would have comfortably accommodated everyone who lived there but for the fact that no one slept in any of the rooms, upstairs or down, that faced the street. The idea was to sleep well clear of any bullets or bomb fragments that might come hurtling in.

Reynaldo, Annie, and their teenage daughters slept in one room. Miguel Angel, Ester, and their four young children slept in another. The large central hallway was partitioned into little cells where the rest of us slept on cots. Celia had one cell to herself. I shared one with Joaquín. Lisa Magarrell shared the other with Susan Greenblatt, a new volunteer from Boston.

At night, everyone took turns on watch. There were three shifts — 10:00 to 1:00, 1:00 to 4:00, 4:00 to 7:00 — and two people on each shift. The commission had wired an automobile battery to a large klaxon that hung by one of the upstairs front windows. If anyone came prowling in the dead of night, that klaxon could be set off to scare the bejabbers out of them. All night, every night, teams took turns standing by that front window, watching every car and pedestrian that happened along, recording everything they saw in a logbook. Reading through the logbook, the commission could determine any patterns in the nighttime traffic. One vehicle did cruise by on a regular basis — the patrol car from the nearby U.S. Embassy, which circulated through the neighborhood from dusk to dawn.

I spent my watches with Lisa or Susan. It was fatiguing losing three hours of sleep every night, but I somehow enjoyed it. It's not often that you have the chance to watch a city at night, watch the dawn from the first graying of the blackness until the sunlight streams over the roofs. Besides, it gave me a good chance to get to know Lisa and Susan better as we chatted the night away while peering through the louvered window slats.

Lisa Magarrell was then in her eighteenth month on assignment with the commission, whose executive committee eventually hired her as a member of the staff and head of the legal department. Her competence as a lawyer, her all-but-compulsive work habits, and her dedication to the commission earned her a permanent place among them. But when she went to El Salvador in June 1987 expecting to stay for three months, I wondered if she would last even that long.

Lisa graduated with highest honors from the University of Iowa Law School in 1979, then worked as staff attorney in a Washington state agency that did advocacy work for farm workers. She also served the director of the Joint Legal Task Force on Central American Refugees in Seattle, where she spotted our notice in the National Lawyers Guild newsletter. But she lacked self-assurance and offered her ideas hesitantly. When she first came to the commission, her reticence stood out amid the generally gregarious atmosphere of the place. Other volunteers complained that she was difficult to work with.

But by January 1989, Lisa had changed. She had won the affection and regard of the commission members, in part, I think, because she had handled herself well under pressure. As we peered out through the window one night, she told me of an incident where she realized someone was tailing her as she drove the car. "It was daytime, so I wasn't sure they were following me at first," she said. "It's hard to tell. Maybe they just happened to be going the same way I was. So I turned off the highway into a hillside neighborhood. Sure enough, the car followed right behind me. I turned this way and that until finally I saw some men working at the side of the road. I pulled over and asked them for directions, while the other car waited back a little ways. Then I made up things to say to the guys on the work crew, anything that came to mind. I just kept talking to them and talking to them. Eventually, the other car pulled out and roared past me. Then I drove home."

Precisely what it was that endeared Lisa to the commission, I wasn't sure. Perhaps it was indeed her coolness under pressure; perhaps it was her competence. All I know is that when they accepted her, it changed her. Her diffidence was replaced with assurance. She gave the clear impression that she was where she belonged.

Susan Greenblatt also had a rocky start with the commission. Self-assured and voluble, Susan bristled at a number of things when she began her assignment. She took offense when commission members neglected to introduce her to various people, which they should have done; she found things to be generally disorganized, which they were; and she thought Lisa Magarrell a somewhat cantankerous den mother, as she sometimes could be. Her irritation deepened to indignation when her complaints went largely unheeded. Years later, however, when I asked Joaquín to name the volunteers who had made the best impression on him, Susan's was the first name he mentioned.

"Susan was an active person, somebody you could talk with. There were confrontations, but they were misunderstandings. I was always on her side. Our cultures are different, you must understand. She was a good person."

After a month on the job, Susan screwed up her resolve and decided to adapt, to take cues instead of giving them. This process of adaptation was something that every volunteer had to go through. Not all of them were successful, and those who weren't had a terrible time, coming home bitter or defeated. One volunteer told me that she had resorted to stepping into a closet every now and then to have a good loud scream. And there was plenty to scream about.

Despite our elaborate and repeated warnings to applicants about the tedium, about having to do as they were told, about the need for security precautions, and about feeling ignored and out of the loop, almost all of the volunteers went down there expecting to be welcomed as instant friends, expecting that their professional skills would soon be put to use, expecting that the interpersonal habits that had served them well in the United States would serve them well in El Salvador. When the commission forbade them their customary morning jog, they fumed. When the members of the *directiva* closeted themselves for hours and hours of secret discussions, they wondered what was going on behind closed doors. When the staff was preoccupied with the business at hand or with surveillance or with finances and other matters, they felt ignored. When the volunteers were assigned no duties and sat around for days on end, they went out of their minds with boredom and frustration.

After a month or so, their egos would crack, and one of two things would happen. For some, the assignment would become an ordeal to be suffered through until it was time to go home. For most, though, personal friendships would begin to form and new ways of thinking and relating would bloom. Not everyone had to go through this adaptation process — some, like Kate Bancroft, understood the situation instinctively and began making friends the very first day — but most did, Lisa and Susan among them, and they rejoiced when it happened.

Watching the volunteers go through all of this brought me moments of terrible anxiety and gnawing frustration — and moments of immense relief and abiding gratitude. Yes, some of the volunteers performed better than others. Yes, we sent a few people who should have stayed home. Yes, every one of them had some quirk that I wished they hadn't. But every one of them stuck a neck way out on behalf of strangers. Every one of them risked death for these people we admired so deeply. Every one of them went to El Salvador.

By the time of my next trip to El Salvador in June 1989, the commission had abandoned the house across the street and, with the exception of Celia and Joaquín, moved home. Celia and Joaquín lived with Lisa Magarrell, Jack Hammond (who had returned to complete his abbreviated first tour), and Lisa Sheehy (a volunteer from Boston) in a house in the northern part of the city. I slept in that house with them and was awakened early each morning when Joaquín, Celia, and Lisa Sheehy cranked up the cassette player to accompany their living room aerobics.

The project was in great shape at that point. We had three solid volunteers — the optimum number — in San Salvador and several more undergoing the application process back home. Herbert's death was receding into the background. We had ironed out the snarls that had plagued us early on. I had met with the leaders of the commission often enough that we were beginning to know one another as people; our relationship had finally moved beyond our respective roles in the commission and at MITF.

It was fortunate that the project was in good shape; trouble was heading our way.

In the months following my June visit, Jack Hammond and Lisa Sheehy came home and four new volunteers replaced them: David Weinstein, who had served as campaign chairman for Mayor Bernie Sanders in Burlington, Vermont; Pat Moreno, founder of the Springfield (Massachusetts) Area Central America Project; Mike MacDonald, a Nova Scotian who was working at The Center for Global Education in Cuernavaca, Mexico; and Larry Ross, a part-time photojournalist from Marin County. Including Lisa Magarrell, we had five people on assignment, our largest contingent ever, and two volunteer houses (the commission wanted Larry Ross to work at arm's length collecting stories and pictures, so they rented him a house of his own where he could set up a darkroom and make contacts with the media on an untapped telephone line). All five volunteers were on assignment by mid-October 1989.

On October 31, bombs exploded in the offices of two prominent popular organizations. In both places, North Americans were present. The bomb at COMADRES wounded four when it went off in the early morning hours. The bomb at FENASTRAS, a union umbrella organization, killed nine and wounded many others. Someone placed the device behind the heavy metal door of the lunchroom at FENASTRAS and timed it to detonate at midday. The force of the explosion reduced the door to shrapnel that hurtled through the crowded room, ripping off limbs and decapitating people as it went. In an instant, the bomb transformed the room into a tangled mass of human flesh, smashed furniture, and slick blood. Chris Norton, a writer for the *Christian Science Monitor* who happened to be conducting an interview upstairs, later found his car thirty feet from where he had parked it, blown clear across the street. Larry Ross went over to FENASTRAS and photographed the sickening and dreadful scene.

The stakes had suddenly changed in El Salvador. With these violent attacks against well-known organizations — one of them in broad daylight and both of them with members of the international community present, several of whom were wounded but none of whom died — the security forces and the death squads had thrown down the gauntlet. They seemed to be saying, "We've tolerated these Commie labor organizers and subversive demonstrators long enough. So what if a few non-Salvadoran heads get whacked? You remember what it was like in the early 1980s? Well, it can be that way again." The commission tightened security measures to the point of suffocation, while in Marin we worried like mad and asked ourselves if we should call the volunteers home.

Twelve days later, the FMLN launched an offensive, bringing the civil war to the streets of San Salvador for the first time. Guerrillas swept down off San Salvador Volcano at night, right through the neighborhood where Larry Ross lived, to attack strategic points all across the city. They stormed into the Sheraton Hotel, stumbling onto a contingent of visiting U.S. military advisors and holding them at bay until the U.S. Embassy negotiated their release. They holed up in the shantytowns and barrios around the city. They launched wildly misfired missiles at the Estado Mayor from the back of a pickup truck. Within forty-eight hours, they disproved the popular notion that they were finished as an effective fighting force.

The army struck back. The Salvadoran air force bombed the shantytowns where the guerrillas went to ground, while the army saturated them with artillery fire. They pounded the campus of the National University in a nighttime artillery and infantry attack, killing scores of people whose bodies were trucked away the following day. They slipped onto the campus of the Jesuit-run University of Central America on the night of November 16, dragged six priests out of their beds, and blew their brains out. Then they killed the eyewitnesses, a housekeeper and her daughter.

David Weinstein called to say that the commission was abandoning its offices. He, Mike, and Pat would be at the safe house and would call in regularly. I had the telephone number for the house but never used it. In case someone was tapping MITF's line, we never wanted to make the mistake of initiating an international call to a safe house. Lisa Magarrell and members of the commission rented rooms at the Camino Real Hotel. Larry stayed in his house alone.

Back in Marin, we were frantic. The television networks were broadcasting scenes of violence from San Salvador — neighborhoods in flames, the bodies of the slain priests, helicopters launching rockets — and Larry Ross was calling on a regular basis, partly just to hear our voices, and partly to relay the scenes of death and destruction he witnessed as he ventured out into the city with his camera. He drove toward the university campus the day after watching the fireworks from his hillside neighborhood, and when his car came under fire, he stopped and squirmed under the vehicle. While waiting for the gunfire to cease, he noticed a cigarette lighter lying on the asphalt, so he picked it up and put it in his pocket. Later, Larry was able to return that lighter to its rightful owner, Phil Bronstein of the *San Francisco Chronicle*, who had spent some anxious moments beneath his car at precisely the same spot the night before.

Larry ventured into the Zacamil neighborhood, where the fighting was intense, and came upon what appeared to be a guerrilla command center. They told Larry that many civilians had been killed in the bombing attacks there and offered to escort him to the far side of the neighborhood, where the bodies had been stacked. Larry turned on his video camera and shouldered it as he dodged from house to house behind two guerrillas, who led him through ruined alleyways while bullets whistled overhead. They paused when they came to an open street, and Larry stayed behind a few yards as his escorts ventured around the corner and out into the boulevard. On Larry's tape you can hear the explosion that followed and see the dirt showering down around him. Assuming that the two guerrillas had been killed by a grenade, Larry retraced his steps.

Meantime, in Marin, we lost contact with Pat, Mike, and David. When the better part of a day passed with no call from the house where they were staying, I decided the time had come to break our rule and call the safe house. I went next door and asked my neighbors if I could borrow their phone, explaining that I didn't want to make this particular call on my own line. The phone in San Salvador rang and rang. No answer.

The three volunteers had decided to abandon the house and seek refuge at the Camino Real Hotel, where others had already holed up. They called me from there several hours later, and I advised them to start looking for ways to get out of the country. Enough was enough.

Meantime the commission members who were at the Camino Real began to worry about materials they had left behind at the office — years worth of testimonies, photographs, and video footage. The security forces could waltz in there and take it away, or simply dynamite the building and destroy it all. They decided to contact Larry, who still had a house and car, and ask him to cart everything over to his place. The next time Larry called me, he told me that he was babysitting the commission's archives — all of their photo albums, more than 100 videotapes, and boxloads of written material. I didn't much like the thought of Larry sitting there alone with that invaluable material. God only knew when someone might come knocking on his door, there to find him keeping watch over the archives of the Human Rights Commission.

For the next week, Larry and I stayed in close touch. He badly wanted to stay on the scene so he could continue to record the fighting; he also badly wanted to get the hell out of there, not knowing as he climbed into bed each night who might come knocking. When David and Mike made airline reservations for home and Pat Moreno flew out to Mexico City with two members of the commission, Miguel Angel and Camelia Cartagena, Larry finally decided that it no longer made sense for him to stay, either. He secured permission from the commission to take the archives to the United States, then arranged with DHL to ship 103 kilograms of material to Marin on December 6. The bill came to $970. Larry's son, Andre, and I met him at San Francisco International Airport several days later. When he wheeled his cartload of personal effects and the remainder of the archives out of customs, I don't know who was the most relieved.

Lisa Magarrell stayed on in El Salvador throughout the offensive and helped the commission reopen its offices when the dust had settled. David Weinstein returned to El Salvador a few months later to complete his assignment and ended up staying on beyond the project's end in May 1991. Brenda

Mueller did a three-month stint beginning in March 1990. Rouge Dezza, a friend of Kate Bancroft's, began an assignment in April and has stayed on to this day. Brenda and Rouge were the last volunteers we sent to El Salvador.

When we initiated the Accompaniment Project with the Human Rights Commission of El Salvador, we agreed that we would continue sending volunteers for as long as they were needed. The project ended in May 1991, four years and ten months after Kate Bancroft's first visit to the men in Mariona. By then, the FMLN and the Salvadoran government were hammering out the United Nations–sponsored peace accords that went into effect on January 16, 1992. The commission's staff had grown from a dozen or so to more than sixty. The UN had placed scores of monitors in El Salvador. The need for accompaniment had ended. Lisa Magarrell had long since made the transition from volunteer to staff, so she stayed on with the commission when the project ended, as did David Weinstein and Rouge Dezza, both of whom were hired to continue their work in the commission's media department.

Of the twenty-eight volunteers who accompanied the commission, I got to know seventeen, either by interviewing them in Marin before they went or by staying with them on one of my periodic trips to San Salvador. Of the eleven I never met, I most regret missing Lisa Brodyaga, the lawyer from Texas who met Kate on her first visit to Mariona, succeeded Kate as our second volunteer, and provided the legal expertise that the commission needed to do the torture report. Lisa was also the one who smuggled the report out of Mariona, interleaving its pages among her other papers so that they would remain undetected by the guards who examined her personal effects as she departed each day. By all accounts a remarkable woman, Lisa had dedicated her life to the people of Central America, long before we bumped into her, by offering legal advice and advocacy to refugees as they poured into the Rio Grande valley in the early 1980s and by training other lawyers to do the same. Lisa referred two of her pupils — Patrick Hughes and Jonathan Jones — to us, and both of them served in the early months of the project.

It was a great privilege for me to have administered the Accompaniment Project. That work allowed me to get to know the members of the commission; it allowed me to get to know the volunteers. We didn't do much recruiting — just the occasional notice in a progressive publication — because we didn't have to. We relied on the nationwide solidarity network for applicants.

Every now and then my phone would ring at the office or at home, and there would be someone on the line, calling from Seattle or Indiana or Boston or Texas to say, "I've heard that you're looking for volunteers to accompany the Human Rights Commission of El Salvador. I'd like to go. I'd like to serve them." After hanging up the phone, I would wander out into the backyard to collect myself, because those calls always messed with my composure.

Those twenty-eight people are great blessings — for me, for the commission, for all of us — and they deserve to be recognized here: Kate Bancroft, Dorothy Barnhouse, Mallorie Baron, Tim Block, Robyn Braverman, Lisa Brodyaga, Libby Cooper, Rouge Dezza, Susan Greenblatt, Jack Hammond, Kathy Herrera, Patrick Hughes, Jonathan Jones, Danny Katz, Mike Mac-Donald, Lisa Magarrell, Pat Moreno, Brenda Mueller, Diane Paulsell, Elaine Porinski, Terry Rayburn, Larry Ross, Lisa Sheehy, Glen Shelly, Vicki Stifter, Jack Tobin, David Weinstein, and Emily Yozell.

_ 6 _

BARBARA

When Larry Ross shipped the commission's archives from El Salvador to Marin in early December 1989, we knew exactly what we wanted to do with the documentation: take it to our congresswoman, Barbara Boxer.

From MITF's early days, Barbara had been an asset and an ally. She was one of the few members of Congress who could be counted on to oppose U.S. funding of El Salvador's military when appropriations bills came up for a vote. Her opposition to our national policy in El Salvador was visceral and dependable. She was appalled at what was happening in El Salvador, could discern absolutely no foreign policy objectives that justified our support of a government that systematically violated the protocols and conventions governing warfare, and expressed her opinion forcefully.

From time to time when she was in the district, we would stop by her office to brief her on the latest developments in El Salvador. She wanted to know what was happening, and through our relationship with the commission, we were able to provide her with their most recent statistics and analyses. That the commission had been branded an FMLN front organization by the U.S. Embassy in San Salvador did not daunt Barbara. She could understand that armed insurgents and unarmed popular organizations might struggle against a common foe without necessarily being affiliated. She could understand that the guerrillas and the commission might even share the same political perspective, might even communicate from time to time, without being one and the same. That such discernment made her look like a dupe in the eyes of her more conservative peers did not deter her. Nor did the specious assertion that patriotic public officials must support the policies of the administration.

Over the years, we got to know the members of her staff, too. They would call us occasionally when they wanted information or perspective on El Salvador. We would call them every now and then to alert them to upcoming foreign aid struggles. Barbara's staff reflected her best attributes. They were consistently accessible, forthcoming, and solicitous — this in marked contrast to the self-assured smugness and ignorance of staff members we sometimes encountered in other congressional offices, people with whom dialogue was simply impossible.

When we initiated the Accompaniment Project for the Human Rights Commission of El Salvador, we made a point of briefing Barbara fully. We fervently hoped that none of our volunteers would come in harm's way while on assignment, but if one did, we wanted to have done everything possible in advance to ensure a prompt and appropriate response from the U.S. Embassy. Barbara understood this perfectly, and she went to bat for us without hesitation when Jack Hammond was captured with Celia Medrano in early 1989.

Even so, in December 1989 we wondered whether Barbara would be willing to do something as drastic as introducing the commission's archives — gruesome, graphic, and horrific as they were — into the halls of Congress. In the commission's archival material we knew we had powerful and persuasive documentation of the Salvadoran reality. We wanted to make as much of it as we could. But first we needed the commission's permission. The problem was that we had no way of reaching them in El Salvador. The offensive was still raging, and everyone was in hiding. Even if we could have reached them over the phone, we couldn't discuss our plans without disclosing to listening ears where the archives had been spirited away.

Fortunately, we got a timely call from Pat Moreno, one of our volunteers. She and two commission members had flown to Mexico City, where they could work in relative safety and freedom. I grabbed a plane for Mexico City, where Pat met me at the airport and took me to meet Miguel Angel and Camelia. Without hesitation, they gave us the green light to use the archives in any way we saw fit.

The month that followed was the busiest that MITF ever had. We made an appointment to see Barbara while she was in Marin for the Christmas congressional recess. Suzanne and I went to her district office in San Rafael, bringing with us the photo albums that I had seen on my first visit to El Salvador in March 1987, the albums filled with photographs of death squad victims, armless corpses, eyeless sockets, decapitations, bodies with slogans carved into their chests, and other horrors.

Putting those albums before another human being is something to give you pause. You hesitate before opening those albums for someone you know and like, knowing you will be etching their consciousness permanently with something dark and frightening and despicable. No one with a heart in her chest could look at those pictures and ever be the same. On top of that, we were preparing to ask Barbara to give those pictures the widest and most dramatic circulation possible, to present them to her colleagues and the U.S. public. As consistent as she had been in supporting our work and opposing U.S. policy in El Salvador, we didn't know if we could rightfully expect her to go that far.

We sat down around a low coffee table and stacked the albums before her. We described how they had come into our possession. We explained the importance we attached to the contents of the albums and to the many hours of videotape that had accompanied them. We described the role we hoped she might be willing to play in broadcasting what the commission had sent to us. We repeated what she already knew — that eight people had died for their work in assembling the documentation before her.

Barbara squared her shoulders, took a breath, and opened the first album. She paged through it silently for a few moments, then closed it and turned to us. "Of course you can count on me with this. You didn't think I might duck this one, did you?" I admitted our uncertainty a little sheepishly. Then, in her characteristic let's-get-down-to-business manner, she asked us what we wanted her to do. We wanted her to call a press conference in Washington to display this evidence exposing the results of U.S. foreign policy in El Salvador.

Barbara didn't miss a beat. Recalling the impact that photographs and film footage from Vietnam had made in the 1960s when the networks had broadcast them into living rooms across the country, Barbara figured that the commission's frightful evidence might have a similar effect. She asked us to keep in touch with her and her staff as we distilled the commission's mountain of material into a usable format. She promised to try to round up some Senate support for her press conference and assured us that she would make herself available when we were ready to bring everything to Washington.

Suzanne and I left Barbara's office in high spirits, drove back to the MITF office in San Anselmo, and launched into one of those hours-long discussions we so often had. How could we assemble and edit this mountain of material into something striking and telling, something that could be conveyed during a brief press conference?

We decided to divide the task. In addition to preparing poster-size enlargements of a dozen photographs, Suzanne would produce a twenty-page booklet of photographs and written testimonies covering the 1980s. I would somehow edit the hundreds of hours of videotape into a sixteen-minute "highlights" film. I would never have been able to accomplish that task in the month we allotted without the help of Alejandro Hernandez.

Alejandro was a classmate of mine at San Francisco Theological Seminary, a Salvadoran national who had been recruited to the masters program in divinity by Jorge Lara-Braud, a professor at the seminary and a member of our advisory board. Alejandro and I had become friends when he discovered that I was director of MITF. Alejandro's advocacy for human rights in El Salvador and his intimate knowledge of the situation there qualified him perfectly for the job I asked him to undertake. Would he be willing to review the hundred-odd videotapes that the commission had sent to us and cull from them a few segments that could be spliced together into a short piece? Alejandro was more than willing. He closeted himself in front of his television set for a week in early January, remote control in hand, to catalogue the footage.

At the end of that week, Alejandro invited me in, showed me the catalogued cassettes, and cued up the footage he thought would be the most telling. Alejandro had done his job brilliantly. We had our raw material; now all we had to do was find a video studio that would be willing to help us splice it all together, frame it with an introduction and conclusion, and lay down the soundtrack. Film and Video Services in San Francisco, with whom we had worked on prior video projects, offered us the use of their facilities for a song. We showed up bright and early on a Saturday morning near the end of the month. Martha Hook and Lonnie Voth came along with Alejandro and me to provide additional dubbing for the soundtrack. By midday Sunday, we had recorded the master, including testimonies of four torture victims.

In the meantime, Suzanne enlisted Jan Bauman to carefully rephotograph everything. She then spent hours at her desk sorting through and categorizing the pictures of the dead, an experience she found profoundly spiritual. After a while, she got past her shock and horror at the mangled limbs and the eyeless sockets and found that she was focusing instead on the victims themselves — people who had simply been people before their brains were blown out. As she carefully mounted their photos on the galleys and recorded the circumstances of their deaths for the captions, she felt she came to know and treasure each of them, to experience — entirely unexpectedly — their sweetness and wholeness as human beings. At the instant of their deaths, they had become disfigured, lifeless flesh, where for years and decades, they had been people who laughed and ate and smiled at their children. By some alchemy of the heart, Suzanne was able to see the people instead of the corpses.

We had set ourselves a monumental task, and we had accomplished it, with a lot of help from a lot of people. We were proud of the results, and we were ready to go to Washington. Suzanne and I flew east in early February 1990. With us we carried enough copies of the booklet to distribute to every member of the House and Senate, as well as fifty copies of the videotape. The poster-size photographs we reserved for Barbara's scheduled press conference.

Barbara was on the House floor when we arrived in her office, so we were greeted by the three members of her staff she had assigned to work with us: Drew Littman, her chief of staff; Rob Alexander, her press secretary; and Lisa Pullen, her Central America specialist. For the next forty-eight hours, these generous people shoehorned us into their busy schedules and made space and phone lines available to us. As we told Barbara when we left, her staff reflected her well. In a city populated by power seekers, Drew and Rob and Lisa distinguished themselves by being nice people.

The press conference had been scheduled for the following afternoon in the Senate Press Gallery, and Barbara had delivered on her promise of securing a Senate co-sponsor. John Kerry of Massachusetts had agreed to join Barbara before the cameras. Drew had conveyed this good news to Suzanne and me several days before we left California, and we had confirmed the details with Kerry's office by telephone. But bad news awaited us upon our arrival. After we had introduced ourselves around, Drew told us that Kerry's office had just called; he had decided not to do the press conference with Barbara after all.

This was a serious blow. Kerry was much more likely to attract coverage than a junior congresswoman from California, and without him we would lose the use of the Senate Press Gallery. Feeling that Kerry had breached his promise to MITF, as well as to Barbara, Suzanne and I marched over to the Senate Office Building and requested an interview with a member of his staff. Maybe we could change the senator's mind. But it was not to be. The woman who met with us expressed exasperation at our effrontery and sent us on our way.

We returned to Barbara's office, where she now awaited us, and confirmed the bad news. Together we decided that the press conference would have to be held in her office for lack of a better alternative. Barbara then dictated a Dear Colleague letter to accompany every copy of Suzanne's twenty-page booklet. Suzanne and I sat down to call the offices of wire services, newspapers, and networks, letting the press know where and when to gather the following day.

Early the next afternoon, we erected easels in Barbara's office and set the photo enlargements upon them. We cued up the videotape and hoisted the television set up onto Barbara's desk. A few minutes before the press arrived, Barbara came in to examine the photos and review the notes she had made for herself. Then the camera operators began to trickle in to set up their tripods and run their microphone cables and test their lights. By the time everything was ready, some fifteen or twenty representatives of the media had squeezed themselves into the room.

Barbara addressed them briskly and forcefully, cited the most current statistics about the numbers of dead and disappeared Salvadoran civilians and about the magnitude of U.S. military support, and declared her resolve to disclose the consequences of that support. She turned to the easels, expressed her regret about the unpleasantness of the images displayed on them, and repeated what she had told Suzanne and me back in December — that people in the United States needed access to images like these if they were to understand what was happening in El Salvador, just as they had needed access to the images broadcast from Vietnam a generation earlier. After fielding questions for a few minutes, she asked that we roll the video and turned to the television with the rest of us. She had not seen it before.

In silence, the assembled crowd watched the images and testimonies that the commission had recorded: torture victims exposing the welts and burns and scars left by electric shocks, acid, and knives; a woman who had been beaten and raped by a gang of soldiers; another woman sobbing at the side of a grave. Halfway through the film, Barbara squeezed her way to the door and ducked out of the room. She had lost her composure and needed to find a tissue. By the time the tape was over, she had rejoined us with eyes dried and poise restored.

Finally, we distributed copies of the booklet and videotape to those who requested them, and then the reporters pocketed their notebooks, shouldered their equipment, and dispersed.

When we flipped through the newscasts that evening and the following morning, nothing of Barbara's press conference was to be seen. The newspapers provided the same amount of coverage — zero. As far as we were able to tell, only the Fox affiliate in San Francisco, Channel 2, and the Spanish language network, UNIVISION, found the commission's documentation of human rights abuses in El Salvador newsworthy. There may have been coverage elsewhere that we never saw, but in the end I think it is safe to say that the booklet and the videotape received wider distribution through the solidarity network than they did through the media.

Later that year, Barbara took the large photos we had left with her onto the floor of Congress during the annual appropriations debate and used them to challenge her colleagues to reconsider their ongoing support of military funding in El Salvador.

In 1992, Barbara Boxer declared her intention to run for the U.S. Senate, and I for one was dismayed to hear the news. I just didn't think that Barbara had enough recognition and stature in the eyes of the electorate to win that Senate seat, and I was chagrined at the prospect of losing our steadfast advocate when she abandoned her seat in the House. In the end, of course, Barbara's political savvy proved as reliable as her moral instincts. She won the Democratic primary and went on to win the general election. Of course, now that Barbara had a whole state to contend with, we lost the ready access we had so prized. But to our great fortune, Lynn Woolsey, Barbara's successor in the Sixth Congressional District, has proven Barbara's equal at championing Central American issues.

Legislative advocacy has never been MITF's long suit. Small and remote from Washington, we have relied on the larger East Coast organizations to keep before Congress and the administration those issues that pertain to

Central America. Besides, we have always had our hands full recruiting volunteers and administering various projects in that region. What felt like a monumental task to us when we rushed to bring the commission's documentation to Washington was in fact just another grain in the sandstorm of opposition to U.S. policy in El Salvador. It was work we simply had to do when it fell into our laps, work we could not have accomplished without Barbara Boxer's gracious and impassioned partisanship.

I like to think that the sandstorm, persistent as it was and still is, eventually helped decrease U.S. support of the war in El Salvador. The very events that prompted the commission to send their archives our way — the FMLN offensive of November 1989 and the assassination of six Jesuit priests and two women that coincided with that offensive — were telling blows to U.S. support of the Salvadoran government. The offensive demonstrated the FMLN's fighting effectiveness despite a decade of U.S.-sponsored attempts to eliminate them, and the killing of the Jesuits exposed yet again the Salvadoran military's wanton disregard for the distinction between their armed opposition and their unarmed critics. As congressional support began eroding and the United Nations began exerting forceful pressure, the Salvadoran government reluctantly dragged itself to the bargaining table and commenced the difficult negotiations for peace.

The FMLN offensive and the killing of the Jesuits finally turned the tide of U.S. support for the Salvadoran armed forces, but not before a lot of faithful people had laid the groundwork on Capitol Hill by consistently disclosing to their elected officials what was happening there. I like to think that MITF played a part in that advocacy, and I am proud that we did what we could.

(Left to right) Sister Bernadette Wombacher, Bill Hutchinson, and Suzanne Bristol. In the fall of 1984, Sister Bernadette convened the meetings that ultimately spawned the Marin Interfaith Task Force on Central America, of which Suzanne and I were founding chairs. *(Photo by Jan Bauman)*

(Left to right) Jesús Campos, Kate Bancroft, and Suzanne Bristol at MITF's fifth anniversary party in 1990. *(Photo by Jan Bauman)*

Bill Hutchinson and Herbert Anaya at the office of the Nongovernmental Human
Rights Commission of El Salvador in March 1987. *(Photo by Suzanne Bristol)*

Herbert Anaya at the office of the Human Rights Commission in March 1987. This is the picture Kate Bancroft carried to Herbert's funeral in October of that year. *(Photo by Suzanne Bristol)*

Mirna Anaya in a San Salvador restaurant in the summer of 1994. *(Photo by Bill Hutchinson)*

(Left to right) Patrick Hughes, Herbert Anaya, and Joaquín Cáceres at the office of the Human Rights Commission in March 1987. Patrick was the third volunteer who accompanied the commission. *(Photo by Suzanne Bristol)*

Kate Bancroft and Joaquín Cáceres at the office of the Human Rights Commission in the summer of 1994. *(Photo by Bill Hutchinson)*

Miguel Angel Montenegro at the office of the Human Rights Commission in the summer of 1994. *(Photo by Bill Hutchinson)*

Reynaldo Blanco at the office of the Human Rights Commission in the summer of 1994. *(Photo by Bill Hutchinson)*

Celia Medrano at the office of the Human Rights Commission in the summer of 1994. *(Photo by Bill Hutchinson)*

Herbert Anaya *(left)* taking a testimony at Mariona Prison. The testimonies gathered by Herbert and other incarcerated commission members were incorporated into *Torture in El Salvador*, a daring report published from within Mariona.

Herbert Anaya *(left)* and Reynaldo Blanco taking testimonies at Mariona.

Joaquín Cáceres *(right)* taking a testimony at Mariona.

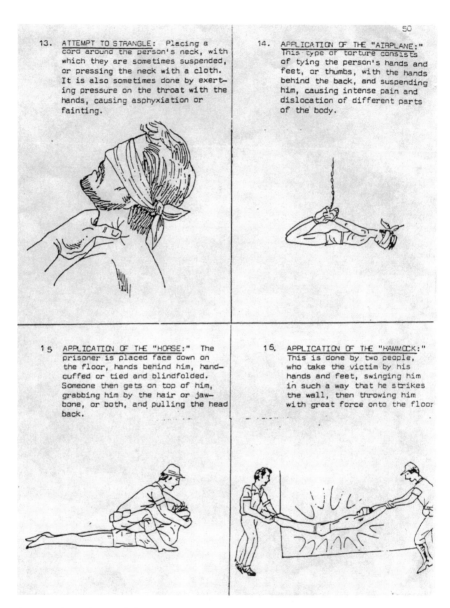

50

13. ATTEMPT TO STRANGLE: Placing a cord around the person's neck, with which they are sometimes suspended, or pressing the neck with a cloth. It is also sometimes done by exerting pressure on the throat with the hands, causing asphyxiation or fainting.

14. APPLICATION OF THE "AIRPLANE:" This type of torture consists of tying the person's hands and feet, or thumbs, with the hands behind the back, and suspending him, causing intense pain and dislocation of different parts of the body.

15. APPLICATION OF THE "HORSE:" The prisoner is placed face down on the floor, hands behind him, handcuffed or tied and blindfolded. Someone then gets on top of him, grabbing him by the hair or jawbone, or both, and pulling the head back.

16. APPLICATION OF THE "HAMMOCK:" This is done by two people, who take the victim by his hands and feet, swinging him in such a way that he strikes the wall, then throwing him with great force onto the floor

Page 50 from the English version of *Torture in El Salvador*. In this report, commission members documented tortures inflicted upon political prisoners.

114

Corpse of José Abraham Menjivar, a student at the National University of El Salvador, discovered May 27, 1988, in the San Antonio Abad neighborhood of San Salvador. Menjivar's eyes were gouged out and his thumbs tied behind his back. *(Courtesy the Nongovernmental Human Rights Commission of El Salvador)*

Corpse of Medardo Ceferino Ayala Pérez, a member of the Salvadoran Association of Telephone Workers (ASTEL). Assassinated in front of his home by four heavily armed men dressed in civilian clothing, he was shot twelve times with a .45-caliber weapon. *(Courtesy the Nongovernmental Human Rights Commission of El Salvador)*

Lisa Magarrell at the commission's office in the summer of 1994. Lisa was the longest-serving volunteer for the Accompaniment Project, and she was eventually hired by the commission. *(Photo by Bill Hutchinson)*

(Left to right) MITF volunteers Ann Dolan and Kit Everts, Congresswoman Barbara Boxer, Suzanne Bristol, and Bill Hutchinson at MITF's fifth anniversary party in 1990. *(Photo by Jan Bauman)*

César Vielman Joya Martinez at a speaking event in Marin. César claimed that the First Infantry Brigade — his unit within the Salvadoran Army — contained a clandestine death squad, of which he was a member. *(Photo by Jan Bauman)*

Mirtala López with her brother Miguel Angel López in 1987. Mirtala was one of the founders and leaders of CRIPDES (Christian Committee for the Displaced of El Salvador). *(Photo by Franklin Rivera)*

Mirtala López in January 1997 during her campaign for a seat in the Salvadoran National Assembly. She was elected as an alternate delegate. *(Photo by Bill Hutchinson)*

Brian Willson in 1987. In September of that year, Brian lost his legs while sitting on the tracks outside Concord Naval Weapons Station when a munitions train rolled over him. *(Photo by Jan Bauman)*

(Left to right) Neto Anaya, Rouge Dezza, and Rosa Anaya at the commission's office in the summer of 1994. Rouge was the last volunteer recruited by the Accompaniment Project. *(Photo by Bill Hutchinson)*

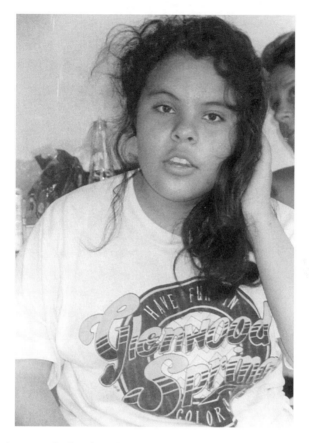

Gloria Anaya at the beach in the summer of 1992. *(Photo by Bill Hutchinson)*

Rafa Anaya at the beach in the summer of 1992. *(Photo by Bill Hutchinson)*

Edith Anaya at the beach in the summer of 1992. *(Photo by Bill Hutchinson)*

1993 gathering of the Anaya children and the families with whom they stayed at various times between 1988 and 1993. *(Photo by Tom Valens)*

The Salvadoran advisors to the El Salvador Archives Project in January 1996. Top row *(left to right):* Benjamin Cuellar, Edwin Rodriguez. Bottom row *(left to right):* Mirna Anaya, Mirtala López, Miguel Angel Montenegro. *(Photo by Bill Hutchinson)*

_ 7 _
CÉSAR

During the years that MITF recruited volunteers to accompany the Human Rights Commission of El Salvador, I often wondered whether we were in over our heads. What did any of us at MITF know about political violence, about appropriate security measures for volunteers in a far-off violent situation, about surveillance and death squads and torture? Next to nothing. We could only hope — perhaps naively — that our project on the commission's behalf was more of an asset than a liability to them and could only trust that they knew what was best for them when they continued to request volunteers.

Unschooled as we were about security risks in El Salvador, we were equally innocent about what risks we might be running at home. We often wondered whether our phones were bugged, and we operated on the assumption that they were. A friend who claimed to know about such things offered to have a listen on Suzanne Bristol's telephone. He dialed a number, listened for a minute, and affirmed that the line was bugged. "As you dial," he told Suzanne, "you'll hear, very faintly, the beeping sound of another number being dialed in the background. That's the electronic equipment dialing up the recording instrument." Sure enough, that background sound was audible whenever we dialed out. We wondered whether it might simply be the telephone company's equipment doing its normal thing, but we didn't hear that background sound on any other telephone lines.

On one occasion, we invited John Stockwell, a former CIA agent who had abandoned the agency in disgust after managing its Angola operations for a time, to come to Marin for a speaking engagement and fund-raiser. We had dinner together beforehand, and I asked whether he thought the CIA had a file on me. "They don't have *a* file on you, Bill," he responded. "They have *files* on you, and on anyone else who by your standards and mine is a patriotic American."

Sometimes at night, when a noise woke me, I would leave Lori asleep in bed to prowl through the house in my shorts and T-shirt, wondering if some operatives of my own government might be out there in my quiet neighborhood, recording my license plate number or doing God knows what else. I would eventually crawl back under the covers, telling myself to quit thinking such foolish thoughts and go to sleep.

Some in MITF have urged me to submit a Freedom of Information Act request to see what my government has in its records on me, but I have never wanted to; I would rather not know. We were operating in an environment about which I knew nothing, beyond what I had read in spy novels, and I sometimes had to laugh at myself for all the elaborate measures we took with phone calls and message couriers, wondering on the one hand whether such measures accomplished anything and on the other whether I was actually enjoying the cloak-and-dagger bit. And then remembering Herbert and the others at the commission and all that they had been through.

Part of our ignorance was intentional and had to do with the commission itself, with the queries we received from many quarters about whether the group might be mixed up in some way with the fighting forces of the FMLN. Having asked the commission members about this when we first met and having satisfied myself that they were the independent human rights monitors they claimed to be, I nevertheless wondered what kind of communications they might have with the guerrillas. They seemed to know in advance that the FMLN offensive of 1989 was coming — or at least that something was coming — and when Herbert Anaya spent the better part of a year in Morazán during 1984 and 1985, it is difficult to imagine that he did so without coming in contact with the ERP (Revolutionary Force of the People), the part of the FMLN that controlled much of Morazán at the time.

Regarding such matters, we decided that the best thing was to remain as naive as possible. The less we knew, the better for our sleep at night and the better for maintaining our stance as a group of well-intentioned, politically uninvolved churchpeople. We applied to ourselves the same standard we invoked in communications with our congressional representatives — that neither we nor our government had any business meddling in the internal affairs of a foreign country. We took our stand on human rights and stubbornly restricted our focus to that area, knowing that our government was providing financial and logistical support to a murderous regime and suspecting that the United States might be providing even more than that.

Then, in the spring of 1990, César Vielman Joya Martinez, a Salvadoran soldier and self-confessed death squad operative, landed on our doorstep and told us that our worst suspicions were true. According to him, the Intelligence Department of the Salvadoran Army's First Infantry Brigade, in which he had been a case officer, had tortured and killed scores of suspected FMLN supporters during his tour in 1988 and 1989 and had received funding for their operations from two U.S. military advisors who maintained desks in the unit's office. Further, he claimed to have personally trained a subordinate, Oscar Amaya Grimaldi, and to have familiarized Amaya Grimaldi with his contacts at the Jesuit-run University of Central America (UCA) in San Salvador. On the night of November 16, 1989, when members of the Atlacatl Battalion entered the UCA campus and assassinated six priests, their housekeeper, and her daughter, Amaya Grimaldi was among them, on loan from the First Infantry Brigade, and later confessed that he was one of the triggermen. If César's allegations were true, if U.S. military personnel could be confirmed to have been involved in death squad operations, if César's intelligence operation had in fact been instrumental in the killings of the Jesuits that had aroused such indignation in Washington, then, we felt, everything possible should be done to ensure that his story received a full and public hearing. If reliably corroborated, it might just raise a hue and cry sufficient to finally halt U.S. support of the Salvadoran regime.

César is a cocky, self-possessed, shrewd sort of guy, short of stature and handsome, with the customary Salvadoran head of sleek, straight black hair. Born on September 21, 1962, he had been raised in a middle-class family until he joined the Salvadoran Army at age seventeen in 1980. He served as a commando in a special naval forces battalion called the Piranhas, patrolling the Gulf of Fonseca in speedboats for two years, then mustered out. Finding little employment and wanting to leave the war in El Salvador behind, he headed for the United States, fell into the hands of the INS soon after entering Texas, and spent seven months in detention before being deported to El Salvador in late 1983.

In November 1987, a friend of his who was a soldier in the First Infantry Brigade persuaded him to reenlist. This friend, Sergeant José Burgos Torres, was a member of the First Brigade's Intelligence Department, and he wasted no time in introducing César to the other officers there. They, in turn, impressed on young César that his quick mind and prior experience as a naval commando suited him well for intelligence work. He was soon recruited to their department. According to the testimony César prepared in Marin County in late 1990, he was quickly readied for an assignment whose nature he only understood much later.

"I was accepted and thereafter assigned as a case officer in what was commonly known as Department 2. I was given the code name Alex. After three months of special psychological warfare and intelligence training within the brigade, I joined the Department of Information Management, where I began my work as a case officer. At this time, I did not know that the Intelligence Department's primary mission was the clandestine elimination of Salvadoran civilians suspected of supporting the FMLN, nor was I aware of the Department's interrogation and execution activities."

He then described his training. "The psychological preparation entailed maintaining a high spirit, keeping the mind sharp, and the ability to feel well although all around you is bad. They made us understand that we were special people with the capacity for facing and resolving any problem. The intelligence training included the evaluation of information received from human resources, the recruitment of informers, review of counterintelligence charts and other materials, and map reading."

When he joined Department 2 in November 1987, he became aware of two North American advisors who worked there. "I personally met them at the time but did not understand the significance of their presence. By the time I completed my training and received my first assignment as a case officer in February 1988, I knew that the U.S. advisors were economically supporting the Intelligence Department and its operations."

The officers of Department 2 had apparently assessed César's capabilities accurately. Over the next eighteen months, he excelled at his assignments. "My responsibilities were in the metropolitan area of San Salvador, as well as in the Chapín and Piedra zones, and began with the recruitment of human sources who would serve as confidential informants, for which they would receive payments from the department. My friend, Sergeant Burgos Torres, was assigned to supervise my work and continue my training. In connection with that work, I was required to formulate reports regarding informant activities and payments, and submit requests for operational funds to the U.S. advisors, who had a private office in the department.

"The names used by the advisors were Mauricio Torres, whose code name or pseudonym was Cana, and Raúl Antonio Lazo, who was known as Chicano. It was my understanding that Torres was a U.S. Army officer with the rank of major and that Lazo was a captain, but both always presented themselves as civilians."

After he had been with the unit for about four months, he began to realize the department's true purpose. "We were capturing, interrogating under torture, and executing most of the suspects targeted by informants. Although I was a new case officer and working only with informants, I became aware of the unit's secret holding cells, and of its department of interrogators who extracted information from the prisoners held there. I knew that a commando squad working directly under Captain Martinez Martinez took some of the prisoners out at night. I could frequently hear them coming back at 2:00 or 3:00 in the morning, making comments indicating that they were carrying out executions."

César divided his time between his duties as a case officer in the city and brief assignments to combat details in the countryside. As a case officer, he recruited informants to penetrate organizations suspected of supporting the FMLN — popular organizations such as the Human Rights Commission of El Salvador and the Mothers of the Disappeared (COMADRES), union organizations such as the National Union of Salvadoran Workers (UNTS) and the National Federation of Salvadoran Workers (FENASTRAS), and the campuses of both the National University of El Salvador and the Jesuit-run University of Central America. In addition to gathering information, the duties of his informants included joining street demonstrations and stirring up trouble. In his combat assignments, César participated in ambushes of FMLN cadres and suspected safe houses.

"As I became more experienced and skilled at developing sources of information and important confidential informants, I began to participate more in the operations that resulted from this process: the capture of identified supporters of the guerrillas, their weapons, and supplies. I also acquired a greater appreciation of the scope of the support provided by the U.S. advisors to the department. It was clear that the entire department operated primarily on the funding they supplied and controlled. Both routine and nonroutine operating costs were paid by the advisors, including gas, vehicle maintenance and equipment, as well as money to pay the numerous networks of informants who were feeding information to the case officers.

"At one point my network numbered approximately eighteen confidential informants who were paid a total of approximately 20,000 *colones* ($3,000) each month. There were seven other case officers running networks with an average of thirty informants each."

In addition to providing money for cars and informants, César claims that the U.S. advisors also occasionally secured ammunition for his unit and that they provided money for the safe house that his department rented in May or June 1989, when the nighttime traffic of vehicles and prisoners in and out of the First Infantry Brigade headquarters became excessive. The activities of Department 2 were kept strictly confidential from other units within the brigade. Only Department 2 vehicles were allowed to pass in and out without being thoroughly inspected.

Though the U.S. advisors paid the expenses and read the intelligence reports, César claimed they went out of their way to avoid hearing anything about the specific methodology — capture, torture, and assassination — employed by the case officers and interrogators. On the few occasions César initiated a conversation with them about his activities, they told him to change the subject. When César and his fellow case officers began discussing specific operations among themselves, the advisors would leave the room.

Gradually, César was sucked deeper and deeper into the clandestine operations of Department 2. Once he came to understand what was going on, he assumed there would be no leaving; anyone who knew what he knew and did what he did would not be allowed to walk away and live. He further assumed that although they bowed out of operational discussions and never committed their suggestions to paper, the two U.S. advisors must have known what was happening.

"The routine of these covert operations was the removal of people from their homes, workplaces, or off the streets, with as few witnesses as possible to their disappearances. They were then brought in to the First Infantry Brigade, where they were kept in the jail cells of Department 2. Because they had been identified as members or supporters of the FMLN following a period of surveillance and reports from informants, the department would interrogate them brutally and efficiently to extract any useful information."

César noted that "the office of the U.S. advisors was only a short distance from the clandestine cells where these methods of extracting information were regularly applied to civilian prisoners — men and women, girls and boys. They passed by these cells all the time, but they never stopped to see what was happening and they ignored what they must have heard."

Eventually, as the scope of the Department 2 operation increased and its pace accelerated, César himself became an executioner. He claims to have killed eight prisoners, some with his .45, one by strapping dynamite to his body and blowing him to bits, others by strangulation or by slitting their throats. He and his comrades took special care to dispose of the bodies where they would never be found, usually dumping them off a cliff into the sea at a place called Majagual near the port city of La Libertad.

"On May 26, 1989, there was an FMLN attack on the First Brigade, and the Belloso Battalion had captured a student of economics who was transferred to our cells for interrogation. The student worked as a car salesman, was dark skinned, 1.60 meters tall, and wearing glasses of the kind that people use who can't see — very thick. He was wearing blue pants and two shirts: a sport shirt and the other white, with long sleeves. The report said he was caught with a 9 mm Luger automatic, a favorite FMLN weapon. I watched as he was interrogated under the control of Sublieutenant Vega Pleitez.

"That night Major Hernandez assembled the members of the special forces group in order to put the student into the van, and he informed us that there were special orders from Colonel Zepeda for him to be eliminated immediately. The assignment was given to Moreno Escobar, myself, our top interrogator — a corporal with the code name Elvis — and the subsergeant of counterintelligence with the pseudonym Flores.

"As we were leaving the department in the van, Colonel Zepeda himself appeared suddenly and stopped us. Elvis and I were in the back seat with the student between us, blindfolded. 'These case officers seem very suspicious to me,' he said. 'We have to put an officer of higher rank in here to verify this operation.' Colonel Zepeda then ordered Sublieutenant Vega Pleitez to accompany us and gave him a direct order, in front of us, that the student was to be killed and Pleitez was to personally verify it.

"Lieutenant Pleitez was shocked. He wasn't part of the special forces group, and he was nervous and frightened. Normally, he was head of the case officers when the major wasn't there; he would take charge of reviewing fees and reports. He was only there because Zepeda ordered him to be there.

"But Colonel Zepeda knew he was an officer we would obey. I believed that the student had very classified information, and that Zepeda thought he could prevent us from interrogating the student further if he sent Lieutenant Pleitez along with us. He read our minds, our thoughts. We would have liked very much to hear what the student had to say. Given Colonel Zepeda's personal interest in his elimination and his extraordinary visit to the department to see him off, the student must have been a key person inside the FMLN.

"On the way to Majagual, the lieutenant was so unconcentrated that he stalled the vehicle a half dozen times, and Moreno Escobar had to drive the rest of the way. As we were driving along, the student asked, 'Where are you taking me?' We told him that he was being taken to the artillery unit. Then he said to me and Corporal Elvis, 'I have money. A lot of money. I'll give it to you. Don't kill me.' Nobody responded, and Moreno turned on the radio to play some music.

"As we got near the place, Lieutenant Pleitez asked if we were close. He didn't know the area. Moreno told him we were very near, then he said, 'Commando, get ready.' I knew he was talking to me, and I got prepared. I had evaluated the student as very dangerous and thought he might try to get out the back window, so I took his hand as we came to a stop. Moreno got out and I opened the middle side door. Elvis and I each took him by an arm and helped him out as Moreno was putting his gloves on. We went out and up a small slope near the cliff, and Lieutenant Pleitez stayed in the van as security.

"Moreno made a gesture that I should cut his throat, and we sat the student down on the ground. His hands were handcuffed behind him and he was blindfolded. I asked him one question as I readied my commando knife: 'Who are you?' He answered, 'I'm an urban commando. Win or die.' I cut his arteries. In that moment he moved forward and swung his arms over his head so that he brought his hands forward, and he threw himself on me. Elvis wanted to shoot him, but he had me down. He fell on top of me, grabbed me, and said, 'Don't kill me.' But I stabbed him several times in the stomach and stood up as he lay there agonizing.

"Corporal Elvis said that a commando shouldn't die like that, and he shot him once in the head with a .45 automatic. His handcuffs were removed, and we were going to throw him over when we remembered the blindfold, with First Infantry Brigade stenciled on it, and removed that first. His lifeless body was then thrown into a ravine that leads to the sea via El Majagual.

"We were sad not to have been able to interrogate him before killing him, to find out what he knew. He was trained to escape handcuffs. He flipped his arms all the way over his head, to his front, to the point where he was hugging me. Only someone who has taken special courses, who has left the country to be trained, can do that.

"We went back to the van, and I said to Lieutenant Pleitez, 'We talked with the boy.' He said, 'What? What did you say?' I said, 'Nothing,' and I showed him the commando knife, covered with blood in my bloody hand. He looked like he was having a heart attack. On the way back, he was in the rear seat, thinking about things I could only imagine, thinking that we might go crazy and assassinate him."

César's testimony includes other gruesome accounts of murder, and through them runs a certain bravado, a certain residual pride at having been selected for these delicate and risky assignments. This is evident in the specificity with which he identifies the weapons used, the gratuitous if not fabricated detail about the student's throwing his handcuffed arms over his head and tackling César just after his throat had been slit, the assertion that only a foreign-trained commando could have done such a thing, and the gleeful speculation about what poor Pleitez must have made of the whole affair. At other points in the testimonies he gave, however, César indicated dreadful remorse at what he had become and the hope that his testimony had already helped halt the activities of his old unit. These feelings are expressed in a journal entry he tape-recorded in Washington, D.C., in November 1989.

"I'm thinking of the acts. The form in which the people died who we took in these vehicles — vehicles with dark windows into which you introduce a civilian person, a person with no hope, a person who is tied up. Their hands tied, their face covered with a mask. To see their expression and to see their chest and their arms and their hands and their feet tremble. I remember this. The memory comes back to me. And that's what gives me the strength [to give these testimonies]. And these dead, these people who died in the direct operations in which I took part, operations which I could not do anything to stop at the time. I had the key to make these declarations and give names and other things, and these operations were stopping simultaneously. How many lives have been saved?"

When informants identified suspected FMLN supporters in areas of guerrilla operation, members of Department 2 would capture them with the assistance of whatever regular army units were operating nearby. According to César, it was through one of these operations with army regulars that he ended up fleeing for his life.

In late June 1989, Major Hernandez assigned César to assist the Sixth Company of the Atlacatl Battalion in an operation to eliminate a squad of FMLN regulars that had been identified by César's best informant, a man known as Tecomate. According to Tecomate, this FMLN squad had been blowing up power poles in the area of Apopa, north of San Salvador. César and Tecomate, dressed as regular soldiers, would accompany the Sixth to identify and interrogate the suspected combatants. On July 1, the first day of the operation, the soldiers captured two of the suspected guerrillas, took them to a storage building on a nearby farm, and began the interrogation.

"Both young men were subjected to extraordinary pain and psychological terror through the night but still refused to give us any information. The following morning, I accompanied a smaller patrol to Camotepeque. Our contacts had told us that one of the leaders, Lucio Parada, was at his home. Despite my concern that captures be covertly conducted, it was decided that we would act immediately, before Parada left the area. We located Parada's house around noon and made an open capture, with many witnesses."

Over the next two days, as the soldiers captured others and discovered caches of arms, they intensified the beatings they gave the prisoners. "From the moment he was captured, [Parada] defiantly announced that we should just kill him because he wasn't going to collaborate in any case. He was treating the soldiers badly, and they gratefully retaliated by badly beating him. The soldiers were not accustomed to somebody like Parada insulting them and telling them that they're dogs and criminals. No civilian ever treats a soldier like that, especially someone who is poor and unarmed.

"Through the rest of that day and evening, the interrogations continued at the base camp, and more captures were made, but little more information was obtained. We took Parada back to his home briefly to search for weapons near there but found nothing.

"The following morning, Monday, July 3, the forced interrogations began at dawn, around 5:00 A.M.. The six captives, including a still-defiant Parada, were beaten and questioned by teams of soldiers who used clubs, bayonets, and boots to inflict pain, alternating this treatment with applications of the *capucha*, a hood placed over the head and tightened around the neck until suffocation occurs. This near-death experience is a dependable, commonly used method of extracting information from difficult prisoners, and it produced results that morning."

Two of the torture victims consented to lead the soldiers to another guerrilla leader, a man named Miranda. Miranda was taken at his home, and he, in turn, led the soldiers to a cache of explosives. When the soldiers returned to base camp, they became angrier than ever with their captives.

"The pressure of the soldiers on Parada went up a lot higher after we found the explosives, which included a device designed to kill large numbers of soldiers. It was manufactured by the FMLN and it was portable. It looked like it weighed twenty-five pounds and could be carried in a food carrier on the shoulders. It appeared to have the explosive power of at least several Claymores, and the soldiers knew it had been intended for them.

"It became clear that the soldiers would beat him to death if I did not interfere with their anger. When we detonated the device and the soldiers saw its tremendous explosive power, they jumped on him. 'Is this the present you wanted to give us?' they screamed at him. And he shouted back, 'Yes! Yes!' And they kept on beating him. He actually wanted to die fast. He was intelligent to conclude this, but the soldiers didn't understand. I told them. 'Don't pay attention to him. What he wants is for you to kill him ahead of time.' "

César, the seasoned intelligence officer, had a different motive than the angry soldiers for torturing Parada. He wanted the information about rebel commanders that he assumed Parada possessed, information he felt he could extract with the patient application of the proper methods. But in the end, despite renewed applications of the *capucha* and continued beatings, Parada disclosed nothing to his captors. Finally, he talked one of the soldiers into giving him a canteen, then sucked the contents into his lungs, suffocated, and died. They buried him on the spot.

The operation was a botch. Parada went to his shallow grave without talking. The civilians who witnessed Parada's capture by uniformed soldiers of the Atlacatl Battalion reported it to the human rights groups, who mounted an investigation. Parada's tortured body was found.

Who was to blame — the Atlacatl Battalion regulars or the imported intelligence experts from Department 2? In the fallout that followed, it seemed to César, scapegoats had to be found, and he and his informant, Tecomate, were chosen. Both were restricted to quarters. Then Tecomate was given permission to visit his family, but he was instead arrested by the National Police.

César got wind of Tecomate's arrest before they came for him. "Early in the morning of July 23, around 5:30, they came and got me out. They personally prepared a vehicle, fooling me, according to them, telling me that we were going on a clandestine operation commanded by Moreno Escobar. We went out with an authorization from Colonel Elena Fuentes. We were going to do a clandestine operation which consisted of going to assassinate my informant, Tecomate. But I had already found out that he had been captured.

"When I was riding in the front seat with Corporal Moreno Escobar and he said, 'We're going to assassinate the informant Tecomate,' he knew that Tecomate was an informant of mine, a confidential informant. 'Why are we going to kill him?' That was my question. 'Moreno Escobar, why are we going to kill Tecomate? Why are you lying to me?' I loaded my .45 and a fragmentation grenade, and I took the pin off the grenade. He knew that I was a special forces commando and that I had, as they say, the 'balls' to kill the two of us. He didn't have the capacity to die, but I did. He told me simply, 'Look, I'm going to tell you. We're going to execute you, and a vehicle was going to come from the guard to pick you up.' "

César held his pistol on Moreno Escobar and the two others who sat in the back seat, then sprang from the vehicle and took off running through a nearby ravine. He emerged from the ravine, found a taxi, and began the two-week flight that took him from San Salvador to the coastal city of La Unión, then on to Honduras, to Guatemala, and eventually to Belize.

Once there, he went to the Human Rights Commission of Belize and gave his story to William Huesner on August 10, 1989. Huesner had him record it all on tape, then called the office of CODEHUCA in San José, Costa Rica, suspecting that CODEHUCA, which represents all of the human rights groups in Central America, would be interested in César's story as well. He had guessed correctly. When Huesner reached CODEHUCA's general secretary, Mirna Anaya, she urged him to send César on to Mexico City, where she would arrange for him to give his testimony to a member of the Human

Rights Commission of El Salvador. From the outset, Mirna and the commission understood the potential value of César's testimony — confirmation of their oft-made assertion that the Salvadoran death squads were not the renegade independents the government claimed them to be, but part of the military structure, operating under its direct command.

César made his way to Mexico City, where he gave a second testimony to a member of the commission on August 28. A month later, he crossed the U.S. border and headed for Washington, D.C. By this time, César had realized that his testimony could have explosive impact on U.S. foreign policy in El Salvador, that the Salvadoran authorities would track him down and silence him in any way they could, and that his safest and most dramatic option would be to put his testimony before Congress. Meanwhile, Mirna alerted lawyers and solidarity groups around the United States that César was on the way and that his story deserved all the attention we could muster.

On October 10, while César waited in the Harlingen, Texas, airport for a flight to Washington, an INS agent approached him for a routine documentation check. César had no visa and was taken into custody.

At this point in César's saga, two old acquaintances of ours entered the picture — Lisa Brodyaga and Bill Van Wyck, the very same lawyers Kate Bancroft had met on her first visit to Mariona Prison in the summer of 1986. The two attorneys were long-standing friends of the commission's. Lisa's office was in Harlingen; Van Wyck's was in Washington, D.C. Mirna alerted them to César's situation and asked them to do what they could to bail him out. Just then, a Mexican newspaper broke César's story on its front page, and Mirna, Lisa, and Van Wyck feared that if the U.S. authorities put two and two together, they would realize just who they had in custody and deny him bail. Van Wyck wired $3,000 of his own money to Lisa, who went down to the INS, as she did so often in her law practice representing asylum applicants and detained refugees, with several pieces of apparently routine business to conduct, including the posting of César's bail. There she discovered that the INS had misspelled his name (Hoya Martinez instead of Joya Martinez) and had therefore failed to make the connection. She bailed César out, and Van Wyck immediately flew to Harlingen to escort him to Washington that same day. César was about to make a big splash in our nation's capital, and things were about to get complicated and ugly.

Among those whom Mirna had alerted to César's situation was Robert White, former ambassador to El Salvador during the Carter administration. White knew full well the implications of César's allegations and offered to represent him and introduce him to interested members of Congress, if possible. On the day after César and Van Wyck arrived in Washington, White sent a member of his organization, the Center for International Policy, to meet with César, Van Wyck, and several representatives of Washington-based solidarity organizations. White's office had planned a press conference, but César thought that going public so soon after his detention in Texas might be a misstep. He then asked Van Wyck to assume his legal representation. Having extended himself thus far on César's behalf only because he knew the value of César's story, Van Wyck reluctantly agreed to become his attorney of record, stipulating that he was willing to do so only if César promised full disclosure. The next weeks were hectic for both of them.

Van Wyck knew that he needed help and therefore called on an old friend, Andrea Primdahl, a filmmaker and activist who lived in Washington. She then turned to a friend of hers, filmmaker Allan Frankovich, whose most celebrated piece of work to date was the damning documentary film about the CIA entitled *On Company Business*. Frankovich had sources of funds, spoke perfect vernacular Spanish, and developed an immediate rapport with César, in whose testimony he saw verification of his long-held beliefs about illegal U.S. covert operations in all corners of the world. Frankovich soon became César's most trusted confidant and interpreter. In the following weeks, he accompanied César and Van Wyck as they visited those with an interest in El Salvador: staff members at the Senate Intelligence Committee and the House Intelligence Oversight Committee, the Washington Office on Latin America, Americas Watch and Amnesty International, the United Nations special rapporteur on El Salvador, and the Organization of American States. Frankovich also contacted the media, and through his efforts, CBS carried César's story on October 10, and the *Washington Post* ran it the following day. Meanwhile, Van Wyck filed an asylum application on César's behalf.

His story was getting out and steps were being taken to prevent his deportation, but at the same time, Frankovich and Van Wyck were alienating organizations that might have proved helpful allies in the days and months to come. Not willing to trust anyone with César's security and concerned about steps the INS might be taking to have him deported, Van Wyck and Frankovich began to freeze Robert White and the Washington solidarity organizations out of the decision-making loop. Van Wyck today regards this alienation of potential friends as a regrettable mistake. "César needed all the friends he could get, but Frankovich and I didn't trust anyone, so we pushed them out."

Van Wyck also began to have doubts about Frankovich's manipulative and seemingly paranoid personality. When Frankovich translated for César before congressional staffers or human rights organizations, he would often dominate the discussion, expanding a simple "Yes" or "No" on César's part into a windy tirade against U.S. covert operations. When I later came to know Frankovich, I observed the same problematic traits. Frankovich stood by César for months and years, found him places to live, found money for his attorney's fees, and worked tirelessly on his behalf, but he always managed to convey the impression that only he knew what was best for César, thereby alienating many potential allies.

Frankovich arranged a press conference for November 1, and it was well attended but generated hardly any coverage. By then, the bombing of the FENASTRAS office in San Salvador and the FMLN offensive that erupted shortly thereafter dominated the news about El Salvador, and when the Jesuits were assassinated at the University of Central America on November 16, César's story was forgotten, which was ironic because Oscar Amaya Grimaldi, the junior case officer whom he had familiarized with the UCA, was one of the triggermen.

Shortly after the UCA massacre, House Speaker Tom Foley asked Congressman Joseph Moakley, a Boston Catholic, to head a congressional task force to investigate the Jesuits' killing. Jim McGovern, Moakley's chief of staff, soon met with César and arranged for him to make a presentation to the Moakley Task Force before they left for El Salvador in January 1990. Prior to that meeting, Van Wyck had had César draw a detailed map of the First Infantry Brigade compound and arranged for Moakley to take a copy to El Salvador. Members of the task force used César's map to bull their way into the Department 2 detention cell area when they visited the First Infantry Brigade. They found the cells right where the map indicated. Van Wyck also provided Moakley with a letter assuring him that César would give full testimony and take a lie detector test if Moakley guaranteed that he would get fair and public treatment.

By the time Moakley returned from El Salvador with his task force, however, Frankovich and César had decided that taking a lie detector test might not be in César's best interest. Van Wyck, feeling that Frankovich's increasing influence on César abrogated his lawyer-client relationship, withdrew as César's attorney, but not before asking the ACLU to replace him, which they agreed to do.

As the weeks dragged by, Frankovich pegged away at members of Congress and the media, some of whom become disenchanted with the whole affair. Close examination of César's various statements in Belize and Mexico and before various groups in Washington disclosed inconsistencies, inconsistencies that he and Frankovich explained by saying that César had not felt free to disclose certain information when he first fled El Salvador, fearing that friends and family members might suffer reprisals. They also confessed that his memory was imperfect. But when these inconsistencies were combined with the furious denials now emanating from the Salvadoran high command (which also alleged that César had been the one to kill Lucio Parada during the botched Atlacatl Battalion operation) and with the self-admitted fact that César was a killer, people began to doubt his veracity.

Nevertheless, Frankovich's advocacy continued to pay off. When the Moakley Task Force submitted its report on the Jesuit killings to Speaker Foley on April 30, 1990, the cover letter contained a statement of continued interest in information about other cases, including that of César Vielman Joya Martinez. Six weeks later, shortly after César's asylum hearing in Alexandria, Virginia, the government indicted him for illegally reentering the United States after having been deported in 1983, a rarely used technical ploy that justified issuing an arrest warrant. A month after his indictment, seven U.S. Senators (John Kerry, Tom Harkin, Patrick Leahy, Robert Kerrey, Paul Simon, Barbara Mikulski, and Alan Cranston) sent a letter to Secretary of State James Baker on July 18, asking that César's allegations be fully investigated before legal proceedings against him began.

At this critical juncture, César and Frankovich burned their bridges with the ACLU by writing an open letter to the U.S. ambassador in El Salvador, William Walker, demanding that César's allegations be investigated more speedily. In that letter, which was circulated among members of Congress as well, César misrepresented his statements as having the blessing of the ACLU. When the ACLU realized what he had done, they withdrew as his counsel.

Frankovich, meanwhile, arranged for César to move into a house in Long Beach, California. There, agents of the INS arrested him in July on a warrant issued in Arlington and flew him back to the East Coast, where Frankovich arranged for yet another lawyer, Dan Alcorn, to take up his case. After Alcorn had César released on bail, Frankovich pushed for one last meeting on Capitol Hill. Jim McGovern of Congressman Joseph Moakley's office arranged the meeting, inviting staffers from the intelligence committees and other congressional offices. Ramsey Clark, former attorney general during the Johnson administration, had taken an interest in the case and attended as well.

This was to be the meeting at which César would make full disclosure in a formal, if not legal, forum. But César's new attorney, Dan Alcorn, advised his client that his testimony might jeopardize his upcoming hearing, and on the strength of that recommendation, César declined to answer anything of substance. With this disastrous meeting, the flurry of interest in Washington all but fizzled out. Jim McGovern knew that César's allegations deserved thorough investigation, and Jim has maintained his interest in César to this day, but he also recognized that a muddle had been made of things, that the people he had persuaded to come hear César's testimony felt burned, and that the chances of César's getting the full and open hearing he so desired were rapidly diminishing.

This is where MITF came into the picture. Mirna had contacted us during César's first stay in Long Beach. She had kept us apprised of the whole affair from the outset, and we had contributed some money toward transportation and other costs. From our perch in Northern California, however, we had not yet become directly involved. I turned to Larry Ross, the Marin County photojournalist who had spirited away the commission's archives during the offensive, asking if he would be willing to go to Long Beach to meet with César. Larry interviewed him there before his July arrest. When César returned to Long Beach after the disastrous meeting on the Hill, Mirna contacted us again and asked us to try to resurrect some interest in his case. Thus for me began the most painful and exhausting chapter in the history of MITF.

There was from the outset some opposition among MITF board members to throwing our time and resources into an undertaking on behalf of a death squad killer. There were also some reservations about the efficacy of the whole enterprise. Having already sent money to pay for airfares and other expenses, we knew that taking a lead role in César's cause might cost us a pretty penny more. Little did we expect, however, that we would accrue $30,000 in César-related expenses over the next fifteen months for cross-country airfares, legal fees, godawful telephone bills, and César's personal living expenses. Amazingly, our faithful cadre of contributors earmarked very nearly that amount in designated donations over the same period.

We knew, too, that we were inheriting a mess, a trail already littered with solidarity groups and individuals who had been rebuffed, who had become disenchanted with César. But we plunged ahead into the dark Salvadoran reality once again, this time to see things from the other side, from the perspective of the killers.

We flew to Los Angeles to meet with Allan Frankovich. We invited César to Marin to give a talk and some press interviews. We checked in by phone with some of those who had already been involved in the saga — Lisa Brodyaga, Bill Van Wyck, Robert White, and Jim McGovern. We hired a publicist to try to reignite some media interest. We made contact with César's new attorney in Arlington, Dan Alcorn, and learned from him just how little time we had. César was free on bail until September 18, the date of his hearing. If convicted of illegally reentering the United States, he might be sentenced to as much as two years in prison. Worse yet, while Alcorn planned César's defense, the Salvadoran government was simultaneously preparing a legal action of its own for César's extradition to face desertion and murder charges.

To further complicate matters, Alcorn evinced little enthusiasm for our strategy. We were pinning our hopes, and César's, on once again fanning the flames of congressional interest so that political pressure might be brought to bear on the Justice Department and its case against him. Alcorn doubted that his client's best interests would be served by putting his full disclosure before a congressional committee, some of whose members would be bent on discrediting César. The final decision would have to be César's, but how could he make a rational determination in his current circumstances? He was in fear for his life and had little understanding of U.S. political institutions and jurisprudence, he had already lost the representation of two attorneys, and he was on the receiving end of constant — and constantly contradictory — advice. And he was enduring a moral crisis of unimaginable proportions.

We turned to Ramsey Clark for guidance. In the years since his career in the government, Ramsey Clark had made a name for himself representing any number of people in predicaments similar to César's. He knew international law backward and forward, still had good contacts in Washington, and enjoyed a rock solid reputation for integrity. When we initially contacted him, he told us that the political angle was still worth pursuing if it was handled properly, and that time was of the essence.

Ramsey was less than sanguine about César's chances at his September 18 hearing, and his hunch proved correct. César was convicted and once again released on bail pending his sentencing, scheduled for November 30. Dan Alcorn wasted no time in entering an appeal.

What a mess. Nobody knew for sure how long it might be before the government acted on the asylum request that Bill Van Wyck had filed before excusing himself as César's lawyer, or whether that asylum request, even if granted, would have any bearing on Alcorn's appeal. And then there was the looming possibility that the United States would honor El Salvador's anticipated extradition request. Expenses — cross-country plane flights, Alcorn's fees, telephone bills — were beginning to mount. Frankovich had nearly exhausted his sources of funds and depleted the credit limit on his American Express card. The financial demands began to sorely tax MITF's resources.

César's conviction persuaded us all the more firmly that his best chance would be to keep hammering away at sympathetic officials in Washington who might be convinced to intercede on his behalf. Ramsey Clark agreed and suggested that we meet with him at his office in New York City. We made a date for October 19. He advised us in the meantime to sit down with César and have him prepare a comprehensive, airtight statement of disclosure. If Ramsey was going to go to bat for César, he didn't want to waste his time fouling off such inconsistencies as had cropped up in prior testimonies.

We needed to find a place in Marin County where César could live and work while we prepared for the October 19 meeting with Ramsey. We turned once again to Larry Ross. Having already met with César in Long Beach, Larry was as familiar as any of us with his case. Though he was not a member of MITF, we felt that Larry's prior experience as a journalist suited him well to help César prepare the comprehensive testimony that Ramsey had requested. In addition, because Larry worked as a self-employed process server out of his home in San Rafael, he could be with César day and night.

César drove up from Long Beach in a car he had somehow obtained, and he settled in at Larry's house to begin the arduous task that Ramsey had assigned. Kate Bancroft, who would act as interpreter, also set up camp there. The work proceeded excruciatingly slowly.

After all he had been through since drawing his pistol on Moreno Escobar some fourteen months earlier, César was somewhat recalcitrant about setting down his testimony yet again in hopes that it would finally accomplish his two goals: freedom from detention in the United States and from deportation back to El Salvador, and a fair hearing. His resistance should have come as no surprise. Dan Alcorn expressed strong doubts about the wisdom of our undertaking. Frankovich, with whom César had maintained frequent telephone contact, felt that César should keep as many balls in the air as possible but evinced no particular enthusiasm for our plan. Larry, Kate, and I probably seemed no better qualified to pull his fat from the fire than any of his previous advisors. So he cooperated in fits and starts, always trying to gauge us and our motives, always trying to discern what course of action might save his hide. What, he wondered, should he disclose? Which details of his past were significant, which inconsequential? Who was running his life, or what was left of it? From time to time he insisted on driving back down to Long Beach for a few days to see his girlfriend.

By the time we headed east for the October 19 meeting with Ramsey Clark, César's testimony was little more than loosely connected fragments that Larry had transcribed as Kate translated. Exhaustion had overtaken everyone. The four of us — César, Larry, Kate, and I — straggled into Ramsey's office and sat bleary-eyed around a conference table, awaiting the former attorney general of the United States. When Ramsey, who was relaxed, genial, confident, and clear-eyed, stepped into the room, my hopes ratcheted up a notch or two. From the moment he began talking, it was clear that he was just the man to handle things.

He told us of similar clients he had represented in the past and made no bones whatsoever about César's peril. He suffered no illusions about the government's desire to discredit and silence César, even if that meant extraditing him right back to the nightmare he had so recently escaped. And then he reiterated the need to adhere to his proposed course of action.

Ramsey disclosed to us that years earlier, he had represented Frank Serpico, the New York cop who dared blow the whistle on the rampant corruption in that city's police force. Knowing back then that powerful political forces would do everything possible to discredit Serpico, Ramsey had insisted that he set down in writing absolutely everything he had to say, then stand on that written declaration, come what may. Serpico had followed Ramsey's advice and ultimately been vindicated. Ramsey told César flat out that without such a statement, César didn't stand much of a chance.

César resisted Ramsey's proposal. Why, he protested, should Ramsey be able to accomplish what nobody else had accomplished for him thus far? I explained to César that the authorities in Washington were like elephants and he was like a fly. Loud as he might yell, they hardly noticed him. What he needed was a bee who could sting that elephant into action. I pointed to Ramsey and said, "Here is your bee."

At the end of the meeting, we all agreed to proceed full speed ahead. With César's sentencing hearing a scant six weeks away, Ramsey told us that we absolutely had to get César's statement back to him in two weeks' time. Anything beyond that, and he didn't know what he would be able to accomplish. Two weeks. It seemed nearly impossible.

We bid Ramsey farewell and headed out onto the streets of New York. Jack Hammond, the Accompaniment Project volunteer who had once spent an anxious night in the custody of El Salvador's National Police, had offered to let us crash at his apartment on Riverside Drive. After a good night's sleep, we would fly back to California and get down to work. We agreed on a division of labor. Larry would handle the interviews with César from which the statement would be constructed; Kate would translate; I would provide organizational and logistical support. Before we left for the airport the next morning, I called MITF to mobilize a team of typists who would enter into a rented computer Kate's tape-recorded translations of César's statements.

But things began to founder the day we got back. What Ramsey asked us to accomplish in two weeks took six, and on the day Larry asked César to sign the freshly completed 100-page document, César refused to do so and departed for Southern California. Just about everything that could go wrong did.

From the outset, Larry had insisted on keeping to a minimum the number of people involved in the process. He and Kate and César holed up at the house and never used the waiting typists. César continued his recalcitrance, and his relationship with Larry soured. Larry got bogged down in the minutiae of César's rambling statements and grilled him at length over points they had covered earlier. César would disappear from time to time, usually in the middle of the night.

Larry and I feuded, each suspecting that the other wanted to control the undertaking, and as a result I had virtually no involvement in the work. Although everything I saw and heard when I stopped by to monitor progress told me that the situation was rapidly spinning out of control, I could do nothing, because it was, after all, Larry's house where things were happening. He wanted to do things his way and told me to butt out; I insisted he abide by the agreement we had made in New York to work on this together. Round and round we went, going nowhere.

As the days, then weeks, slipped by, my frustration grew. I could hardly think of anything else, day or night. Eventually, I backed out altogether, hoping that matters would somehow set themselves to rights. In the end, Larry became completely overwhelmed, reaching the point where he couldn't write another word, and sent the incomplete statement — and thickets of notes — to me. By the time I had tied it all together several days later, our window of opportunity had passed. We had missed it, and now César's fate rested with the courts.

On November 30, 1990, César was sentenced to two years' incarceration at Atascosa County Jail in Texas, where the INS housed prisoners from time to time. Out there in the middle of nowhere, César whiled away his days until he was released and immediately rearrested on May 29, 1991. The extradition request from El Salvador had come through. When the courts finally denied César's petition for asylum two months later, nothing stood between him and a forcible return to his homeland. The INS shipped him back to El Salvador, where the Salvadoran authorities took him directly to Mariona Prison.

Eventually, Mirna Anaya secured his release from Mariona, employing as a legal lever the 1992 amnesty law passed by El Salvador's National Assembly indemnifying armed forces personnel from prosecution for offenses committed during the war. Mirna arranged for César to live in Costa Rica, where he stayed until returning to El Salvador in late 1993. The last I heard of him, he was living in La Unión.

Did we plunge in over our heads when we agreed to go to bat for César? Did we serve him well? Those questions are hard to answer. We may well have been unqualified to represent César, but by the time he came our way in mid–1990, other offers of assistance had dwindled almost to nothing, and we had little choice but to fall on our own resources or simply decline Mirna's request for help. Preparing him to make his case as best he could in

Washington seemed the best course of action, both to us and to Ramsey Clark, but we failed to accomplish what we had set out to do. Should we have taken another tack? I don't think so. Once we stepped into the morass surrounding César, the best thing we could have done — for him and for his cause — was to stay our course.

We spent a great deal of time over the years getting to know Salvadorans who suffered from the violence inflicted by death squads. But César was the only Salvadoran we came to know whose suffering arose from inflicting that violence. If he is any indication, the same oppressive system that chewed up so many in El Salvador's popular organizations and Christian base communities also tore up the soldiers and security force troops who were sucked into the whirlpool of destruction and allowed themselves to become cold-blooded killers. Kill or die.

How does one judge the Césars of this world fairly, if at all? If there is forgiveness to extend, is it mine to proffer, or can it only be granted by the surviving wives and husbands and children? Unlike the other killers, who stayed within the system, César will spend the rest of his days looking over his shoulder. But at least he will know that he was one of the very few who emerged from the whirlpool to name it for what it was. And though I admire him for that, my admiration for César is nothing to that which I hold for those who stood up to the worst that the Césars had to offer. Among them is Mirtala López.

_ 9 _

MIRTALA

Whenever I went to San Salvador to visit the commission and monitor the Accompaniment Project, commission members introduced me to other people who participated in the Salvadoran popular movement — people like Hector Barillas of National University, María Isabel of the small religious community called la Pequeña Comunidad, and Guillermo Rojas of the labor federation UNTS — all of whom had opinions about the events of the day and all of whom had stories to tell.

But none had a tale like Mirtala's. Still a teenager when I met her, Mirtala López had already suffered firsthand the terrible devastation and deprivation visited by the Salvadoran Army on rural communities where the guerrillas operated, had lived off the land while on the run from the army for almost two years, and had helped form the Christian Committee for the Displaced of El Salvador (CRIPDES) while living in a San Salvador refugee camp. Still before her was her worst ordeal.

Mirtala would be memorable even if her life were commonplace. She is that pretty, that vivacious, that self-assured. She is also a great storyteller. When I interviewed her during two extended sessions in June and July 1993, once in San Francisco and once in San Salvador, I was barely able to squeeze a word in edgewise. Once she began reliving her childhood, rolling out her voluble descriptions of the hamlet where she grew up, creating scenes with her hands and eyes as well as her words, I felt as though I was being treated to a private screening of the movie of her life. Later, when I sat to compose this third-person account, I discovered that my narrative skills were no match for hers. Most of the words that follow are Mirtala's.

Mirtala López was born on April 19, 1969, into a large campesino family. One of the youngest among fourteen brothers and sisters, Mirtala lived her early years in the small village of Los Naranjos — so named for the orange trees prized by the villagers — in the northern part of Chalatenango Department. The family was very poor. Her father earned his living as a day laborer; her mother spent her days caring for the youngsters. The lessons of Mirtala's youth were those of hard work and survival.

She and her siblings contributed to the family's welfare as soon as they were old enough. By the time she was eight, Mirtala was washing clothes, making tortillas, and minding the younger children. Her father taught her how to plant and tend their vegetable garden while the older brothers and sisters handled the heavier work of cutting firewood, planting corn, and laboring for wages. She brought lunch to her father and older brothers in the fields, an hour's walk each way, carrying a basket of food and a string bag full of drinks. "I had to pass a bull along the way," she remembers, "and I only had two dresses, one red. When the bull saw my red dress, its eyes would open wide, and I would run, provoking the bull and dropping the food as I ran."

By the time she was eleven, the army's campaign against the guerrillas was underway. When the short-lived political reforms of the late 1970s were quashed by the army, FMLN fighters took to the hills in the northern sections of the country, and the army pursued them, making little distinction between the guerrillas and the civilian population among whom they operated. The counterinsurgency campaign that followed was essentially a repeat of the counterinsurgency campaign designed by the U.S. military in Vietnam. It even bore the same name — Operation Phoenix.

The operation's objective was to deprive the guerrillas of their base of civilian support, using any means necessary. Although the Geneva Accords specifically enjoin military action against civilians — even those who support guerrillas operating in their communities — the army and its collaborators targeted their reprisals indiscriminately. Relatives of guerrillas died. People who fed or sheltered guerrillas, even under duress, died. Labor organizers, co-operativists, and catechists who had no contact with the guerrillas but whose community organizing was perceived as consonant with guerrilla demands died.

The cycle of community resistance and savage reprisal swept across the mountainous rural landscape. When peasants organized to express legitimate demands for self-determination, they were labeled Communists and eliminated. When the violence spread and communities organized to protect themselves, such organizing was perceived as ideological activism rather than simple self-defense, and its leaders were slain. When fugitives from the army's reign of terror sought shelter in neighboring villages, those villages were destroyed for harboring insurgents. And as the violence narrowed options for an already poor and desperate peasantry, its sons and daughters began picking up arms to resist, further justifying violence in the minds of the army and its advisors.

The military cultivated a network of informants in as many villages as possible. As a result, people soon learned to speak in code and to conduct conversations and meetings clandestinely. Army press-gangs rounded up campesino teenagers and forcibly recruited them. Fields were burned, villages bombed and mortared, villagers sent fleeing into the night with only the clothes on their backs. Meanwhile, the most rabid elements of the Salvadoran Army and security forces formalized their network of informers under the name ORDEN and operated ORDEN outside the normal chain of command.

To all of this Mirtala bore witness. "In 1980 I began to see signs of violence — fingers on the ground, parts of bodies, heads impaled on sticks. We would see these things when we went to get water. My parents said they didn't believe me when I told them about it. They said it was just children's stories. But gradually they realized there were bad people in the village. That was when the Christian Federation of Salvadoran Peasants was formed."

Mirtala's family members began attending meetings, and she became curious about what was going on. "One afternoon they went to a meeting in a nearby *cantón*. I was left at home to watch my little brother, so I put him to sleep and I followed them. My mother and father didn't know I was following them; I was afraid they would hit me if they knew. I wanted to tell about the corpses I had seen. They went to a house of a man called Adam. I stood behind the house and listened. The people inside studied on how the campesinos could keep the land (some big landowners wanted the land). They decided to train people about first aid and health for whatever might come up. They formed support groups and decided to look out for suspicious people in the villages. They said that the children could support, too, as spies. I said to myself, 'I can do that.' "

As the rural people began to organize themselves, however, larger events crashed in on them.

"Then we heard that they had murdered Archbishop Romero. My mother had gone to San Salvador once to hear him give the Mass, and I had heard him on the radio. We always listened to his Mass on the radio. In our village at the Mass, the priest would always pray for Archbishop Romero's life. We cried. If they could kill him, they could kill us, too. We had no knowledge, no support.

"The Christian Federation of Salvadoran Peasants and the Union of Countryside Workers asked if we wanted to go to his funeral. But ORDEN was already going around with sharp knives, and they told us that we would get killed on the way to the bus. So we went by different ways, all of us who went from my village. We walked six or seven hours to the bus place. I went with my mother. I had never been to San Salvador until then.

"I wanted to go to the funeral, but I also wanted to see the cars; I was totally fascinated by all the cars. I stood there in the city, looking at the cars, trying to understand how they made them and how they ran and how they avoided hitting each other. Eventually, we made our way to Romero's funeral.

"There were thousands of people in the square outside the cathedral, where they held the service on the front steps so everyone could see. I had never seen so many people. Then we heard shots and everybody ran. We got knocked down again and again. My mother was all bruised and dirty, and I lost my shoes. We got separated from all our friends from Los Naranjos, so everybody made their way home as they could, some in days, some in a week.

"After Romero's funeral, we began to do more organizing in the region, but we had to be careful because the death squads had spies among the people. The spies would tell the Guardia about anyone doing organizing work or anyone who supported the guerrillas. One boy in the village whose father was a death squad man, he came to our house and asked if he could live with us because he couldn't stand what his father was doing. He became like our adopted brother.

"In the second week of May 1980, displaced people came from other places nearby, from other villages where the Guardia had come. The Guardia was conducting a big operation then, creating the first of what became Chalatenango's displaced populations. The refugees came around 6:00 P.M. to our house, in the middle of a rainstorm, so they were all drenched. Lots of children, naked, drenched, covered with mud, crying. Mothers, too. A huge group of people.

"My father said to go tell people in the village to give them food and shelter. We went to all the houses asking for tortillas and beans, and Father started cooking food for all the people who had come. Tortillas and beans and coffee.

"The children were so cold that they lay down with the pigs to keep warm. It was really sad. We took off what clothes we had to give them, because it was raining really hard. People kept arriving until 11:00 or 12:00 at night, so we kept making more tortillas and more coffee.

"They said if they stayed, they would be killed. They said they had to go to Honduras. So they left and headed off in the direction of the Río Sumpul at 4:00 or 5:00 in the morning. At 6:00 A.M. we heard shots in that direction, from the ridge of the mountain where they walked. We could see them as they ducked and ran and dispersed. Father said, 'Who knows, because we support-ed these poor people, they may come to kill us. If we die, I will know that I gave food to these people.' "

Los Naranjos lies about ten miles south of the Río Sumpul, the border between El Salvador and Honduras in northern Chalatenango. The refugees Mirtala's father had fed and sheltered fled into one of the bloodiest massacres in the history of the Salvadoran conflict. The Salvadoran Army had called a secret meeting with Honduran army officials at the Salvadoran town of El Poy on May 5 to notify them of the operation they were about to conduct in Cha-latenango and to propose that the Hondurans establish positions on the far side of the Sumpul to prevent refugees from crossing over. Elements of El Sal-vador's First Brigade, of the National Guard, and of ORDEN then swept through villages on May 13 and pursued the fleeing populace. When the ref-ugees reached the river, ground troops and helicopters mounted with machine guns mowed them down in a murderous crossfire, killing more than 600 peo-ple, most of them women and children.

The Diocese of Santa Rosa de Copan in Honduras conducted an inves-tigation and issued this statement on June 24: "Women were tortured before being killed and babies were thrown in the air and shot. People who crossed the river were forced back by Honduran soldiers. In the late afternoon the kill-ing ended, leaving a minimum of 600 cadavers."

As the refugees fled to their bloody doom on the banks of the Sumpul, violence came to Mirtala's family. "Around 8:30 a helicopter came and hovered over us until around 9:00. Then some children came and said the Guardia was coming to kill everyone in the village. We were upset. There were around thirteen of us there, including my older brothers and sisters, and four of my sisters' children.

"When we heard the first barking of the dogs in the houses at the edge of the village, my father said they might be coming for us, because the dogs never barked at anyone but strangers. He had a rifle for hunting animals. He threw it and the fumigating pump in the stack of firewood and covered them over.

"When the soldiers came, they came from all sides of the house. We heard the first kick on the wooden door. 'Does Juan López live here? Open the door or we'll kill you all.' Mother opened the door. I started crying and shaking. We got all together in a group. They said, 'Juan López should come out.' My mother said, 'What do you want him for? He doesn't know anything.' They said, 'Tell him to come out or we'll kill you all.'

"Then they cocked their guns. Father was trembling. He told us, 'I don't know anything. They're not going to kill me, so don't cry.' Mother wanted him to stay, but he told her, 'I prefer them to kill me and not the children; they are just starting in life.' And so he said to them, 'Look, I'm going to go out if you assure me you won't kill my children.' 'Don't worry about that,' they told him. 'That's not your problem.'

"When he went out, they grabbed him by the neck of the shirt and dragged him around to the back of the house. There was a tree out there. I got up on the table so I could look out and see what they were doing to him. They were asking him questions. 'Are you a guerrilla? Where are your children? If you don't turn over your sons who are organizing people, we will kill you.' Then they grabbed his head and hit it against the tree. They brought the other men from the village there, too — six men in all — all the men who were in the village at that time.

"Father must have had a premonition of death. Before they came, he said, 'I don't want to die without eating *güisquiles* once again, so cook some *güisquiles* for me.' We had a *güisquile* bush by the house, so we began to cook them, and while my father was lying in the hammock waiting for them to cook, they came for him, and he never got his *güisquiles*.

"After they had the six men there, they tied their thumbs behind them with wire. As soon as they did, their thumbs began to swell horribly. Then they put them in a line, with their hats pulled down low so we couldn't see their faces. They began to take them away. We went outside. There were a lot of us. It was horrible.

"I hugged my father. I told him I would go with him. I touched his hands. His two thumbs were swollen, purple, bleeding. The others were in the same condition. Father said, 'No, daughter, stay here, take care of your mother. And if I don't come back, you leave, because they'll kill you, too.'

"My brother Pablo, who was fifteen, and my adopted brother, the son of the death squad guy, said, 'Why are you taking my father? What has he done?' The soldiers said, 'We want to investigate him. The people are accusing him of being a guerrilla. But if you want to come and be a witness, then come.' My adopted brother said, 'Let's go,' even though his father was right there. He said, 'Here, take my earnings. I will pay so the six of them can get off.' The Guardia said, 'Okay, let's go together.' So they put my brothers in front and walked away.

"All the children and my mother ran to follow, but then a soldier came back and said to my mother, 'Señora, if you go with us, you're going to die. So stay. The children can't be alone.' So my mother came back to the house with us.

"Half an hour later, we heard four shots. We said, 'Okay, they've killed them. What else can they do to us?' About forty minutes later, we heard other shots, louder.

"Then, at about 5:00 in the afternoon, I said to my older sister, 'Let's go ask the neighbor people what has happened.' So we went to the house of a good friend of ours, and she said, 'What are you doing? Don't look for your brothers or your father, or the soldiers will kill you. Your brothers and your father they have already killed.' They pointed to what looked like packages hanging on a tree. It was the bodies of my two brothers.

"The women told us they tied their hands and legs and told them to run along the path. When they were running, they shot their legs to break their legs, and then they started to pull out their eyes and cut off their ears while they were still alive. Then they slit their throats. When they were in their death agonies but still moving, they put the daggers in their backs and opened a hole and then stuck them on a tree and left them hanging there. My little brother, they left him hanging on a tree with his shoes tied under his mouth so they were filled with his blood from where they slit his throat. They gave two coups de grace to each of them. They were the first they killed.

"When we went back to our house that night and told my mother they had killed them, all the people were in our house. We prepared to pray around 7:00 at night.

"May 14 is when they killed my father. A friend of my mother came to say, 'Juan López has been killed.' We arranged the altar in the house a little bit and called all the people in the village, and we prayed for the eight people they killed. There wasn't a single man left in the village. The few other men had run away.

"The next day the soldiers came to the house again to tell us they would kill our relatives, and us, too. My mother was four or five months pregnant. When my mother asked them why they were so murderous, one of them grabbed a piece of wood and threw it at her. If she hadn't ducked, it would have killed her for sure.

"Afterward, we kept on sleeping in the village. Then the Guardia came to tell us, two days after the massacre, that we had to come with them to Las Vueltas. We made food. 'Who knows what they're going to do with us?' we said. So they took us to Las Vueltas, but they said that since we were guerrillas, they wouldn't give any food to us, and they made us sleep in the street. All the families of our village were told that we were not allowed to sleep in Los Naranjos any longer. This was to ensure that we had no contact with the guerrillas and to punish us for our organizing work. So they made us walk back and forth every day, two hours each way.

"They would get us up at 4:00 A.M. and make us walk back to the house. It was kind of a sacrifice, kind of a torture for us. If anyone sat to rest, the guards would come up with a club and beat us. And with a lot of children, that was always happening. That lasted for about two months — being forced to go back and forth to Las Vueltas every night.

"Then my mother said we should go into the mountains. Not into other houses, but into the bushes. It would be better to be in the mountains then to continue to suffer in this way. She didn't have any money, so she went to borrow some from a friend. But she was under surveillance. I was the oldest at home then, with six other children, and we were playing in the yard. Two men came and asked where my mother was. I told them I didn't know, so they left.

"My mother had left at 6:00 in the morning and said she would be back by 11:00, but by 1:00 in the afternoon, she hadn't come back. My godfather came then, and he said, 'Daughter, what are you doing here with these children?' I told him, 'I am waiting here for my mother.' He said, 'Don't wait for your mother because your mother has been killed.' He said they had an ambush set for her near Los Chorritos, which is where she was going.

"We started to cry because they had killed my brothers and my father, and now my mother was murdered, too. And I didn't know what to do with the children, what with all of us crying, so my godfather told us to come to his house. And then my mother turned up.

"We were so happy. She had realized they were following her, so she came back by a different path than she went on, or else they would have killed her. That same day, about 2:00 in the afternoon, we got dressed in the clothes we had and prepared food. It was better to die from hunger than to keep suffering what we had. We left and began walking, but the death squad saw us and began shooting at us up on the hill. There were some huge rocks where we hid so they wouldn't hit us. It was raining really hard because it was around July.

"My mother said, 'Look, I have a relative in another village, Sicahuite, so we will go there.' So we went, and three days later we got to that place. We got there around 8:00 at night, and they got upset. 'What are you doing here?' they said. 'The Guardia came looking for you here, saying that you asked for protection and they're coming to give it to you.' It wasn't true, of course.

"They knew my mother very well, and they asked for her everywhere. After two days, my mother said, 'I don't want you children to die because of my fault. I would rather die of hunger in the mountains. But I want you to live.' So what she did was give us away to different families. I went to a family with my little brother. She said to us if we didn't see her again, we should not acknowledge that she was our mother. It was hard for us to know she was going to suffer in the mountains while we stayed in the houses. We couldn't accept that. Imagine, if they killed my mother, we wouldn't see her again.

"Later, a Guardia came to the house where I was staying. I was milking a cow, and he said, 'Little girl, what's your name?' I said a name, some name I just made up. And he said, 'Your mother, what's her name?' And I just kept milking with my head down. He said, 'Little girl, do you like sweets? I'll give you sweets, but tell me about Magdalena Mejia from Los Naranjos.' I said,

'No.' He said, 'Does she come around here?' I said, 'I don't know her.' He said, 'If you hear the name Magdalena mentioned, let us know, because we are looking for her.' It hurt me a lot to say I didn't know her, and I didn't show my face because I was afraid he would recognize me. It was my mother he was asking about. Then he left.

"After that, the military operations started, and all the population decided to go to the mountains to flee from the operatives. During that period, we found that my mother was alive. For a while, we hadn't heard anything about her, but she had hidden in a cave where the entrance was behind a big rock and the soldiers could walk right by without seeing her. So my mother came back to the village to pick us up to go to live in the mountains. And even though it was a difficult time, it was a happy time — so much joy after you don't know if they have killed your mother, if she even exists, what happened with her. We were happy even though we decided to flee.

"From then, maybe July of 1980 through 1981, we lived a year and a half in the bushes. I wasn't fighting, but I was always working in what we called expansion work, recruiting work. We would meet with other refugees and people in the communities to explain to them the reasons for the war and to urge them to work together. We distributed pamphlets and things like that.

"There was no food there. We cut bananas. We ate bananas, *jocotes*, coffee beans to get rid of the hunger. Any weed. We ate so many things, snakes even. We were far from any villages, near Honduras. And the soldiers militarized the towns, so we couldn't go there, but sometimes people would bring us food. Sometimes, if someone would get sick, they would take us to their homes to recuperate. Just in the group we were in, there were 200 to 300 people, and we divided into smaller groups, one going one way, one another, so when they bombed us, we would separate.

"We carried our nine-month-old baby sister with us. But one day my sister who was carrying her laid her down on the ground and went to get some water. Just while she was away, a plane came over and dropped a 500-pound bomb, which landed where the baby was lying on the ground. When my sister came back, the baby was gone.

"There were great sacrifices. One time, there were 100 of us hiding in a coffee grove in Chalatenango when the patrols came. The children were crying, so their mothers had to cover their mouths to silence them. It was horrible. So painful to tell the things that happened in the war. A very palpable reality.

"One time, we spent two days and one night with constant bombardments, throwing ourselves on the ground all the time. I didn't want to live anymore. I wanted them to kill me. I lost the desire to live. I don't know why. So I stood up and leaned against a tree, waiting for my death. When mortars come, they make a soft sound before they explode, and when I heard that sound, I felt a chill, so I knew I wanted to live, and I threw myself on the ground. I had a little skirt on — a full skirt, like for dancing.

"When the mortar exploded, I was hit by shrapnel here on the leg, and I thought it had blown my leg off. My leg went all numb, and since I had my face buried in the weeds, I couldn't see anything. I felt something hot running down. I thought I was going to be with one leg. So I told the children, the people, that I didn't want to be with one leg so that they would have to carry me around.

"About twenty minutes later, I started to pinch myself here on the leg to see if I had my leg or not. And I felt my heart beat; I was getting really excited. Then I could feel my toes, and I was really excited, so I shouted out. It was one of my few joyful moments — to discover that my leg was still there. Then the *compas* came and scolded me for shouting out, but fortunately, no one heard me.

"I started looking at my leg. It was all purple from the impact, and a little bit scratched. My skirt was all blown away, and I had a little wound on my shoulder, too, from the shrapnel, that I didn't even notice. I was just there in my underpants. If it had hit my leg instead of the skirt, it would have taken my leg. They treated me, and then I was okay, even though my leg nearly got infected. There is a scar there now.

"I was barefoot there in the hills of northern Chalatenango for two years, always on the move from one place to another. I had two blouses, one skirt. We each carried a piece of plastic that we slept under. The plastic was light to carry and kept us dry and warm. But after two years, it got so that we couldn't stand it anymore. We had skin diseases, all sorts of things. My feet got infected from being exposed to cuts all the time, and there were worms growing in my feet, but I wouldn't let my mother burn out the worms with a cigarette.

"At the beginning of 1982, the church took us out of there to give us medical attention, food, and shelter at the San José de la Montana Seminary in San Salvador. That seminary is where Romero graduated. Some of the men hiked out of the mountains to make the arrangements with the church, then they came back for us. We walked for fifteen days, only at night, to reach the place near the town of Chalatenango where the buses came for us. Anyone passing by could tell from our dirty clothes who we were — the displaced — so we got water in little jugs and cleaned our clothes as best we could.

"The buses got us to San Salvador in the afternoon. At the seminary, they received us and took our information and gave us mattresses. They had set up a camp for us on the soccer field — big rooms with laminated roofs where about 100 people could sleep, with no privacy for family groups. In all, there were about 1,000 refugees at that camp. It was frustrating being there, and we were afraid. Our surroundings there were limited, and I remember thinking, 'Where will we flee if they come after us?' In spite of the hardships, we missed the mountains and feared we would be trapped there. It was like a persecution psychosis. At night I dreamed of planes bombing us, and I would wake up and cry for my mama. I was thirteen years old. Even now, whenever I hear a helicopter or a plane fly over, it reminds me of those days in the mountains.

"All this time, I was thinking, 'When can we go back to our village? What is happening there?' So we began to think of organizing ourselves. We got together a singing group and education groups and community organizing groups. And we talked about creating an organization for the displaced. Some were afraid, but we were joyful, too, because we wanted to go home. So for two months we met, trying to figure out how to promote our struggle and trying to come up with a name for ourselves. Finally, out of several heads came the name CRIPDES — Christian Committee for the Displaced of El Salvador. Our objectives were to get the government to stop the war and the evictions of thousands of families, to stop the forced recruitment of young campesinos, to return to our places of origin, to gain respect for living in our communities and for freedom of movement, to obtain respect for human rights.

"We sent our requests to the government but got no response. So we started to march and demonstrate in the streets, demanding cessation of oppression and of human rights violations. Everything was militarized. That was in 1984, when the war was at its apogee, and the government didn't want to give in. So we started to bring delegations from North American churches to support us and to provide solidarity with us in our demands.

"After two years of this work, we did the first repopulation — of San José las Flores in Chalatenango on June 20, 1986. First we spent two weeks in the streets demonstrating with a good group of campesinos and North Americans, then we went back to Las Flores with 200 families. We rebuilt the huts there and cleaned the place up. And immediately the army erected a roadblock at Conacaste, just outside Chalatenango, to make sure that no food, medicine, or construction materials could get through to Las Flores. From then on, the delegations always had to get *permisos*. That roadblock stayed there until the end of the war."

San José las Flores is a town in northern Chalatenango Department not far from the hamlet where Mirtala grew up, and like Los Naranjos, it was evacuated by its residents when the army conducted its sweeps of the region in the early 1980s. With the support of the United Nations High Commission on Refugees and a number of religious groups in the United States, CRIPDES caravaned residents back to their homes in San José las Flores from the refugee camps where they had resettled.

"By now we had our first little office in a little room at the Human Rights Commission of El Salvador, at the back of the garage. We had room for one desk and three chairs and a cardboard box for our files. Herbert Anaya would always laugh at us because of our little office and tell us that we wouldn't leave there until we had an office of our own. We had met the commission when they came to the refugee camp and when they went into the *campo* to investigate abuses, so we asked them for a place.

"Our success in repopulating San José las Flores impressed the refugees at the Mesa Grande refugee camp in Honduras, so they sent us letters through the churches asking us to help them return, too. In this work, we had help from Medardo Gómez of the Lutheran Church, Luis Serrano of the Episcopalian Church, and Monseñor Urioste and Father Octavio Cruz. With them we discussed the repatriation for Mesa Grande, and we went with them to Mesa Grande to have an assembly. We agreed to have them return in October 1987.

"There were 4,300 refugees there, and we were a little worried about how to do it. But we organized a lot and had a lot of international support. In the United States the churches organized the Going Home Campaign to support us. Lots of bishops accompanied us, and we did a lot of fund-raising campaigns and organized accompaniment delegations. There was something about that repatriation that made me very happy: my two sisters were in the Mesa Grande camp, and they were able to come back to Las Vueltas.

"The people in that first return from Mesa Grande went to Las Vueltas, Guarjila, and other places. We made four caravans and did it little by little. Then in 1988 we began the return from the Colomoncagua refugee camp in Honduras. And finally the return from San Antonio to Cuidad Romero in Usulután. In total, 30,000 people were repatriated. It was a lot of work."

I first met Mirtala López in June 1988 while she and the rest of the CRIPDES staff were working on repatriating the displaced to their places of origin. At the time, I knew nothing of her work or her background, but she made a strong impression on me nevertheless. By then, CRIPDES had its own office in a building some blocks distant from that of the commission.

Remembering the *pupusa* dinner that Suzanne and I had so enjoyed on our first trip in 1987, I proposed to commission members that we repeat that feast once we had concluded our meetings. As always, a long discussion ensued about where we should go, and they finally decided on a place called Los Planes de Renderos up in the hills near the city, where there were a lot of little *pupuserias*. Lisa Magarrell drove the decrepit BMW near which Herbert had been killed the previous October, and I drove an equally decrepit Peugeot. Ten or twelve of us squeezed into the two cars and headed off through the city toward Los Planes. Joaquín Cáceres rode shotgun with me, and after we had driven a few blocks, he asked me to pull over to the curb so we could pick up an additional passenger — Mirtala. She was nineteen at the time.

Mirtala was then and is now a lovely young woman, slender, lively, outgoing, bright, animated. But what struck me most about her was her eyes. On that evening in Los Planes and again when I visited El Salvador the following January, their clear sparkle was what stood out about her.

Knowing now what I did not know then — about the loss of her father and her siblings and about the many months she scrambled to survive in the far reaches of northern Chalatenango — I am amazed that her demeanor revealed nothing of what she had been through. She looked like somebody's kid sister, eager and full of life, only prettier. Little did any of us know that her most terrible trials still lay ahead of her.

The Salvadoran authorities frustrated the work of CRIPDES in every way possible, but they were forced to put on a good face about the return of the refugees to the communities from which they had been ousted several years earlier. The army was in a public relations bind, and military officials knew it. The U.S. Congress was becoming increasingly restive about the tales that trickled north of army atrocities. The United Nations High Commission for Refugees sponsored the repatriations that CRIPDES organized. The Salvadoran churches — Catholic and Protestant — threw their full weight behind the repatriations and were joined in this by endless delegations of North American churchpeople who accompanied every caravan of buses and trucks that crossed over from Honduras. The whole repatriation campaign irritated the authorities to no end, but they couldn't prevent it. Instead, as Mirtala relates it, they threw sand in the gears of those repatriations whenever possible.

"Then the repression began against the repatriated communities — bombings, crop burnings, murders, captures. And always there were the roadblocks everywhere to block food and medicine and merchandise. When the repression increased, I proposed a human rights secretariat in CRIPDES to document violations. I was constantly in the communities to investigate, and I had an active presence at the public level, conducting press conferences. We took people to the Human Rights Commission, to the Red Cross, to Tutela Legal, and even to the Governmental Human Rights Commission. We made contact with affiliated human rights organizations in the United States and with the United Nations and with Americas Watch. We became a reference point for this kind of work.

"It was not easy always having to argue with soldiers at the roadblocks. They took our cameras and our notebooks and would always say, 'We've seen you before. It is a pity you're with these gringos, otherwise we would have your head hanging in that tree over there.' So I always went with others and I told little white lies and I discovered alternate routes that would bypass the roadblocks. We would tell the soldiers that we were geography students doing field research, anything that would enable us to pass back and forth to the repopulated communities.

"The work was hard, but I'm proud of having left my youth to work with the people — my people — who had suffered. It was a great joy for me that they were able to be in their places of origin. They had the courage to struggle and to get home. So they inspired me to keep on without getting weak in my commitment.

"I was captured three times. The first time was in 1988 in Chalatenango by the First Military Brigade. They released me after one day because of the pressure they received from solidarity organizations.

"The second time was on April 19, 1989, my birthday, when they militarized the CRIPDES office. There were sixty-four of us there, mostly children, including a day-old baby. We had a small clinic there, and we distributed food and all kinds of things. At 2:00 in the afternoon, I was in a meeting with a German doctor, a British volunteer from Peace Brigades International, and a U.S. woman named Stephanie. The military came and rang the bell. Nobody answered it, so I went to see. I looked through the window and saw a fat soldier there and a member of the Treasury Police. They said, 'Open the door. We want to search the building.' I said, 'Why? Do you have a *permiso?*' They said, 'We are the authorities. Open the door, or we will kick in the windows.'

"I was scared. I went to get the key, but instead of opening the door, I double-locked it and threw the bolts. They said, 'When are you going to open the door?' I told them, 'We are just keeping you out.' They began to hit the door with their rifle butts. We armed ourselves with clubs and stacked bags of rice and beans in front of the door. We took the megaphones to the window and used them to cry out that we were being attacked. We kept that up until 11:00 at night. They got a good look at four of us. And they told us they would kill us all.

"They cut off the phone, blocked off the street, and brought in forty antiriot police and others. Then they got up on the roof and began to break the roof in. Our megaphone was so loud that they brought in sound equipment to drown us out. They didn't want the soldiers or the policemen to hear what we were saying. But our megaphone was still louder, and they shouted in anger because their equipment was bad. Finally, they cut the bars on the kitchen windows with saws and started to come in. All of us went into the living room to hold hands. Outside, lots of solidarity groups had assembled in the street, including the Human Rights Commission and some press.

"They came in with grenades and tear gas and cameras to take pictures. They beat us with clubs and rifle butts. But we continued to shout with the megaphone even when they were inside. They grabbed one end of it and we held the other, fighting over it until finally it broke. Then they grabbed me by my hair, me and Inocente Oriano, Jorge Olivedo, and Isabel Hernandez. They wanted to take us out another way so the press wouldn't see us. We all hugged each other and told them they would have to kill us all or we would go together — all sixty-four of us. When they couldn't get us four out, they said, 'We'll show you. If you get out of the Treasury Police, you'll be dead.'

"So we all went out by the front door. TV 12 has footage of this. They grabbed me by my arm, and when I grabbed on to the others, they clubbed me in the back. They had three trucks there to take us away, but we made them put us all in one. When they drove us to the Treasury Police, we shouted all the way there, 'The Treasury Police have caught us, children and women. They have threatened to kill us.' Then we sang to overcome our terror. People were fainting from terror and crying.

"We got to the Central Barracks around 12:00 at night. They greeted us by saying, 'Ladies and gentlemen, welcome. We will do nothing to you if you behave. We have food and showers for you. This is just an investigation. How soon you get out will depend on you.' An old man and woman got out of the truck. They handcuffed them, so the others wanted to stay in the truck. I was very tense and afraid. I got out of the truck, and they handcuffed me, too, and then the others. They separated the women from the children.

"Then they blindfolded me, and when they took me inside, a soldier kicked me in the chest, knocking me against the wall. He said, 'You have finally fallen into my hands. Now you will tell the truth.'

"They took my documents and dragged me by the hair. I don't know where. It was a big place, and they put us all in there. It was hard being blindfolded, and if we moved, someone would hit us. They began to take us out, one by one, one to the left and one to the right. They would grab someone by the hair and drag them out, and then five minutes later that one would come back screaming and vomiting.

"When my turn came, they took me by the hair, which was longer than it is now. They said, 'Now it's time to tell the truth. Are you a guerrilla?' 'No. I work with the displaced.' 'Tell the truth, or we'll show you who we are.' Then they grabbed my head and pushed it into a toilet filled with urine and feces. I screamed and vomited because of the filth. They hit me in the chest, hard, and then took me back to another room.

"I was separated from the others. They isolated all of us, and then the interrogation started. 'Where are the FMLN people? Who gave the orders to CRIPDES? What are your political activities? What is the FMLN plan to defeat the government?' So I told them, 'First, we are not with the FMLN. Secondly, you know where the guerrillas are, since you send your bombs against them in the countryside. Third, we know nothing about guerrilla strategy. We work with the displaced, and if you want to confirm that, you can go to the communities where the people are.'

"Then they beat me harder, and they stripped me to my underwear. Then they threw me on the floor and stood on my body. They said they would rape me and drug me. 'You'll never get out except to go to the cemetery, where there is a tomb for you. We have made the FMLN *comandantes* talk. We'll make you talk, too, or we'll pour acid on you.' They were putting psychological pressure on me.

"They stripped me completely and began to touch my breasts. I was shouting, 'If you rape me, I'll tell the whole world. Many people know me. You'll have a serious political problem.' They said, 'No. We did not put your name on the list of people we captured. People think you are dead already. You'll be here forever.' Then they said they would take me to the basement, and this really terrorized me because of the things I had heard about the basement. But I didn't want to sign any papers.

"At that point I was completely naked, and five men took me down a lot of steps. I felt that two had stayed with me and the others had gone ahead. Then they said, 'This is your last chance to answer questions. There are two questions. Answer them and your life will be saved. If you don't answer them, the animals in the basement will eat you. There are knives to fill your body and destroy you.' Then they said, 'Here is the first question: Who gave the orders to CRIPDES?' 'Nobody.' 'Here is the second question: Turn over ten of your *compañeros* to us.' 'I would rather you kill me then that ten should suffer like I am suffering. Kill me if you must, but I'll go proud that I have struggled for these people.'

"Then one took me by the hands and another by the feet, and they swung me as they counted, 'One, two, three!' Then they threw me through the air, and I fell on something with points, maybe plastic. It felt like knives, and I began to bleed. They said, 'You can't die yet. Tell the whole truth, or now we'll rip off little parts of your body.'

"Then they took me to another place that smelled like chemicals. They poured some liquid on my breasts and took off the blindfold. Then they held daggers in front of my eyes, touching my eyelids with the points, while another looked for the vein in my throat to slash my throat. They told me to open my eyes, and I screamed, but I was pressed against the wall. I thought they would take out my eyes. They told me to open my mouth, but I was afraid to. All five men wore black hoods over their heads, but they were dressed as soldiers. I closed my mouth tighter. They told me they would rip my tongue out.

Then one of them punched me in the jaw, dislocating it so that I couldn't close my mouth. They grabbed my tongue and pulled and then sawed on my tongue with a knife blade. My mouth stayed open because they had dislocated it. They tried to put it back in place, and when they couldn't, someone said, 'That's easy. Hit her on the other side.' So they hit me on the other side, knocking my jaw more or less back in place. The pain was horrible. In cold weather, my jaw hurts to this day.

"Then they hung me by my breasts. They tied threads around my nipples and pulled me by my breasts. It is one of the most sensitive parts a woman has. I was screaming a lot. Each time, they would pull me up more — the whole weight of my body. They pulled up more and more until I was only touching the ground with the points of my toes. They threatened me with a knife. I may have fainted. I was not reacting; I felt far away. They beat on my breasts, and I could feel blood on my breasts, but they had poured a warm liquid on my breasts that felt like blood. Then they carried me somewhere else.

"They threw me on the floor and pushed on my chest to make me react, because I was still semiconscious. I asked for water, but they wouldn't give me any. I couldn't feel my breasts, and I thought they had been cut off. After some time, I started to move my body and sat in one of the corners of the cell. They asked me, 'Do you want to tell the truth now?' 'You already know the truth. You know where I work. Why do you ask me so much?' 'You rebellious little girl. With us, everyone says everything.'

"Then I heard someone saying, 'Bring la Toñita.' I thought Toñita was the name of a woman. Then they sat me up straight, and someone put his knees behind my back, and they told me that when I wanted to say something, I should move my head. It turned out that la Toñita is the *capucha*, a plastic bag filled with lime and gas. They pulled it over my head and tied it over my neck, then pressed it against my mouth and nose. Then they took it off. 'What do you have to say?' 'Nothing.' Then they put it back over my head again and again, always the same thing, six or seven times. The powder and gas burned my throat. I coughed and felt asphyxiated. I gave no reaction.

"Then something happened. I felt my body had changed, and I felt tranquil in all my body. I felt I was in a very green place, and I was very happy about the place I was in. I saw from a mountain the sunrise coming out softly. When the sun came up, there I could see three white crosses were sprouting. I felt happy and calm. I wasn't thinking anything about the past. I was happy about this atmosphere I was in. I feel like at that moment I had contact with death. I'm not capable of believing much in these things, but this experience left me moved. I believe at that moment I felt myself die. Maybe I did die. I entered into a moment of rest.

"Then I felt them move me, interrupting the happiness of that moment. And then I started to think of soldiers, to return to what was happening. When I woke up, I asked for water, but they brought me urine. I could smell the bad smell, but I was so worried about my throat that I drank it. Then they put me in a cold room, very dirty. And I was still naked. I couldn't react because I was definitely bad, bad off.

"There I was with them until another came in and began to drag me by the hair, and someone said, 'If we fuck her, she'll die, and then it really will be harder for us, because we will have to face a big campaign and there will be trouble.' So he threw me down again.

"Later, they took me out again and threw me in the air and let me fall. I hit the corner of the desk with my head. It hurt my brain and gave me a terrible headache. Then someone kicked me with his boot in the upper part of my stomach. It caused an internal injury that still gives me problems. I tried to remember where I was and what was happening. Then they took me to another place with a bad smell, really bad. They held my head so I was facing forward and removed the blindfold. In front of me was some kind of machine with blades around the outside. Hanging from the blades was women's hair and blood. They said, 'Remember the basement. Remember the knives.' I had chills, and I started to cry from nervousness. They said nothing, just showed me the machine. It was a psychological torture. Even after I got out, I remembered that machine. All told, I was there for seventy-two hours.

"They gave me clothes on the day they were to free us. I was isolated until then. They took me to where there were more people, and I heard familiar voices. They put on loud music when they started to beat us so they wouldn't hear our screams. I couldn't dress myself, so the soldiers had to dress me. I couldn't move my arms or my body. Then they gave us bad, rotten food, and when we didn't eat it, they threw it in our faces. But now I felt the other people around me, and I began to say their names. They responded and I felt happy — not because they were there, but because I knew I wasn't alone, they hadn't disappeared me.

"They took us to another room and removed the blindfold but left the handcuffs on. The soldier who was there said, 'I am in charge of keeping peace from you. Wherever I see you, I am going to put twenty bullets in you. I will come to the jail to visit you, and I'm coming with a knife to slash your throat.' That scared me a lot when he said that, of course, because in a jail it's not difficult to get a knife. And besides, they are capable of that.

"After seventy-two hours, they put us on a military truck. I was traumatized. I started to know who I was as I recognized the people around me. I touched them to see if it was really them. Then I touched my breasts to see if they were there. Then I found my breasts. It was one of the great emotions of my life; I thought they had torn them off.

"They drove us to the court, but it was late and the judges were gone. This made the soldiers happy. They could take us back to the Treasury Police because the judges had gone. Now there were just six of us; they had released the rest. It was Friday afternoon. If a judge didn't receive us, they would have us for another seventy-two hours until Monday morning. This terrified us. But there were a whole bunch of people waiting for us — the Human Rights Commission, the archbishop's office, lawyers. So they went and got a judge, and we testified. I couldn't walk into the court because when they had stood on my legs when my legs were crossed, they dislocated my hips and stretched the tendons or something. So they helped me in. They tell me I started to scream in the court: 'Don't put the *capucha* on me. Don't beat me.'

"That night, they put us in jail. I slept on the second floor with two other women at the women's prison. They had to carry me because I couldn't walk.

"It was very hard, very difficult. I was five months in prison. The first two months, I was in bad, serious condition. I passed out several times for as much as an hour, without reacting at all. The judge wouldn't let me go to the hospital. But afterward I recovered, and I came out of jail with even more energy. I reconfirmed my commitment to keep on struggling. Nothing or nobody, no matter how difficult it could be, would stop my struggle, my commitment, my decision to work for a more just and human future for Salvadorans. I saw a doctor who gave me some treatment for the blow to my brain. I'm embarrassed to say I didn't follow it.

"My third capture happened a month later during the fourth return of refugees from Mesa Grande on September 26, 1989. They captured me at the border after I had been two weeks at Mesa Grande organizing another return. The Treasury Police and National Police crossed into Honduras, to the Mesa Grande camp, in civilian clothing as a delegation with the minister of the interior to detect who was organizing the return. One of those who came was one of my torturers. When he saw me in front of the assembly, he came and stood in front of me and sentenced me with a nod of his head, like saying, 'You're going to regret it.'

"Later, when we got back to the Honduras/El Salvador border, they had our names there. Colonel Ciro López Roque of the Fourth Brigade ordered the capture of five of us. His name appears in the Truth Commission Report. They took us to Fourth Brigade Headquarters and took pictures of us, but the archbishop sent lawyers from Tutela Legal to free us. So instead, they sent us to the National Guard in a stake truck. We got there around 6:00 P.M.. The whole way, we shouted to everyone we passed that they had captured us. They had eight soldiers, well armed, guarding us, but they would hide their weapons whenever we passed the buses.

"At the National Guard, they blindfolded us and handcuffed us to interrogate us. But immediately, the United Nations High Commission for Refugees started to do the procedures to have us released. Right at the border, meanwhile, the people being repatriated decided not to advance until we were released. So the people spent two days sleeping in the street and said they would stay there a month to achieve our release.

"Monseñor Rivera y Damas sent a letter to the director of the National Guard, to Colonel Machuca, to ask for our immediate release, explaining that we were people who worked for the rights of the displaced, repatriating refugees to their places of origin. They released us the next afternoon. The UNHCR had to lend us their radios so that we could communicate with the refugees to tell them that thanks to the pressure they had brought, at that moment we were coming out of the National Police. They were happy. They had a party. Then they started their march to their communities. It stimulates your work knowing that the people are always with you, that they don't abandon you."

During the period of Mirtala's torture and incarceration in April 1989, and again during her brief captivity the following September, the U.S. urgent action networks flooded switchboards in El Salvador and in Washington with calls of protest. Mirtala had told her torturers the truth: lots of people did know her, and we were heartsick imagining what they might be doing to her when she was first taken in, then outraged to hear what she had actually suffered. When she got out of prison and went straight back to work at CRIPDES, it was an almost unbelievable act of defiance and courage. Mirtala López is one tough person, and that toughness — as well as the residue of her suffering — is now visible in her eyes.

I next saw Mirtala in June 1990, fourteen months after her ordeal with the Treasury Police. On June 20, the town of San José las Flores planned a big celebration to commemorate the fourth anniversary of the town's repopulation. CRIPDES was in charge of ferrying the international delegations and Salvadoran popular organizations up to San José las Flores, deep in the mountains of Chalatenango. When I arrived at the commission's office at the beginning of my seven-day visit, they asked me if I would like to go along with Lisa Magarrell to represent them. This would be my first opportunity to visit the zones controlled by the FMLN, so I was honored by the invitation.

On the night of June 19, Lisa and I and several other North Americans who were going along slept at the commission's office. A van from CRIPDES would pick us up at 3:00 in the morning and head north in time to cross the bridge at the Río Lempa, where the army maintained a roadblock, before the soldiers awoke.

When the doorbell rang, Mirtala stood before us, pretty as ever, smartly outfitted in a bright yellow dress and heels, smiling her dazzling smile in greeting. But the glitter was gone from her eyes, and etched there instead was the suffering she had endured and the strong defiance with which she had endured it. Not many people could bounce back from what she went through, then step right back into the risks she ran as part of her daily job.

Mirtala had to take us the back way to San José las Flores on that very long, very hot day. The roadblock at the bridge was manned when we got there, so we had to backtrack and take one of the muddy, tortuous alternative routes that Mirtala had pioneered years before when she began working with the displaced communities. The fourteen of us spent the day levering that van out of mudholes and creek bottoms with tree branches, shoving it up muddy inclines while its spinning wheels coated us with goop from head to foot, and sweltering for hours in the midday heat when we got mired to the axles in a quarter-mile-long brown puddle between cornfields.

At that point, when it became clear that no amount of pushing would get us out, Mirtala tripped back up the road in her heels to find help while the rest of us squeezed into the single dab of shade cast by the only scrawny tree within a mile. An hour later, we heard a distant rumble that materialized around the bend as a huge Massey Ferguson tractor bearing two men, Mirtala, and a case of warm Coke. These were the guys who had originally shown her this lengthy detour around the roadblock, guys who knew the consequences to themselves if an army patrol helicopter happened to drone over while they were looping a chain around our front axle to help us complete the journey we had been forbidden to take at 5:00 that morning by the lieutenant at the road-blocked bridge. They hauled us for the better part of three miles, through that first mudhole and the several others that followed.

By late afternoon, we reached the town of Chalatenango, where we scooted into a nunnery to await the dark and our opportunity to run the second roadblock, just east of town. Suddenly, a torrential rain squall swept over the town, and Mirtala hustled us back into the van, knowing that the soldiers at the roadblock would be heading for dry quarters. We whistled past undeterred, lugged up the twisty mountain roads as dusk gathered, and rolled into San José las Flores fifteen hours after the journey began, just in time for the party that lasted until dawn.

I saw Mirtala again when she came to Marin on a U.S. speaking tour the following year, and I was glad to see that some of her sparkle was back as we greeted each other. She chuckled along with the crowd when I told the story of our muddy odyssey to Las Flores as I introduced her. That same year — 1991 — Mirtala was honored by the Rothko Chapel in Texas with its Human Rights Award for Truth and Freedom and by the Reebok Corporation with its annual Human Rights Award. Then, as the peace process wound to a conclusion in El Salvador, Mirtala moved on to a new stage in her life.

Having worked at CRIPDES for seven years after helping found it at age fifteen, she resigned her post and took a position with the now legally constituted FMLN political organization.

"In March of 1992, I started to work with the FMLN. I never had worked with the FMLN before, despite accusations. Now, with my head held high, I work there to build the young peoples' movement. I like working with the youth a lot. But it will not be easy for me to forget the things that have happened to me in my short years. They are marks which stay with you. I will try to be happy in my personal life, but I'm never going to forget everything I went through."

Mirtala López lost eight family members and one unofficially adopted brother during the civil war: her father, a brother, and the adoptive brother, who died on the day the Guardia came to their home; the baby who perished when a bomb landed on her in the mountains; and five other siblings who were at one time or another FMLN combatants. Of these, one brother was wounded near Las Vueltas, then captured, doused with gasoline, and burned to death. Another little brother died in combat near San José las Flores in 1991. A fourteen-year-old brother died under bombing in Chalatenango in 1989. Her sister María, assassinated doing organizing work, was beheaded and left on a pile of stones with garbage stuffed into her vagina. Another brother, a *comandante* in the west, died in Santa Ana on November 17, 1989.

When I met with Mirtala just before writing this account of her life, I asked what her childhood had been like. This is how she answered: "When I was a little girl, I didn't know what it was to be happy. I worked. I felt a need for having a childhood, without a lot of pressure from my parents. I didn't enjoy my childhood as I would have liked to. When I see the way things are in these times, I say, 'Gee what a privilege for the children.' I'm happy that today's children have an opportunity to enjoy their childhood, but my situation was entirely different. I'm not ashamed. On the contrary, I'm proud that I became a witness since the time I was a little girl, that since that time, I dedicated myself to community tasks, helping others.

"I was upset and mortified to see bodies around, and to know that the security forces and the military didn't respect people, even children, and I was afraid. I saw how the landowners treated my parents, and I didn't like it. I saw how they treated my father because he couldn't read. So I became conscious. And the same way I saw it with my father, I saw it when they were that way with anybody else. The same with children. So by the time I was ten years old, I understood the situation. By the time I was fourteen, I had this deep knowledge of the situation. So I spent my youth in this way and in the bushes and working with young people. When I was fifteen years old, I was one of the founders of CRIPDES, working and facing the challenges of life.

"I can't get my father out of me. Whenever I'm going to do something, I think of my father and I think of my brothers. And also my mother is an inspiration. I'm proud of her. She's a very strong woman, and she has also gone through her struggle. It has been very painful for her. And we are real friends. Today, I feel closer to her, and we're both political, so we discuss a lot of things. She still lives in Las Vueltas, where I visit her every two weeks. She is the coordinator of the community, and she is in charge of the land transfer in Chalatenango.

"I have come to a conclusion — that I live to struggle, and I struggle to live. I don't know what I would do if I didn't struggle beside these people."

_ 9 _

BRIAN

In the mid-1980s, MITF was by no means the only U.S. solidarity organization confronting public officials with concerns about Central America. Solidarity organizations took root all over the map — the Chicago Interreligious Task Force, the Springfield (Massachusetts) Area Central America Project, the Southern California Interfaith Task Force on Central America, the Wisconsin Interfaith Community on Central America, and a number of groups with Washington, D.C. offices, among them the Central America Working Group, National Agenda for Peace in El Salvador, Neighbor to Neighbor, SHARE Foundation, and the Ecumenical Program on Central America. The 1987 *Directory of Central American Organizations*, published by the Central America Resource Center in Austin, Texas, ran 290 pages, three or four listings to a page. In addition to those who served as volunteers or staff for this extensive solidarity network were individuals who acted more or less on their own initiative. Brian Willson was one of them.

From September 1 to October 10, 1986, Brian Willson, Charley Liteky, Duncan Murphy, and George Miso consumed nothing but water. Every day during that period, they sat on the steps of the U.S. Capitol conducting what they called the Veterans' Fast for Life. All four had served in the U.S. military — Murphy in World War II, and Liteky, Miso, and Willson in Vietnam, where Liteky earned the Congressional Medal of Honor. All four had come to the conclusion that as veterans, they had a special obligation to resist those uses of U.S. military power that killed and maimed innocent people in faraway places to advance U.S. foreign policy. They were particularly outraged at U.S. military involvement in Nicaragua, where, despite the express prohibition by Congress of U.S. support, the U.S.-trained and -funded Contras were then conducting a terrorist war against the duly elected Sandinista government, and in El Salvador, where the U.S. military was advising and the U.S. Congress funding a Salvadoran military apparatus that killed and tortured civilians with impunity.

Brian Willson remembers the time he spent on the Capitol steps as a remarkable and vivid period. He and his friends regarded their country's policies as policies of terror, and they resolved to resist that terrorism in the most peaceful and dramatic way they could imagine. When they began their fast, they resolved that it would be open-ended; they would go without food until they died or until they determined that the response to their action was sufficient to merit eating again.

Brian attributes the vividness of his experience in part to the response the men received during their hunger strike — the friendliness of the Capitol guards who spoke with them on a daily basis, the crowds of people who assembled around them as the weeks passed and it became clear they were prepared to give their lives so that others might live, the words of encouragement they received from other veterans who came to talk with them, the reporters who interviewed them, and the visits they received from members of Congress whose consciences were moved. Of the twenty elected officials who stopped by to see what they were up to, or to offer words of encouragement, Brian best remembers John Kerry, Don Riegel, Christopher Dodd, and Tom Harkin. But what he recalls most clearly about those forty-eight days of increasing hunger and weakness is the extraordinary and unexpected sense of freedom he and his three friends experienced once they had decided they were prepared to die. The man who emerged at the end of the fast was different from the man who began it.

As the days went by and the response to their fast increased, the four former soldiers began to think that perhaps they were indeed achieving their goals. They had received 20,000 letters of support, and some eighty senators and representatives had signed a statement of support as well. But time was running out. George Miso's health had deteriorated to the critical point, and the three others were forced to confront some difficult questions. What if the response became clearly sufficient a day or two after George died? Would their deaths call any more attention to Nicaragua and El Salvador than their hunger strike had already achieved? Resolving that they could accomplish more alive than dead, they broke their fast. George Miso lived, but he will never recover his health. Still suffering from heart problems, he has started a hospital in Germany for children from around the world who are victims of war.

After the Fast for Life ended, Brian traveled to Nicaragua, where he met a midwife from San Francisco named Holly Rauen. He followed her back to the Bay Area and moved with her to the Canal area of San Rafael. They rented an apartment there, which they shared with Holly's thirteen-year-old son. It was during their courtship in the spring of 1987 that I first met Brian.

He and Holly had chosen the Canal, as this out-of-the-way community is known, because it was home to the greatest concentration of Central American refugees in Marin County. Four thousand refugees, most of them from El Salvador and many of them undocumented, crowded into Canal apartments, slept in cars or on the street, scrounged for jobs, and tried to steer clear of immigration authorities. In those days, Jesús Campos and his family were also living in the Canal and had observed the same desperation and miserable conditions that Brian and Holly had. Through Jesús, the Marin Interfaith Task Force was beginning to support programs for these refugees, and it wasn't long before Brian crossed our path.

We had heard of Brian from the press accounts of the Fast for Life and soon came to know him well. Suzanne Bristol and I taped a television interview with him on the San Rafael cable access channel. On that and other occasions, we talked at length about all kinds of things — the ongoing tragedies in Central America, our spiritual lives, what it was like to live in a society that resolutely turned its back on distant suffering caused by its own government, and baseball.

Brian made quite a figure — tall, commanding, engaging, bearded, and always sporting a St. Louis Cardinals baseball cap, regardless of his attire or the weather. His militant pacifism, and the extent to which he was willing to dedicate his life to the principles of that pacifism, had by that time moved him well outside the mainstream of American society. To many people, Brian seemed just plain weird, a longhaired hippie two decades out of sync with the rest of the world. That separation from his cultural roots was painful for Brian, dedicated as he was to his ideals.

He knew that his actions affronted most people, just as most people's apathy affronted him. He had burned his bridges to most of the friends of his youth, to most of his military comrades from the Vietnam War, and even to some activists whose lifestyles and life choices had not taken them as far as Brian. About all of this he was philosophical and in many ways joyful. He told me once that when he awoke in the morning, he asked the Great Spirit what he should do with the day ahead of him and then did what the Spirit directed.

Brian fascinated me. By the summer of 1987, I had decided to enter the ministry and enrolled at the San Francisco Theological Seminary for that September. Over the past two years, I had realized I was far more passionate about and engaged in the work of the task force than in my duties as an organizational development consultant, and I pondered a career change. I wanted to steer my life permanently toward the passion I felt and the faith that fueled it. As I proceeded with this self-inquiry, the ministry emerged as the obvious answer.

My Central American journey had sprung, after all, from my faith and from my friendship with my pastor, Bill Eichhorn. In what little I knew of liberation theology at the time, I recognized a theology that exalted what most parts of the church have for so long ignored — Jesus's passionate advocacy for those who see life "from below" (to borrow Dietrich Bonhoeffer's term) and his passionate resistance to the earthly structures that subject these multitudes to the lots they suffer. I wanted to be part of that, and ministry seemed to be the way.

I was fortunate in pursuing my newfound vocation. I already knew two professors at San Francisco Theological Seminary, which despite its name is located in San Anselmo in the heart of Marin County. Marvin Chaney, professor of Old Testament, and his family worshiped at Mill Valley Community Church with me and Lori and Kate and Tucker. Jorge Lara-Braud, professor of theology and ethics, had helped us recruit our advisory board when we started the Accompaniment Project for the Human Rights Commission of El Salvador.

Jorge had known Salvadoran archbishop Oscar Romero and had attended his funeral in 1980, nearly getting killed in the process. Jorge had been on the steps of the cathedral with other dignitaries when the National Guard opened fire on the multitude of Salvadorans assembled in the great square outside. Thousands jammed through the doors of the cathedral, stumbling over the wooden benches of the sanctuary, wailing and trampling one another underfoot, urgently pressing forward to escape the hail of gunfire emanating from the roofs of the buildings ringing the square. The desperate tide of humanity filled the cathedral from wall to wall, squeezing tighter and tighter until breathing became nearly impossible. This frantic mob drove Jorge clear through the nave and up against the back wall of the chancel. He was saved from being crushed to death by an old woman who was jammed between him and the wall. Seeing his clerical collar and not knowing that he was a Protestant minister, she gasped out a request for the last rites moments before she was crushed to death. Jorge administered them over his shoulder to this woman whose inert body then saved him from a similar fate.

Jorge had a deep knowledge of liberation theology and a deep commitment to justice in Central America. So did the seminary's interim dean, Walt Davis, who was among those Jorge had helped recruit to our advisory board. San Francisco Theological Seminary was the right place for me, and I was anxious to begin my studies.

Headed into the ministry as I was, Brian Willson held a special fascination for me. He subscribed to no creed or organized faith, but his path most closely approximated what I imagined Christ's to have been. That which Brian called the Great Spirit, Jesus called Abba, or so it seemed to me. Brian's willingness to sever ties to the traditional lifestyles of his day paralleled Jesus's willingness to abandon family and village in favor of his peripatetic ministry. So I liked to talk to Brian about these things, as well as about baseball.

Baseball was the one area of conventional American life for which Brian's zeal remained undimmed. A Cardinals fan from an early age, Brian clung to this one last vestige of his past and wore a Cardinals cap at all times. I am a Giants fan and, having grown up in Philadelphia, a Phillies fan as well, so we talked baseball when we weren't talking politics or organizing or spirituality.

In July, Brian and Holly married in an unusual and wonderful ceremony at a small community center in Mill Valley. Joel Scholefield, minister of the Marin Fellowship of Unitarians, presided over a service that drew upon Native American spiritual practices, and it was a happy occasion for the hundred or so of us in attendance.

By the time they married, Brian had found a suitable and fateful new focus for his devotion and energies: the Concord Naval Weapons Station across San Francisco Bay in Contra Costa County. Peace activists in Contra

Costa had discovered that Concord Naval Weapons Station was one of the armories from which the U.S. government sent weapons to Central America, weapons with which the Contras and the Salvadoran military were slaughtering and bombing campesinos. On a regular basis, freight trains rumbled forth from the weapons station gate, crossed a public highway, reentered government property, and traveled the few miles down the track to Port Chicago on San Francisco Bay, where the armaments were off-loaded onto ships headed for Central America. The freight trains did not leave federal property during their short journeys except for the 100 yards of highway and right-of-way between the weapons station gate and the fence on the other side of the road. That stretch of public land afforded an opportunity for resistance and demonstration.

East Bay activists began to keep vigil alongside the tracks, intending to draw attention to the connection between the contents of those boxcars and the deaths of our brothers and sisters to the south. Peace groups, student groups, church congregations, and members of religious orders came from as far away as Nevada to man round-the-clock shifts so that no munitions train passed unnoticed. The project organizers designated this sustained effort the Nuremburg Actions, and they couldn't have chosen a more suitable name, reminding us as it did of the principles promulgated at the Nuremburg Tribunals in Germany after World War II — that citizens are responsible for atrocities carried out with their knowledge and in their names, even if they do not commit those atrocities with their own hands.

The Nuremburg Actions attracted Brian Willson, and he soon became one of its leaders. The equation was simple yet profoundly compelling: stop those trains and we will ultimately save innocent lives, just as German citizens would have saved innocent lives had they stopped the boxcars rolling toward Dachau and Auschwitz. For Brian, and for a few others, simply protesting the movement of munitions trains was not enough. These few actually intended to stop the trains, by whatever means necessary.

I went out to Concord a time or two, but I did not participate in the demonstrations consistently. I was busy with my life, with recruiting volunteers for the Human Rights Commission project, with preparing to enter seminary in a few weeks. Among Bay Area peace activists and religious people, I represented not the exception, but the rule. Most of us had other things to do, and it was rather boring to stand out there in the hot sun all day, waiting for a train to come rolling out. Of course, the vast majority of Bay Area residents were entirely ignorant of the Nuremburg Actions or, if they had heard of them, remained indifferent or hostile.

The automobiles and pickup trucks that passed the protestors at the tracks expressed the attitude of the general populace. A few drivers waved cheerily or tooted their horns; most cruised past stony-faced; some rolled down their windows to shout insults or give the demonstrators the finger.

Brian and a few others determined that it was time to raise the stakes — and possibly risk their lives. They decided to position themselves on the tracks instead of alongside them, and to hold these positions when the next train rolled out of the weapons station. They notified the base commander of their intent by letter and alerted the press in accounts that were subsequently published and broadcast. They also requested an interview with the base commander, but their request was ignored.

Duncan Murphy, one of Brian's companions from the Fast for Life in Washington, had driven out to California to join him in the Nuremburg Actions. Brian and Duncan and David Duncombe, a veteran of World War II and the Korean War, resolved to sit on the tracks when the next train approached, hoping to force it to a halt. They knew that base policy and long-standing practice permitted the trains to travel at no more than five miles per hour as they crossed the highway. The engineer would have plenty of time to bring such a slow-moving train to a halt.

On the morning of September 1, 1987, a year to the day after the Fast for Life had begun, the three men assumed their positions on the tracks. Brian has no memory of what happened next, but one of the other protestors recorded events on a handheld video camera. The freight train rumbled out of the gate at nineteen miles per hour, almost four times the permitted rate of speed. Two guards stood above the cowcatcher on the front of the train. Brian sat near the righthand rail, Duncan Murphy crouched alongside him, and David Duncombe crouched behind Duncan. When the train was still a couple of hundred feet away but not slowing, David tapped Brain on the shoulder and asked him how he was feeling. "A little nervous," Brian responded. As the train bore down on them, David dove off the tracks. Duncan Murphy held his position, springing up at the last second onto the cowcatcher of the onrushing locomotive, where he hung on for dear life. The train finally slowed to a stop some 300 feet down the tracks. Duncan would say later, "We said we weren't going to leave those tracks, so I didn't leave those tracks."

Brian's body had begun to move when the train was almost upon him. He grasped the rail with his right hand. Was he trying to get out of the way? Trying to lie flat so the train would pass over him? Trying to solidify his position? To this day, he has total amnesia and can only speculate about what he was trying to do in the moments before the train struck him. He does remember how adamant he was about doing what he had said he would.

The locomotive struck his forehead, flung his body backward, and passed over him. By the time the freight cars came to a halt, screams and confusion filled the morning air. Holly rushed forward, thinking that her husband must surely be dead. Her son, Gabriel, cried out again and again, "They've killed my father. They've killed my father." While others cradled Brian's bleeding head, Holly crouched by his mangled feet and legs, stanching the profuse flow of blood with her denim skirt. Appalled witnesses embraced and wept while they waited for the authorities to summon an ambulance.

While the weapons train battered Brian's body in Concord, I was participating in orientation week activities at San Francisco Theological Seminary across the bay. At lunchtime, I drove from the campus across town to the task force office at the Marin Peace Center in San Anselmo. As I parked my car and walked up to the front door, a friend, Don Carney, stopped me to share the news he had just heard over the radio. Don didn't know if Brian was alive or dead.

Shocked and heartsick, I drove back to the seminary, scanning the radio dial for news bulletins. No information was available beyond what Don had told me: peace activist Brian Willson had been run over by a train outside Concord Naval Weapons Station and had been taken by ambulance to John Muir Hospital. I sought out Jorge Lara-Braud in his office and told him the news. I needed consolation. Jorge offered to drive over to the hospital with me at dinnertime.

At the end of the day, we drove over to Concord and found the hospital. As we walked in the front door, Holly was coming down the corridor. We embraced, and she told me that Brian was still in surgery and would probably lose his legs, but he would in all likelihood survive. Jorge and I waited with some of Brian's other friends in the conference room that the hospital had provided, then decided to drive out to the tracks where the protestors still maintained their vigil by candlelight. We told them what we had learned from Holly. After I drove Jorge back to his house, I went home myself to share with Lori the terrible events of the day.

Early the next morning, I got a call from Holly, who was at their apartment in San Rafael. Her car battery was dead, and she needed a jump start before she could visit Brian. I went over to help, but we couldn't get her car started, so I drove her across the bay. When we reached the hospital, she took me upstairs to the intensive care unit, where Brian was lying on a bed, looking, in fact, like he had been hit by a train.

The top of his head was wrapped in gauze to protect the hole at his hairline from which doctors had picked bone fragments the previous afternoon and evening. Cuts and scrapes and abrasions disfigured his face and torso. Both of his legs, crushed beyond repair between the track and the wheels of the train, had been amputated below the knee. After Holly hugged him, Brian reached out and drew me down for a hug, too. I remember feeling that he was consoling me more with that hug than I was consoling him. As battered as his body was, there could be no doubt that his spirit was intact. After some brief conversation, I said my goodbyes and left them together. Brian remembers nothing of my brief visit that day.

Brian made a remarkable recovery, according to the physical therapists who taught him how to walk on artificial limbs. I visited Brian in the hospital about ten days after what he calls his assault by train, then didn't see him again until eight weeks later, when he joined former U.S. ambassador to El Salvador Robert White as co-speaker at an MITF-sponsored event at the College of Marin on the evening of October 30. He swung into Olney Hall on crutches and feet of steel, and when I embraced him, I realized that he was shorter than he had been. He smiled ruefully when I commented on his diminished height and explained that patients start out on short legs because learning to walk is easier with a lower center of gravity. As his therapy progressed, he would gradually be restored to his former physical stature.

After the program, several of us asked Brian how he was coming along, and he decided to give us a demonstration. He hauled himself out of his seat, handed someone his crutches, and clumped proudly back and forth in front of the platform with his arms outstretched. It pleased him greatly that he had progressed so rapidly. The therapists had told him that he had learned to walk in half the time it usually took other amputees, a fact he attributed to his easy acceptance of his loss of limbs. Because he had decided to risk his body and had suffered the consequences of his own decision, he experienced none of the depression and denial that typically hampers those who have lost their legs unexpectedly.

In the months that followed, Brian received mail and gifts from all over the globe, including one book he was particularly proud of — the biography of Soviet fighter pilot Alexei Maresyev, who had lost his legs in World War II. It was sent by Maresyev himself. In Brian, this Russian veteran recognized a kindred spirit. In the letter that accompanied the book, Maresyev congratulated Brian for his brave action and lamented the worldwide militarism that required such heroic acts of resistance.

Three men sat on the tracks at Concord that day, surrounded by perhaps sixty others. But the train that maimed Brian reached its destination, as did the trains that rolled out of Concord Naval Weapons Station in the months to come. Had three million people faced that munitions train, its armaments would never have reached Port Chicago, then Central America. Three thousand would have been sufficient, or three hundred. Perhaps even thirty.

Brian sat on the tracks for all of us.

_ 10 _

MIRNA AND THE VALLEY PEOPLE

On the morning Herbert Anaya was killed, Mirna couldn't bring herself to tell the children right away. She told them that he had been injured, that he might die, and that she would have to take them to her mother's house while she found out what had happened. Her mother had never approved of Herbert's work.

As Mirna remembers it, "First I called the commission and told them to send a doctor, just in case, and to send a judge. Since the children were already dressed, I took them out to the back parking lot so they wouldn't see his body and had the woman who took care of them drive them over to my mother's house. When I got there, my mother told them that they shouldn't cry, because their father hadn't loved them, or else he wouldn't have talked so much. It was a very difficult situation. All the children, especially Gloria, were very angry with her. So I took the children to school. I told the priest there to help me because they had killed Herbert and I needed to find a good way to tell the children so that it wouldn't be so traumatic for them. The priest took them to their classes and told their teachers, who tried to calm them."

In January 1992, Mirna's sons told me about the morning that Herbert was killed. Actually, they told my son Tucker, who was six years old at the time, but I was there, too. The four of us were driving back from the beach house in Sonsonate, following the pickup truck with Mirna and Lori and the girls. After spending a few days on the coast swimming in the surf and sleeping in hammocks strung up on the porch of the beach house, the ten of us had packed up and headed back to San Salvador. We drove past the sugar plantations that carpeted the coastal plain, then into the higher land cut by ravines and dense with blossoming trees, and finally into the capital city.

Rafa, then eleven, sat next to me on the bench seat of our pickup. Tucker sat in fourteen-year-old Neto's lap. My son began asking Neto and Rafa about their father and how he had died: had they seen it happen? What had it been like for them that day? I had often wondered the same things but had refrained from asking. I didn't want to dredge up painful memories for these boys. But inquisitive, unrestrained Tucker went right ahead and asked. As Neto and Rafa disclosed their recollections of that day, I drove the truck and held my tongue, thinking that this innocent interlocutor might give them a chance to share those memories in a safe space.

Their memories were imprecise and dreadful. They remembered the commotion at the apartment, the neighbors suddenly bundling them back inside, their confusion as Mirna rushed back in to call the commission, and their fear as she sent them to her mother's and then on to school. They thought — though they weren't sure — that Rosa had known from the beginning that Herbert was dead. They all knew that something terrible had happened to him. They remembered their anxiety when the priests ushered them to their classrooms, and they remembered when Mirna appeared at lunchtime to tell them that Herbert had been shot and killed.

"When I came back at noon," Mirna recalls, "I told them. It was a very difficult moment. They were hoping that he had survived, and when I told them he had died, they started to cry. I told them not to cry because Herbert had the possibility to work more now, and they couldn't do anything more to him. I told them that Herbert wouldn't want them to cry, that they should think about helping the people and keep on working in what he was doing. Finally, they calmed down and I took them home. I had them change their clothes, then left them with the woman who takes care of them while I went to see how the wake was going to be done.

"I tried to organize everything that had to be done. María Isabel came, from the Pequeña Comunidad, with some women from the Mother's Committee, to propose that they do the vigil in front of the United States Embassy. I thought there was nothing bad about that idea, but that it might be dangerous for the people to be in front of the embassy, because they might massacre them. The people were afraid, and they were very outraged. So they told me they would think about it as long as I had no objection. Finally, they did the wake at the commission office until 6:00 in the evening and then took him to the cathedral. On the following day, a march was organized, around 3:00 in the afternoon, to take his body to the embassy. All the people stayed in front of the embassy all night.

"I remember that I marched with them from the cathedral to the embassy, but I was carrying Edith and she was very tired, so we went to drink a soda in a cafeteria. I decided to take her home, so we got a taxi. The taxi driver said we would have to go the long way around because the marchers were in front of the embassy with Herbert Anaya's body, who was the president of the Human Rights Commission who had been killed. He said that the popular movement was very angry, that that day they were going to burn buses, and that the people were right. I didn't tell him anything, just to take me home.

"There were people waiting there for me around 7:00 at night who wanted to pray with me in the place where Herbert was killed. They were very outraged, but they were afraid, too, because the police were around there in plain clothes. But even with the fear, each person said a prayer, talking about the murder. The reaction of the people was incredible — a lot of fear but a lot of decisiveness also to protest about the murder.

"On the third night, when Herbert's body was back at the cathedral, there was a priest there, Father William, a North American of the Maryknoll Order. It seems that he had insisted a lot on celebrating a Mass, and he was the only one who was allowed to do that because Monseñor Rivera y Damas was very angry with the attitude of taking over the cathedral to do Herbert's wake. He said no priest should celebrate Mass because Herbert was an atheist, and he also threatened to excommunicate anyone who came into the cathedral. He said that all those at the commission were atheist, Communist child eaters, but it seems that the nuns and the priests told the Monseñor not to excommunicate the people who came because he would end up without any Catholics. So he didn't give the excommunication declaration, but he forbade everyone from coming to the Mass. But Father William insisted that Herbert was a member of his parish in Zacamil, so he had an obligation to say the Mass.

"It was pretty strange in those days. There was an effervescence in the popular movement, a strange strength, a strange force, full of a lot of anger but with decisiveness not to allow that that act would go unprotested. I remember that there were an awful lot of people who I never thought would come to the cathedral. People came who worked with me in the courts, with whom I used to talk only about judicial work, very conservative people. [Mirna had been a judge of the first instance since 1983]. I met a lot of people I did not know, people who were very insistent on staying there the whole time. A lot of very poor people came and said they wanted to help, giving all the money they had on them. I talked with a lot of people who had had some help from Herbert at the commission.

"When the last Mass was conducted, the one with the body present, the cathedral was full of people, very humble people from the countryside and a lot of foreigners. Seven or eight priests co-celebrated the Mass even though they didn't have permission. It ended up being a Mass that was full of life and very strong. That's when Kate showed up, in the middle of the Mass.

"On the day of the funeral, the UNTS [a labor federation] made the arrangements for the transfer of the body from the cathedral to the cemetery. Reynaldo and I went to ask them that they not do anything disruptive in the streets because the commission had invited delegations from the outside, and we believed it wouldn't be good if they did violent acts. The people from UNTS said that they could not control the people who were participating in that march and that they knew the people were very angry. When the march began, I saw that they burned several cars, and it was very obvious that the people were angry.

"In the days after the funeral, I had a big problem with the children. They knew that I was very involved in what had motivated Herbert's death. During the whole time of the wake, people would talk about that, and the children would hear it, so they were afraid that I would be killed, too. Every time I went out, they would say, 'Don't let them kill you.' It was very difficult to be in that situation where they had a lot of insecurity and also when the danger was real that they would kill me.

"Then there was also the situation that the police were trying to find a motive to set me up as the person who ordered Herbert's death. I knew of two previous cases where public attention was very strong when the police used a scapegoat to cover up the murderers. So I didn't have any doubt that they could capture me and present evidence saying I was the one who killed him, and in that way neutralize me while covering up the murderers. They went to my mother and to my in-laws to ask if I had motives to kill him — another lover, whatever. That showed me that they wanted to blame me.

"They started investigating me on the day I went to court to accuse Colonel Golcher and the Treasury Police of having killed him and of having used the media to justify the murder. That same day, the police went to the Civil Registry to get my picture, the data about who was my mother, who was my father, and began to investigate me. They came to my house — I think it was October 30 — to interrogate Herbert's brother and the woman who took care of the children. When I arrived, they began to interrogate me.

"These people were from the Investigative Commission of Criminal Acts, a special commission of the Ministry of Justice funded with USAID [U.S. Agency for International Development] monies to improve the administration of justice. But they were all ex-members of the police, so I told them I would tell them absolutely nothing about what had happened because I was sure they were not investigating the criminals but that they wanted to know the details of the crime so they could put up an innocent person as the guilty one. I told them, 'Why don't you go investigate Golcher?' They said they were investigating those who no one suspected it could be. I told them that that was absurd and that I was sure they had no authority to investigate the murderers because the murderers were their bosses. Even if they knew who the murderers were, they would never arrest them.

"They left after some other men came in civilian clothes, men with rifles who drove a car with covered license plates. Kate went out and saw them, so I called the media and they left. But we pushed things against the door. We barricaded the door because we thought they would machine-gun us."

During the first days after the funeral, Kate Bancroft stayed with Mirna and the children at the apartment, but as surveillance there persisted, Mirna decided they all needed to find other quarters. They moved around for a time, staying with various friends and relatives, before Mirna farmed the children out to relatives. She went about her business, working with Kate and wrapping up what details she could as she prepared to take the children to Canada.

"After all those incidents, I went to Canada to let a year pass. When I was in Canada, I worked a lot denouncing the case, giving declarations to the press, going to the United Nations in Geneva, making a tour of the United

States. I remember I talked with Senator John Kerry, who was a big friend of Duarte's. I explained the way Duarte's government justified the incident and how Duarte himself had accused Jorge Miranda even though Miranda had been tortured before he declared that he killed Herbert.

"We were in Canada for seven months. It was a very hard period, in spite of the fact that we had a lot of help and a lot of attention. They were very kind and attentive. The whole program they had for people like us was very good. However, there was a kind of invitation to simply forget about El Salvador and to learn to live as Canadians, and that was impossible. When I went to Canada was when I started to work officially for the commission."

Rosa, Mirna's eldest daughter, remembers the welcome given them by Canadian authorities when they reached the airport in Toronto. While television cameras recorded their arrival, officials gave each of them warm jackets and other necessities of life in the North. As soon as Mirna had the family settled, she returned to her now official work for the commission.

"When I went to Geneva, I got to speak before the United Nations for ten minutes [the United Nations Commission on Human Rights holds its annual meetings in Geneva]. But it was horrible in Geneva, a kind of nightmare. You have to use very diplomatic language. You have to smile at the people who don't understand anything about human rights, who are not interested, but on whom many important decisions depend. I would rather face the National Guard, tanks, and antiriot police than those people. I even got sick with the flu and went to the doctor for the first time in my life to be treated for the flu. But I did learn a lot. I met a lot of people who told me of the injustices in First World countries. I found out about the struggles of all people, and of the need to establish a reciprocal solidarity between the people of the First World and the people of the Third World.

"In June of 1988, I went to Costa Rica to take up the position of general coordinator of CODEHUCA [the umbrella organization of all Central American human rights groups]. On my way to Costa Rica, I had to do a tour of several countries, so I sent the children to Kate in Marin, then stopped by to visit them for a few days on the way."

When Mirna called Kate from Toronto to ask if she could leave the kids in Marin while she went on her tour, Kate called some friends in the San Geronimo Valley, where she lives. Rosa had already been to the valley several times, coming up from El Salvador for her annual visit to Shriners Hospital for adjustment of her prosthesis, and on those earlier occasions, Kate had temporarily enrolled Rosa in the Open Classroom of the Lagunitas School District, where Rosa had made friends with a girl her age, Lhasa Charne. So in May 1988, Kate called one of the Open Classroom teachers, Amy Valens, and Lhasa's parents, Alan and Lynn Charne, seeking homes where the Anaya children could stay. The Charnes invited Rosa to stay with them, Amy and Tom Valens took in Neto and Rafa, and Cathy and Tom Eller opened their doors to Gloria and Edith.

Amy Valens once told me how simple it had been to find host families. "When word came of Herbert's death, it wasn't abstract to people around here — it was Rosa's dad. Everybody knew Rosa and loved Rosa from her earlier visits. That's why it was so easy to get families to say yes."

After her tour, Mirna stopped in Marin to check on the children before preceding them to Costa Rica. While in town, she met Marty Meade and her husband, Bud. Marty, a valley artist and therapist, had lived in southern Mexico as a teenager and had recently seen the movie *El Norte*, a film about Central American refugees in flight from their countries of origin to safety and employment in the United States — the North. "I had been very moved by *El Norte*, so I started a painting which I called *My Prayer for Central America*, and just then I heard from a friend about these children who were living in the valley. I called Tom Valens and asked him if I could meet some of the children, so he agreed to bring them over to my place for a visit. When he brought Neto and Rafa over, Mirna came with them. At first, Mirna was kind of quiet and withdrawn. But then I took her down to the chicken coop to show her the baby chicks that had just hatched, and suddenly she began to laugh and talk and become the Mirna we all now know."

Mirna and Marty struck up a friendship there by the chicken coop, and Mirna ended up staying with the Meades until her departure for Costa Rica. Before she left, Mirna asked Marty if the valley people might be able to provide financial help for the family. When Mirna told Marty what her salary at CODEHUCA would be, Marty knew that no family of six could live on that, and she began to raise funds from many other valley residents, wonderful people who sustained their support for the next three years.

Bud Meade told me that when the children flew on to Costa Rica at the end of the school year, he knew that they would be back, and next time, they would be staying with him and Marty. He was right. When the five Anaya children returned to Marin eighteen months later, Gloria and Edith stayed with the Meades.

Mirna and the kids set up house in Costa Rica while she began her exhausting duties at CODEHUCA. The children's situation in Costa Rica was less than optimal. Mirna's duties kept her on the run, and she lacked the extensive network of family and friends she enjoyed in El Salvador — family and friends who could help with child care and transportation (because of their ages, the children attended different schools with different schedules). She cobbled things together as best she could and relied on the five children to watch one another much of the time. This arrangement became untenable, however, when the United States invaded Panama in January 1990. When CODEHUCA mobilized to study human rights abuses inflicted on the Panamanian population when U.S. troops bombed and strafed their shantytowns, Mirna knew she could not leave the children unattended in Costa Rica while she headed south to conduct the investigation. So she called Kate, and Kate spread the word in the valley.

Marty Meade hustled up money for airfares from the network of supporters she had cultivated, and she rearranged furniture to accommodate Gloria and Edith. Amy Valens prepared for another influx of Salvadoran children into the Open Classroom and asked other friends, Teryl and Bob Densmore, to take Rafa (Neto would stay with Amy and Tom again). The Charnes invited Rosa back into their house. The children arrived in time to begin the spring term at school.

Among the five of them, only Rosa spoke more than rudimentary English, having begun to pick it up in January 1987 when she first came to stay with Kate for her annual Shriners visit. But it didn't take long for the other four to learn English, or to make friends at school. Bob and Teryl Densmore signed the boys up for Little League, which they loved. Through the Valens's son, Jessie, Rafa became friends with Jessie's best friend, Woody Stinson. When Jessie went over to spend the night with Woody, he would take Rafa along, and Rafa began to insinuate his rascally self into the Stinson household. Elizabeth Stinson, Woody's mom, became very fond of him. "If the kids ever have to come back to Marin again," she told Marty, "I'd like Rafa to stay with us."

The Lagunitas School District counselor told Amy Valens of a therapist in Berkeley who worked with children traumatized by repression, and

Amy called that counselor — Adrian Arons — to arrange a session for the Anaya siblings. Adrian took the kids out to eat at a restaurant and observed more or less what everyone else had — that these kids were outgoing, noisy, squabbling, and affectionate; in other words, they were pretty much okay. There was considerable discussion among the families in the valley about how these kids could have suffered what they had and still seem so normal. Of course, although the five Anaya children have shown a remarkable resiliency in the wake of Herbert's death, despite having been jerked around from place to place in the years immediately following it, they have by no means escaped suffering, as the poems several of them wrote in 1993 so eloquently attest.

Mirna came up for a visit in the spring of 1990, and Marty arranged a big reception for her, inviting all the parents involved with her children, as well as Kate, Adrian, several schoolteachers, and me. We gathered after dinner one evening in Marty's studio. While the kids watched TV in the house, the valley people introduced themselves to Mirna and shared their impressions of her children. Several expressed concerns — about schoolwork, about what seemed like withdrawal symptoms, about sibling frictions. The two oldest — Rosa and Neto — seemed the most well adjusted.

When it came time for Mirna to speak, she had difficulty at first. Between tears, she told us how she missed her kids and tried to find words to express her gratitude to these people who had opened their hearts and homes and pocketbooks to them. She told us that CODEHUCA had elected her for a second year-long term as general coordinator and that she had invited her mother to move in with her in Costa Rica. She was ready to have the children rejoin her. I had already planned a trip to El Salvador for June, so at the end of the meeting we all agreed that the kids would fly south with me on June 17 and that Mirna would come up from Costa Rica to meet them at the airport in El Salvador.

On departure day, all of the families met me at the airport and bid their charges tearful and prolonged goodbyes, with repeated hugs all around, before we trundled off down the jetway. All of the children had some regrets about leaving, especially Rafa, who had formed the closest friendships with buddies at school. He had become the most Americanized of the five of them and would have loved nothing better than to stay in Marin. He moped around dejectedly for the first few days in El Salvador.

Mirna greeted us at the airport in El Salvador and told us she would be taking the kids to visit her father that evening. Mirna's parents had divorced years ago. Mirna invited me along, and I was glad for the opportunity to meet her dad, who lives in a village an hour outside San Salvador. It is from him that Mirna inherited much of her social conscience and her penchant for activism. After dinner that evening, her dad loaded us all into his truck and drove us to his nearby *finca* — several acres of rainforest where he had erected a tile-roofed cabin and planted some banana and papaya trees. We hiked down the muddy path to the cabin in a drizzle, then sat on the porch for an hour, singing songs and telling stories, when the heavens opened up with a typical evening thunderstorm.

Mirna took the children back to Costa Rica later that week and settled them in with her mother, the same mother who had so disapproved of Herbert. That next year in Costa Rica was not a happy one for the children. Separated once again from relatives in El Salvador and from informal family in Marin, they now had to put up with this old woman they so disliked. And then that year stretched into two when Mirna's contract with CODEHUCA was extended a second time. Eventually, all of them accustomed themselves to Costa Rica and even came to like it, except for Gloria. In time, Mirna sent them all back to El Salvador to live with various relatives before returning to El Salvador herself in 1992, where she became general secretary of the National University and resumed her work at the commission.

Mirna's high-profile duties at the commission kept her on edge. She engaged the Salvadoran authorities on three fronts, any one of which would have ensured her their enmity. First, Mirna became César Vielman Joya Martinez's legal advisor once he was extradited to El Salvador. She and other lawyers working on his behalf eventually obtained his release under terms of the general amnesty extended by the peace accords and arranged for him to leave the country. Second, Mirna, now a commission member, helped irk the senior military establishment when the commission published full-page newspaper ads listing human rights abuses committed under the command of senior officers during the war. Those officers subsequently filed a defamation suit against the commission. The commission members would welcome a day in court but have not yet had one. Third, Mirna continued to press for a full investigation into Herbert's death and to insist that both the Salvadoran high command and their U.S. advisors be held accountable.

Even though the peace accords went into effect on January 16, 1992, death-squad-type killings persisted in El Salvador. Mirna's high-profile activities continued to make her a likely target, and she knew it. She took security precautions most of the time, but not always.

On January 3, 1993, Mirna took two of the children and a U.S. nun out for a visit to the town of Suchitoto, near Guazapa Volcano. They stayed there until nightfall, then decided to return to the city. While driving along the dark, narrow road from Suchitoto, they were flagged down by a group of men standing at the roadside. Mirna slowed the car, noticed that the men carried rifles, then hit the accelerator and sped past them, not knowing if they were bandits or perhaps a death squad sent to intercept her. The men opened fire as Mirna sped away; several bullets hit the car, and fragments from one of those bullets struck Neto, ripping open his hip and frightening him badly. Mirna called Marin several days later to see if the children might be able to return. They arrived on January 26, moving back in with their now familiar U.S. families (all except Rafa, who this time stayed with Elizabeth Stinson and her son, Woody). They stayed through the school year and returned to El Salvador in early June, this time for good.

During their third sojourn in Marin, the five children often assembled on weekends at Elizabeth Stinson's house, where a Lakota friend of Elizabeth's had erected a sweat lodge in the backyard. They loved to jam into the lodge together to sweat and chant and pray. I never made it to a sweat, but Elizabeth tells me that those sessions were remarkable, that the children prayed there that no other children would ever have to suffer what they had suffered, prayed there for peace in all the world.

On the last weekend of their stay, all of the children came to our house with their families for a farewell barbecue. While the hamburgers were cooking, we sat around the table with the tape recorder on, patching together the chronology of the Anaya children's three visits to the valley, laughing with them as they recalled boyfriends and baseball games, and crying with them as they recalled the day Herbert died and the tears their mother shed when she looked up and found Kate standing beside her at his funeral. Mirna was not with us that day, nor, of course, was Herbert, except in all of us.

Before they flew home, Gloria and Neto gave me copies of the poems they had written here, several of which appear at the end of this book.

I have learned a lot over the years, trying to decipher Mirna. I'm not sure how well I have succeeded even now, limited as I still am by who I am. By my conventional standards — those of middle-class America — Mirna ranks low on the parenting skills inventory. She has shipped her children off to live with perfect strangers in a distant land. She has devoted so much energy, time, and passion to her work that her children rarely see her except in the early morning and the evening. She has placed them under the supervision of a grandmother who drives them out of their minds.

In addition, she seems careless of their physical safety. Several years ago, we all went out to dinner one evening in San Salvador. Mirna asked me to drive her pickup truck while she rode shotgun and navigated. The kids perched in the back. I followed Mirna's directions through the traffic-choked streets and noticed as I did so that the truck simply died every now and then. It stopped cranking all of a sudden but restarted if I quickly depressed and popped the clutch before we lost momentum. "It always does that," Mirna explained.

We were lugging up a long grade in traffic when the evening rains came bucketing down in torrents. It was dusk, almost dark, and I could barely see the buses booming past as the wipers skipped and thrashed back and forth on the windshield. Just then, of course, the engine died. As the car lost speed, I popped the clutch a couple of times without success, then braked to keep from coasting backward while I turned the key. No ignition. What to do?

Mirna told me we would have to turn the truck around, get a rolling start downhill in the other direction, and try the clutch again. She would take the wheel. We both hopped out and dashed around the front of the pickup in the deluge as the kids clambered out to ask what was happening. We were in midintersection. Buses, trucks, and cars careened around us from all points of the compass, flashing their lights and blaring their horns as the kids dodged wildly through the storm, Neto playing traffic cop, several helping me push the truck over the curb and back across the lanes to point downhill, others simply dancing madcap in the rain. It was a wild scene.

My friends in Sonoma would have had their kids back in the truck right away, before some rain-blinded driver flattened them in the street. Had my kids been there, I would have had them at my side every second, might have even left the truck at the curb and taken a cab. But Mirna plowed ahead, intent on the task at hand. She got the truck restarted, then stopped in traffic yet again while everyone climbed on board. Mirna gets things done.

I described her once to another North American as a benevolent manipulator. She always has more balls in the air than you will ever see, and you sometimes discover that when you are doing one thing for her, you are in fact doing something else of which you are completely unaware. That night the truck stalled, as we dried out over dinner, we started talking about basketball, and I somehow found myself telling the boys that if we found some time that week, we would have a game. Mirna looked up from her *pupusa* and said that Wednesday night would be a good time. "Okay. If it works out, Wednesday," I said, knowing full well that in El Salvador, Wednesday might mean Thursday or Friday or maybe never.

Wednesday came, and with it another dinner date with the *tornada* Anaya and a half dozen others at a restaurant near the home of friends. We talked and talked, ate and ate. The night stretched on, and I was getting tired and ready to trundle off to bed when Mirna announced that the time for the game had come. I noticed small heads drooping on folded arms, looked forlornly at my watch, and demurred. But Mirna scooped us up, and off we drove through the humid night air to a nearby park. We took the court and began a trash-talking game of two-on-two under the lights, Neto and Rafa against Edith and me. Up and down the asphalt we raced, laughing and feinting and shooting. But then I noticed that Mirna was nowhere to be seen.

I asked Neto to fetch her from the truck, figuring she must be waiting there, motherlike, while we had our fun. But no, said Neto. She was not there. She had walked to a party at her boss's house three blocks over. There I was, thinking I was having the time of my life — which I was — but what I was actually doing was babysitting the kids while Mirna popped in at a reception given by the university chancellor for a delegation from Italy. Edith and I routed the boys that night (they avenged the loss in the summer of 1993), and then we went off in search of Mirna. Neto knew the way.

And so it goes with Mirna, invariably squeezing the most out of every situation but seldom leaving resentment in her wake, because she is up earlier and abed later than anyone else, and she is always busier in between. Just ask any of the valley people if they minded Mirna's imposing her children on them, on three occasions, for a total of twelve months. On another of my trips to El Salvador, she rose at dawn and drove for two hours to save me cab fare to the airport.

This is how life is for her kids — never knowing when she will swoop in or out, nor whom she will drag along when she goes, nor where they might be headed, nor where they will lay their heads down that night.

On some wider inventory of parenting skills — the big one in the sky, maybe — Mirna likely scores much higher, perhaps right off the scale. Her children are the evidence of that. Anyone who meets them falls in love with them, and not just because they have endured so much so young — though this surely enters the equation — but because they are delightful to be around. They are funny, engaging, unintimidated by yet respectful of adults, bilingual, forthright, and possessed of a depth of understanding about the human condition beyond that of any other children I have ever known. As deeply wounded as they have been, Mirna has not made the mistake of dragging them off into seclusion for therapy but has instead dragged them straight back — on the very day of Herbert's death — into the popular struggle that defined their father and defines their mother.

When Mirna told me she had enjoined her children's weeping when they learned their father was truly dead, my inner voice said, "Good God, woman, you should have let those children cry, should have let them keen and curse and howl, at least for a while, before asking them to button up their feelings and pick up Herbert's cause." But those children show little evidence of repressed or crippling grief, and much of youthful life. What any California therapist would have ordained — a course of healing ventilation — may simply not have been appropriate in their situation.

In this connection, I reflect on Mirtala López and Joaquín Cáceres. Mirtala's torturers very nearly accomplished on her the object of their depredations — the separation of the tortured one from his or her deepest inner belief, from his or her very self — but they found their work undone the moment Mirtala, still blindfolded, heard and touched her *compañeras*. In that instant, by her own testimony, she recovered herself and so emerged from prison five months later to resume her place at CRIPDES, reintegrated and more deeply Mirtala than ever. From this, and from the way she presents herself today, I must conclude that the healthiest thing for her to have done (even from the narrowest perspective of her psychological recovery) was precisely what she did — defiantly reclaim that which they tried so hard to torture out of her. She reclaimed her cause, and with it her human solidarity. She reclaimed her life.

And so it was, I think, with Joaquín. When, after torture, he was reunited with the men in Mariona — his colleagues and the hundreds of others — he began what he considers the best experience of his life, an experience for which he longs to this day. The last thing the security forces should have done, from their perspective, was throw those men into prison together, into the very place where they might most permanently and searingly experience their solidarity, where they might partake of the communal life that is greater than the life of any individual. So in that life they now dwell, having chosen upon release to resume their work for life instead of choosing, any one of them, for their own individual lives by leaving El Salvador, as they contemplated doing.

The preacher in me cannot resist the eucharistic aspect of this. When we gather around the loaf and chalice, we gather to celebrate and remember the choice that Jesus made — our lives over his. It is no mistake that we call this celebration Holy Communion.

So cry if you must, Mirna might say, but don't for so much as a minute let them separate you from the people or from your struggle for them. Those people, that struggle, is who you are.

Not all of those in the valley network were mentioned in this chapter. These few, at least, deserve recognition: Judy Voets, another Open Classroom teacher who handled all the visa application paperwork for the Anayas' last trip to Marin; Peter and Sheila Laufer, in whose home Neto often stayed; and Sandy Dorward, yet another Open Classroom teacher who helped in many ways.

As I have learned over the years, it is hard — if not impossible — to say no to Mirna. Every one of the valley people rejoices in having said yes.

CONCLUSION:
MITF AND BEYOND

I don't like riding in airplanes as much as I used to. When I was in my twenties, I enjoyed it when the plane banked steeply as it came in for a landing or rocketed off from the ground; then again, I also used to enjoy roller coaster rides. Now I prefer boring plane trips, and I search the faces of the flight attendants for any signs of anxiety when the air gets bumpy and the seat belt sign flashes on.

So I absolutely hated the flight I took from El Salvador to Guatemala on January 16, 1992, the day the Salvadoran peace accords finally went into effect. In celebration, our pilot winged the plane low over San Salvador instead of heading straight for Guatemala City after takeoff. As the plane bucked and bumped over the sprawling tropical neighborhoods and dipped its wings in jubilation, I peered nervously out the window at the peak of San Salvador Volcano — now above us — and silently implored our cockpit cowboy to gain altitude. On the ground below us, the people snaked through the streets, unfurled gigantic FMLN banners from the spires of the cathedral, and danced the night away. My queasiness was tinged with regret: having booked my ticket weeks in advance, I had scheduled my departure twenty-four hours too early. I was missing the party.

In the years after the accords took effect, the Salvadoran struggle moved from the battlefield to the ballot box. On March 20, 1994, national elections were held to fill a whole spectrum of political offices — mayoralties, assembly seats, the presidency — and this time, the FMLN participated. As a condition of the accords, the FMLN had been granted status as a legally constituted political entity, thereby exacerbating the ever present tensions among its five constituent political factions: the FPL (Popular Liberation Forces), the RN (National Resistance), the PRTC (Revolutionary Party of Central American Workers), the PC (Communist Party), and the ERP (the Revolutionary Force of the People, now known as the Renovated Expression of the People). The FMLN managed to hang together for the elections and to form a broader coalition with two other leftist parties, the Democratic Convergence and the National Socialist Movement, around the presidential candidacy of Ruben Zamora. This fractious coalition gained 20 percent of the presidential vote in the first round of balloting, forcing a runoff on April 24 between Zamora and ARENA Party candidate Armando Calderon Sol, which Calderon Sol won handily. The FMLN also won twenty-one seats in the National Assembly — enough to surpass the centrist Christian Democrats but not enough to deny ARENA control of the legislature. ARENA's forty-two seats represented exactly one half of the total.

FMLN regulars I met with immediately after the elections expressed a mixture of satisfaction and dismay. Their very participation in the election represented the most tangible accomplishment of their years of armed struggle. They were pleased at having started from scratch less than two years before election day only to emerge as the second strongest political force in the country, and they had denied Calderon Sol the first-round victory he had so confidently predicted. They were dismayed, however, that the ARENA-dominated Supreme Electoral Tribunal had somehow failed to enfranchise some 300,000 Salvadorans, omitting their names from the electoral rolls or neglecting to issue voter identification cards. This was not enough to have changed the outcome of the presidential elections, but it was surely enough to have changed assembly and mayoral races.

Meanwhile, the indigent campesinos who constituted the fighting forces on both sides of the civil war have found themselves desperately scrounging for employment in a devastated postwar economy whose architects embrace a neoliberal paradigm for jump-starting production and exports: suppression of wages and of the unions that might organize to increase them, favorable conditions for foreign investment and foreign start-up businesses, and renewed emphasis on the traditional large-scale production of export crops on privately owned latifundia. As a result, banditry has assumed frightening proportions. Former combatants, many of whom still have an AKA or an M-16, stick up motorists and pedestrians at gunpoint, both night and day, in rural communities and in the heart of San Salvador. Virtually everyone I know in El Salvador has a harrowing holdup tale to tell. North Americans who never ventured forth without their passports in case of military detention now stash those passports — and most of their cash — before stepping out for a cup of coffee. The war is over, but the grinding economic disparities that fueled it remain, as does the perception that the authors of the repression of the 1980s have retained the economic advantages they enjoyed at the outset.

The authors of the peace accords did what no prior peace negotiators in a Latin American conflict had done: they created two mechanisms for identifying the guilty — the Ad Hoc Commission and the Truth Commission. Both bodies were configured under the auspices of ONUSAL, the United Nations peacekeeping force, and both were staffed with distinguished international jurists and scholars. In the annals of repressive Latin American conflicts, these truth-discerning mechanisms are a great step forward. In none of the other countries that suffered "dirty wars" and fanatical military regimes in recent decades (among them Argentina, Brazil, Chile, and Uruguay) has the transition from military rule toward democracy included officially sanctioned devices to identify perpetrators of human rights abuses.

The task of the Ad Hoc Commission was to identify and remove from their positions those Salvadoran military officers responsible for the most reprehensible wartime violations of human rights. This task was largely accomplished. President Alfredo Cristiani nearly dismantled the Salvadoran high command, but he did so in part by posting former incumbents to Salvadoran embassies and in part by heaping praise for their heroic contributions to Salvadoran national integrity on those whose retirement was due in any case. Most of the 100-odd officers named in the Ad Hoc Commission's report landed on their feet, fulminating indignantly all the while against the foreigners who so tarnished their individual reputations and the reputation of the glorious Salvadoran Armed Forces, as if the peasants who died at the Río Sumpul, El Mozote, San José las Flores, Los Cerros de San Pedro, Las Hojas, Copapayo, and scores of other massacres had been legitimate military targets.

The task of the Truth Commission was to examine evidence submitted by any interested party — civilian or military, leftist or right-wing, individual or collective — concerning human rights abuses committed during the conflict. The FMLN came in for its share of censure for ordering the kidnappings and assassinations of ARENA-appointed rural mayors whom the FMLN regarded as agents of the counterinsurgency campaign, for the killings of two U.S. military advisors whose helicopter crashed near Lolotique, and for the deaths of several U.S. military personnel and others during a shoot-up in the Zona Rosa district of San Salvador. But the vast preponderance of violations investigated by the Truth Commission were attributed to the armed forces, security forces, and death squads. All went scot-free and will never be prosecuted, thanks to the blanket amnesty pushed through the National Assembly days before the release of the Truth Commission's report.

The killers of 50,000 were marginally shamed but remain fiercely unrepentant and essentially unpunished. Whether a civil Salvadoran society can now be constructed on a foundation so riddled with gross violators of basic human rights remains to be seen. Among the popular organizations, or at least among those members of the popular organizations with whom I have spoken, the desire is not for punishment — prison sentences, executions, fines — but for two less tangible yet more enduring goals. They want the truth to be known in every detail, and they want the guilty to be permanently removed from Salvadoran civil life — from electoral or appointed positions and from the military. Because the Ad Hoc Commission and the Truth Commission have fulfilled their mandates and been disbanded, the chances of achieving these objectives are effectively nil.

In other words, despite the conclusion of hostilities, despite the enlightened role played by the United Nations under Secretary General Javier Pérez de Cuellar in first wrestling the antagonists to the bargaining table and then monitoring the peace, and despite the political access now enjoyed by the FMLN, the inescapable conclusion continues to be that the broad outlines of Salvadoran society remain essentially unchanged. The poor who constitute the vast majority of the population remain indigent; if anything, their situation has deteriorated. The oligarchs whose vast agricultural holdings were whittled down as a condition of the accords still own a hugely disproportionate share of the land that their ancestors stole from the indigenous peoples 130 years ago. Despite the dismantling of the Treasury Police and the National Police stipulated as yet another condition of the accords, many personnel were reshuffled to other uniformed assignments, among them the Border Police. Despite the downsizing of the army, its relative power in Salvadoran society remains undiminished; its former opponents were disbanded as a military force altogether. No observer of the Salvadoran scene predicts a resumption of the hostilities in the foreseeable future, but as El Salvador now reconstitutes itself along familiar lines, one wonders how far distant another eruption of civil disorder might be.

The last time El Salvador's underclass rose up to demand its rights, during the 1930s under the leadership of Farabundo Martí (for whom the Farabundo Martí National Liberation Front — the FMLN — was named), the army effectively quashed that uprising by killing 30,000 people. This episode in Salvadoran history is referred to as La Matanza (the Massacre). Savage repression can, and indeed does, take the wind out of revolutionary sails. But when another generation, and then another generation after that, grows up under the same conditions of marginalization and dehumanization, the time often comes when the oppressed begin organizing once more, invoking the names of their fallen grandfathers and grandmothers as they do so. Repression may seal the crater, but the magma continues to flow beneath the volcano until, superheated by the day-to-day oppression that continues to build, it erupts again. People get angry when their children starve.

When the Reagan administration began to crank up U.S. logistical support and training of the Salvadoran military in the early 1980s, it did so out of the conviction that the Salvadoran conflict was simply an aspect of a much larger struggle between East and West. This analysis, however, completely misses the deeper, ongoing calculus of poverty and marginalization that delineates much of human history, and it ignores the reality that the conflict is at heart more between North and South than East and West.

This is not to say that the Salvadoran conflict lacked an East-West component. The struggle within El Salvador did indeed reflect global tensions brokered in Washington and Moscow alike. The FMLN was armed and funded by Nicaragua and Cuba, although on a much smaller scale than the U.S. support of the Salvadoran Army. But this is a superficial analog. The deeper analog is disclosed when one compares the vertical structure inside El Salvador — a small upper class of people dominating a large underclass — with the vertical structure in the Western Hemisphere — a single country (the United States) dominating a large underclass of countries. Sweep away the worldwide threat of Communism, as recent events have done, and the underlying reality remains. From this perspective, the interests of U.S. national security and those of the Salvadoran oligarchs are nearly identical.

Every now and then, U.S. foreign policymakers actually articulate these interests without cloaking them in ameliorating rhetoric, as U.S. diplomat George Kennan did in these oft-quoted remarks of 1948:

> We have about 50% of the world's wealth, but only 6.3% of its population. In this situation we cannot fail to be the object of envy and resentment. Our real task in the coming period is to devise a pattern of relationships which will permit us to maintain this position of disparity without . . . detriment to our national security.
>
> To do so, we have to dispense with all sentimentality and day dreaming. . . . We should cease to talk about vague and . . . unreal objectives such as human rights, the raising of living standards and democratization.

If our relationship with El Salvador during the 1980s is not a perfect example of Kennan's "pattern of relationships," I can't imagine what one might be.

And so, at long last and with enormous reluctance, we must ask ourselves what specific responsibility the United States must bear for the slain archbishops and human rights leaders, for the tortured young women, for the orphaned children, for the massacred civilians, the bombed houses, the burned crops and livestock.

When the Reagan administration took office in 1980, it was confronted in El Salvador with a client state whose zeal had done more than simply dispense with sentimentality and daydreaming about vague objectives like human rights. The Salvadoran government had created a messy, unrestrained, and embarrassing debacle of horrific proportions and, significantly, inefficient methodology. Though the Salvadoran Army laid waste to huge swaths of countryside, bombing villages out of existence and exterminating the occupants of those villages in the course of an afternoon, it did not disable the fighting effectiveness of its armed opposition, the FMLN. And although the Salvadoran security forces (about whom Jesús Campos once joked, "You can tell who they are in this way: they are precisely the ones who make you feel least secure") were sweeping through urban neighborhoods, torturing and disappearing the people they swept up, assassinating unionists, human rights leaders, priests, catechists, and even an archbishop, they were not impairing the nonviolent effectiveness of their unarmed opposition, the popular organizations. The army couldn't catch the FMLN in their mountainous redoubts, and the security forces, who were able to catch popular organizers, nevertheless watched in frustration as others stepped forward to replace the captured and assassinated.

Meanwhile, the United Nations and the European community condemned the Salvadoran atrocities with vigor. Something had to be done. Someone had to restrain these jerks and show them how to do the job right. It took a while.

During Ronald Reagan's first term as president, the killings continued unabated — and even increased — despite gargantuan infusions of U.S. cash, matériel, and training. But by 1985, after an expenditure of some $1.3 billion, Yankee ingenuity began to pay off. Units of the Salvadoran Army obtained transmitters whose signals were relayed through San Salvador to the U.S. Southern Command in Panama for computer calculation of coordinates, then on to Ilopango Airport, where jets were scrambled to drop their loads on concentrations of guerrillas spotted by ground troops only minutes earlier. Thereafter, the FMLN had to learn how to conduct its campaigns without ever amassing significant numbers of soldiers.

Regular army intelligence units learned to computerize information gathered from paid informants and torture victims so that they could then capture or kill specific, useful targets. U.S. military advisors provided training in the field, and Salvadoran officers received training at the School of the Americas in Georgia. As a result, the gross numbers of human rights violations indeed declined and the Salvadoran Army indeed seemed to gain the upper hand, at least for a time.

What is yet unknown, however, is the extent to which U.S. advisors were actually involved in any given operation. Did U.S. advisors, as Mirna Anaya suspects, give the green light to her husband's killers? Did U.S. advisors oversee and fund the clandestine death squad apparatus within the Salvadoran Army's First Infantry Brigade, as defector César Vielman Joya Martinez asserts? Was Major Buckland, the U.S. officer whose reluctant testimony disclosed that Salvadoran regulars had killed the Jesuits, the only U.S. advisor in the course of the Salvadoran conflict to learn of such complicity, or was he the only one among many who knew of the atrocities to go public? Did State Department officials lie to Congress about the human rights situation in El Salvador? Were U.S. advisors present at torture sessions, as some victims have claimed? When the U.S. Embassy sent one of its officials, Todd Greentree, to Morazán Department to investigate the Atlacatl Battalion's massacre of civilians at El Mozote and he returned without conclusive findings, was every effort made to query the ten U.S. military advisors assigned to the Atlacatl about what they knew, about what they had possibly witnessed?

We will never know the answers. When the Truth Commission released its report in March 1993, Robert Torrecelli, chair of the House Subcommittee on Hemispheric Affairs at the time, instructed his staff to examine every sentence of testimony given by administration officials during the Salvadoran conflict to see what distortions they may have promulgated. No word ever emerged. Further, the records of U.S.-run covert operations, civilian or military, are simply beyond the reach of Congress. But I believe that the real reason we will never know about the extent of U.S. involvement — who knew what, and when; whether we directed things, simply observed things, or possibly even remained ignorant of things — is that we don't want to know. No groundswell of popular sentiment will force full disclosure. No member, or members, of Congress will muster the political will to pursue the truth, assuming that such pursuit could ever expose it in the first place.

These are distressing and troubling thoughts, suggesting as they do a certain disinterest among citizens of the most privileged nation on earth, if not a willingness to choose our national interests over those of the suffering victims of El Salvador — the war in El Salvador is over; it was a messy and unfortunate affair in which mistakes perhaps were made; let's forget it and move on.

Even in myself I detect an impulse to move beyond my decade-long obsession with Central America, to relinquish this cause that has strained friendships and family alike and return to the normal pursuits of happiness and security. But against this impulse I measure the spirit that has been kindled in me by the Salvadorans I have come to know and by the North Americans who formed, and still constitute, the solidarity movement.

This movement on behalf of the peoples of Central America is, as far as I can tell, unique in U.S. history — a sustained, nonviolent grassroots effort of national proportions that sprouted and blossomed on behalf of distant people in countries where no U.S. ground troops were engaged. At the heart of this movement, repentant love and fierce hope are present. One small subset of that movement is particularly dear to me: those members and friends of MITF who noticed the suffering on the American isthmus, then rallied to take action. They sat through interminable board meetings; attended task force working committees; assembled four times annually to fold, stuff, and address the newsletter; loaded tons of materials onto trucks headed for Nicaragua and El Salvador; peddled crafts; sold tickets for events, then passed the baskets; loaned MITF money when funds ran short; went to Central America, where they befriended individuals and communities; recruited their friends; and sustained MITF with their pledges. The list is endless. Their work was seldom exciting and often tedious. They suffered each other's foibles, and mine. And still they are at it.

Only a few of these people were mentioned in this book, but all deserve recognition: Rosemary Ackerman, Bill and Melba Anderson, Lillie and Peter Anderson, Beth Ashley, Kate Bancroft, Jean and George Banning, Ruth and Alan Barnett, Cate Bauer, Jan Bauman, John Belz, Suzanne Bristol, Clare Broadhead, Elmer Brunsman, Diane Buchignani, Jesús Campos, Larry Carlin, Don Carney, Carl Carter, John Cook, Carol Costa, Hannah Creighton, Jim and Doris Crittendon, Irene Croft, Cathy Culhane, Luz Elena Diaz, Alix and Eugene Doherty, Ann Dolan, Roger Douglas, Ruth Downing, Jean Drake, Ann Dunbar, David Eames, Bill and Ann Eichhorn, Liz Erringer, Tom Etter, Frank Evans, Kit and Bill Everts, Leslie Fleming, George Friemoth, Pat Friday, Virginia and Fran Geddes, Sheret and George Goddard, Charlotte Goldwyn, Maria Gracia, Carolyn Grenier, Shannon Griffon, Laura Hall, Karyl Hendrick, Faye and Lou Hinze, Betsy Holmes, Shirley and Don Holmlund, Martha Hook, Kevan Insko, Helen Jacobsen, Barbara Jay, Karen and John Klingel, Dave Klinger, Penny Leigh, Gail and Keith Lester, Ceil Mattingly, Barbara Mayer, Alexandra McDonald, Berta Mendoza, Lucienne O'Keefe, Dave Nelson, Lori Norby, Elizabeth Page, Judith Peck, Janet and Robert Pence, Alice Preston, Linda Robins, Adina and Gordon Robinson, Lynn Rolston, Dave Sarvis, Scott Schaeffer, Rosemary Schneider, Sue Severin, John Siemens, Ellie Simmons, Renee Soleway, Dale Sorenson, Linda Spence, Frances Steadman, Nancy Sutter, Wendy Tanowitz, Mimi Tellis, Don and Colleen Trudeau, Lonnie Voth, Dave Wahler, Becky Watkin, Marjorie and Jud Weller, Gordon Williams, and Bernadette Wombacher.

Like the volunteers who accompanied the Human Rights Commission of El Salvador between 1986 and 1991, these people define as neighbors the distant others who struggle for life in places like El Salvador. I was privileged to journey among them for a decade of my life, and collectively, they have given me gifts beyond reckoning.

POEMS

POEMS BY MIGUEL ERNESTO ANAYA PERLA (NETO)

POEM 1

I see the knife cutting through my flesh
I see the blood flowing fast
the wound is deep
the wound in my soul

This wound does not heal
the wound keeps on growing
I'm afraid my soul will die
and I will die with my soul

My blood boils at the thought
Death is a mysterious shadow
everybody has to die
only god lives forever

Death is not totally bad
I also wait for it
I see myself joining my father
or suffering and crying in hell

I would like to heal my soul
or kill it once and for all
I would like to cut the pain
the wound is big
the wound in my soul

POEM 6

I ask for one minute of silence
For those who shiver

I ask for one hour of silence
For those who are in pain

I ask for a day of silence
For those who have wasted their lives pointlessly

I ask for one week of silence
For those who we have left dying

I ask for one month of silence
For the rivers that run with blood

I ask for one year of silence
For the child that was never born

I ask for one decade of silence
For the child that had to fight

I ask for a century of silence
For the Earth we are destroying

I ask for a millennium of silence
For those who have given their lives for others

I ask for an eternity of silence
For ourselves

POEM 10

He was a brave
He was a man
He was a hero
But they tortured him

He wasn't afraid
He didn't hate them
He tried to give them his hand
But they killed him

His blood was spilled
But he is alive
alive where they can't hurt him
alive in the hearts of my people

He was a brave
He was a man
He was a hero
He was my father

POEMS BY GLORIA MARIA ANAYA PERLA

WHERE IS GOD?

Maybe God is with a very few people,
which is better than nothing.
Or maybe he is deaf and blind.
I'm afraid that he doesn't exist,
that a very bad and intelligent person invented him
because they wanted us to believe in something.

They make us believe in a God
and they make us afraid of him
But I think that if he exists,
he is our friend.
But what makes me wonder is that they
kill my people and then they say,
"In God we trust."

NIGHT

It's getting closer to the space that I hate of life.
"The Night"
I'm afraid to be by myself in the dark.
It's only me and my horrible thinking
of what is life.
Me and my words,
Me and my story,
I feel lonely and without knowing I start to cry.
The night is short when you just marry the one you
    love.
But the night is an eternity when you are alone
and afraid of the world.

I learned the meaning of the word "afraid"
that day when you left this world.
And now I'm afraid that day appears in my
dream like my enemy.

THE LOST LOVE

She smiles, she was just a happy child.
She quit being a kid when she saw her dad being
    killed.
She prayed, but nobody answered,
She felt alone.
She cried, she knows that she has to be strong,
but then she saw her people without anything
except strong love.
She knew there was her father she had lost.
She understands that love was being responded with
    love.
She cried once again.
She knows her father was gone.
but he had left his love,
and she knew that she will never be alone.

I DON'T KNOW PEOPLE

I see people that love me,
they don't know me,
but they know who I am.

I know about people that hate me,
I don't know them,
but I know who they are
and some day soon
they will know who I am.

AFTERWORD

During the civil conflict in El Salvador, some 50,000 civilians were killed or disappeared. Many additional thousands suffered torture, rape, expulsion from their villages, and destruction of their homes, livestock, and crops. During the 1980s (roughly speaking), several Salvadoran organizations sprang up in response to these terrible human rights abuses. Three of them — the Nongovernmental Human Rights Commission of El Salvador, Tutela Legal, and Socorro Jurídico — are mentioned in this book.

At considerable risk to themselves, the members of these organizations did what they could to document what was happening around them and to report it to a largely indifferent world. They established exhaustive files of newspaper clippings. They photographed the victims. They conducted interviews and videotaped events as they unfolded. They also transcribed tens of thousands of testimonies given by victims or by these victims' friends and relatives. The original documentation is stored in El Salvador, but in that steamy climate it has begun to deteriorate, a precious legacy literally moldering away in rows of filing cabinets.

In 1994, a number of U.S. and Salvadoran citizens organized themselves as the El Salvador Archives Project, intending to preserve these records that so many had given their lives to compile. We had the great good fortune in 1995 to receive an offer from Bruce Montgomery, chief archivist at the University of Colorado, to house the records we intended to preserve. In January 1996, Bruce accompanied me to El Salvador, where I introduced him to staff members at the Nongovernmental Human Rights Commission, Tutela Legal, and the University of Central America, where the records of Socorro Jurídico now reside. Thereafter, the University Archives of the University of Colorado reached agreements with all three Salvadoran institutions to copy and preserve their records.

At this writing, hundreds of thousands of pages of original testimonies are being copied in El Salvador and shipped to Boulder, Colorado, where they will be organized, cross-referenced, catalogued, and preserved indefinitely. Through this monumental undertaking, Bruce Montgomery and his staff have ensured that the record of Salvadoran repression will never be lost. For their wonderful technical competence, their generosity, and their commitment to the documentation of human rights abuses worldwide, I am as grateful as I can be.

BILL HUTCHINSON
Sonoma, California
January 1997

SUGGESTED READING

For those interested in further reading about El Salvador, especially regarding various aspects of the civil conflict during which this narrative takes place, I suggest the following resources.

Among the complex roots of the war in El Salvador was the spiritual phenomenon known as liberation theology, a phenomenon that can be traced back at least as far as the Second Vatican Council of Pope John XXIII. For an overview, these titles may be useful: Phillip Berryman, *Liberation Theology: The Essential Facts About the Revolutionary Movement in Latin America and Beyond* (New York: Pantheon Books, 1987) and *Stubborn Hope: Religion, Politics, and Revolution in Central America* (Maryknoll, New York: Orbis Books, 1994); Jon Sobrino, *Jesus in Latin America* (Maryknoll, New York: Orbis Books, 1987); and Scott Mainwaring and Alexander Wilde, eds., *The Progressive Church in Latin America* (Notre Dame, Indiana: University of Notre Dame Press, 1989). The voices of important Salvadoran religious martyrs are heard in John Hassett and Hugh Lacey, eds., *Towards a Society That Serves Its People: The Intellectual Contribution of El Salvador's Murdered Jesuits* (Washington, D.C.: Georgetown University Press, 1991), and Michael J. Walsh, trans., *Archbishop Oscar Romero: Voice of the Voiceless, the Four Pastoral Letters and Other Statements*, with introductory essays by Ignacio Martin-Baro and Jon Sobrino (Maryknoll, New York: Orbis Books, 1985). I especially recommend this wonderful biography: James S. Brockman, *Romero: A Life* (Maryknoll, New York: Orbis Books, 1989).

For an understanding of the political and revolutionary aspects of the Salvadoran conflict, consult James Dunkerley, *The Long War: Dictatorship and Revolution in El Salvador* (London: Verso Books, 1985), or Robert Armstrong and Janet Shenk, *El Salvador: The Face of Revolution* (Boston: South End Press, 1982).

For more generalized overviews of both El Salvador and the region, you may find these sources useful: Walter LaFeber, *Inevitable Revolutions: The United States in Central America* (New York: W. W. Norton, 1984); Phillip Berryman, *Inside Central America* (New York: Pantheon, 1985); and Tom Barry, *Roots of Rebellion: Land and Hunger in Central America* (Boston: South End Press, 1987).

The following titles provide insight into the Salvadoran conflict itself: Jenny Pearce, *Promised Land: Peasant Rebellion in Chalatenango* (London: Latin American Bureau, 1986); Tommie Sue Montgomery, *Revolution in El Salvador: Origins and Evolution* (Boulder, Colorado: Westview Press, 1982); Mark Danner, *The Massacre at El Mozote: A Parable of the Cold War* (New York: Vintage, 1994); and John L. Hammond, "Popular Education in the Salvadoran Guerrilla Army," in *Human Organization* 55, no. 4 (1996): 436–445.

For a broader human rights perspective than that offered in *When the Dogs Ate Candles*, consult Americas Watch, *El Salvador's Decade of Terror: Human Rights Since the Assassination of Archbishop Romero* (New Haven, Connecticut: Yale University Press, 1991); the Interamerican Commission on Human Rights, *Report on the Situation of Human Rights in El Salvador* (Washington, D.C.: Organization of American States, 1979); the International Human Rights Law Group, *Waiting for Justice: Treatment of Political Prisoners Under El Salvador's Decree 50* (Washington, D.C.: International Human Rights Law Group, 1987); Maria Teresa Tula, *Hear My Testimony: Maria Teresa Tula, Human Rights Activist*, translated and edited by Lynn Stephen (Boston: South End Press, 1994); and John L. Hammond, "Organization and Education Among Salvadoran Political Prisoners," in *Crime, Law, and Social Change* 25, no. 1 (1996): 17–41. The torture report I frequently refer to in *When the Dogs Ate Candles* is the Nongovernmental Human Rights Commission of El Salvador, *Torture in El Salvador* (San Salvador: CDHES, 1986). The most complete listing of Salvadoran massacres available is in the Ecumenical Program on Central America and the Caribbean, *Condoning the Killing: Ten Years of Massacres in El Salvador* (Washington, D.C.: EPICA, 1990). Finally, an exhaustive human rights overview is provided in the following report prepared by the Salvadoran Truth Commission, which was assembled to investigate human rights abuses during the Salvadoran conflict: *From Madness to Hope, by the Salvadoran Truth Commission: Twelve Years of War in El Salvador* (San Salvador and New York: United Nations, 1993).

Here are several titles for those who are able to read Spanish: Carlos Enríquez Consalvi, *La Terquedad del Izote: El Salvador: Crónica de una Victoria* (Mexico City, Mexico: Editorial Diana, 1992); Francisco Emilio Mena Sandoval, *Del Ejercito Nacional al Ejercito Guerrillero* (San Salvador: Ediciones Arcoiris, 1991); and Nidia Díaz, *Nunca Estuve Sola* (San Salvador: UCA Editores, 1988).

INDEX